The Masquerade

BRIELLE JOY

Scripture quotations marked NIV are taken from the Holy Bible, New International Version. NIV. Copyright 1973, 1978, 1984 by International Bible Society. Used by permission of Zondervan. All rights reserved.

This book is a work of non-fiction. Unless otherwise noted, the author and the publisher make no explicit guarantees as to the accuracy of the information contained in this book and in some cases, names of people and places have been altered to protect their privacy.

LifeRich Publishing is a registered trademark of The Reader's Digest Association, Inc.

LifeRich Publishing books may be ordered through booksellers or by contacting:

LifeRich Publishing
1663 Liberty Drive
Bloomington, IN 47403
www.liferichpublishing.com
1 (888) 238-8637

Because of the dynamic nature of the Internet, any web addresses or links contained in this book may have changed since publication and may no longer be valid. The views expressed in this work are solely those of the author and do not necessarily reflect the views of the publisher, and the publisher hereby disclaims any responsibility for them.

Any people depicted in stock imagery provided by Thinkstock are models, and such images are being used for illustrative purposes only. Certain stock imagery © Thinkstock.

ISBN: 978-1-4897-1256-1 (sc)
ISBN: 978-1-4897-1257-8 (hc)
ISBN: 978-1-4897-1255-4 (e)

Library of Congress Control Number: 2017909311

Print information available on the last page.

LifeRich Publishing rev. date: 8/11/2017

Preface

My name is Brielle Joy. Or at least that is what I have chosen to name myself for the purposes of this book you are about to read. I write under a pen name for both the protection of myself and the protection of those around me who are recorded in this memoir. Hence, all names and places have been changed.

The story, however, is true. And it's a story that needs to be told. Some of you may identify strongly with the events and emotions that I reveal throughout these pages. Some of you may recognize loved ones and friends around you that are going through similar trials. Wherever this finds you, I hope, and pray, that you will recognize the Truth that is written throughout the book: you are not alone, there is hope.

There was pain in this journey. There were many days I didn't know how I was going to make it to the next. There were many days I wanted to give up. There were many days where the pain seemed so unbearable I thought I couldn't go on. But I did. By the grace of God, I did.

And I continue on. My healing did not stop at the end of this book. It continues today. And though things aren't perfect, God has been right beside me each step of the way, even when I don't always see Him, always leading me into greater peace and freedom.

The hope I found on this journey came from my heavenly Father. In a time where I was broken, lost in darkness and unable to continue, it was there I found a strength that did not come from me. I named myself Brielle Joy, for Brielle means, "the Lord is my strength" and Nehemiah 8:10 says, "The joy of the Lord is your strength".

I wrote this book for you. Yes, you. Whoever you are. This wasn't written so that you could know my story, but so you could know the hope there is for yours.

Thank you for walking through this story with me,

Love,
Brielle Joy

Dedication

This is for you, child of the One True King

"Praise be to the God and Father of our Lord Jesus Christ, the Father of compassion and the God of all comfort, who comforts us in all our troubles, so that we can comfort those in any trouble with the comfort we ourselves have received from God." 2 Corinthians 1:3-4

PART 1

*The tide drags me farther and farther away from land. The beach now looks like a speck on the horizon. Around me the expanse of dark water seems unending. Its murky depths have entrapped me, and my arms and legs fight to keep my head above water. But why fight? Why not just succumb to the downward pull of the ocean? Surely death would be easier. I've been fighting for too long now. My arms slow and my fluttering feet start to relax; I take a deep breath as I allow my body to sink beneath the surface. How peaceful it is below, I think, as I mentally prepare myself for my fate. Silence fills my mind for the first time in what seems forever, leaving only the sound of my blood rushing in my ears. Suddenly I hear a voice. Not from the ocean, but a voice deep inside me. "**I am with you.**" A peace like none other fills my mind, and a new burst of energy rejuvenates my weary limbs. I must keep fighting. Arms and legs flailing, I propel myself upward toward the light, and with a gasp of fresh air, I break through the surface. "Don't give up, Brielle. Don't give up." And so I battle on.*

Chapter 1

Survivor. For me, a survivor is one who has lived through an event that could have been fatal, such as going to war and making it out alive. Or living through an earthquake that destroyed an entire city. Or surviving a shipwreck, like those few people found after the sinking of the Titanic. I am not a survivor. I am merely drowning slowly. Too slowly.

With a jolt, I wake up. Beneath my clammy skin my heart races. I glance at the illuminated clock. 4:30 am. Ugh. I sigh; another hour or so of sleep would be nice, but the idea of falling back to sleep sends a wave of fear through my body. In one swift movement I climb out of bed and gently pace across my bedroom floor so as not to wake my parents. I flick on the light and my eyes squint as they try to adjust to my surroundings.

Once again, the dream had felt so real. In the dream I was in my old house in New Hampshire, wandering the hallways. I stopped at my bedroom door, my mind willing me to open it, but a much larger force stopping me. The rest of the dream fades into darkness. I try to shake the uneasy feeling growing deep in my mind as I begin my daily routine of getting ready for school.

It's Thursday – I had been good so far this week. Only 313 calories consumed on Monday, 426 on Tuesday (not such a great day) and 257 yesterday. Hopefully today I could continue my relatively good trend. Getting up early and leaving before my mother woke up would save me the breakfast and lunch grilling.

"Brielle, aren't you going to eat breakfast?" she would ask.

"No, Mom, you know how it makes me feel sick eating so early."

"Well, what about lunch, did you pack yourself one?"

"Nah, I'll get something at school; gotta go or I'll be late..." I would scoot out the door before any further inquiry could take place.

It is already getting light outside as I step out the back door into the mild May morning air. The birds have begun their morning chorus and a peace settles deep within me but quickly fades as I think about the day ahead. I silently go through the gate and climb into my Corsa. Pushing play on my iPod sends heavy metal music blasting into my car, pushing last night's dream further and further out of my mind. With the noise numbing my mind, I set off to school.

I can see it in their eyes. That look of concern as I rattle off some excuse as to why I'm not eating lunch. I guess I'm beginning to run out of novel reasons. But today I go with, "I had a big breakfast, I'll get something later." They don't seem convinced, but carry on talking about Amanda's latest crush, Gavin. She sure does go through them. It seems only a couple months ago she was dating a guy she met at a local math event. I try to remain engaged in the conversation, but my mind seems to have a will of its own.

"Brie, Brie!"

A small poke on my arm and I jump back into reality.

"You were spacing out again," Amanda tells me.

As if I didn't already know. The feeling of just waking up is a telltale sign. That plus the dryness of my contacts. I don't know why I space out so much, but I always have, so I'm not too concerned. Right now, I can't handle the mundane conversation that's taking place, so I retreat to the gym as I have my third period free. Once there I pound out my tension into the treadmill. My sheer self-hatred drives me on until my legs protest in pain.

Pain. That is what I crave, the pain of a starving stomach, or the deep muscle ache after pushing myself too far in the gym. Either way, it calms a much deeper pain.

I arrive home to an empty house. My mother and my stepfather, Charlie, must still be at work. I walk through the house doing my usual check of all closets and rooms, just making sure I am truly alone. As I open the last closet with a jerk, I release the air I've been holding in. With the satisfaction that there are no monsters in the closet, I go to my piano and turn it on - our house is too small for a real piano, an electronic one had to suffice. I can feel the darkness closing in on me. I've only eaten 145 calories today, but I still feel out of control. A ripple of panic runs through me. Playing the piano is one of the most effective ways to calm me down. I start playing the lullaby I've been writing. The notes resonate through the room, calming me from deep within. My hands fly over the keys, blending notes to make a beautiful sound. I close my eyes as I play and imagine myself far away, floating over the darkness in my life. However, as the last chord plays and the notes drift away, the darkness once again invades my mind. I rattle through the list of homework I need to do, trying in vain to distract myself from my own thoughts. Realizing most of my homework can wait until later, I decide to switch on the TV.

CSI. One of my favorites. There's nothing quite like a decomposing body surrounded by a load of fake blood to take your mind off reality. Within a few minutes I'm thoroughly into the plot, trying to work out what I think happened before the CSI team does.

"Have you found the cause of death yet?" the head investigator asks the coroner.

"No not yet, but there are definite signs of rape."

My mind freezes and begins to shut down. I can no longer feel the couch beneath me. The room fades and I am plunged into darkness. My body feels compressed and I can't breathe. I try to call out, but no sound comes out. The sound of heavy breathing gushes into my ears. My body feels like it is on fire. Somewhere a door slams shut, wrenching my screaming body back into reality.

"Hello!" Charlie's back from work.

I shake myself, trying to rid myself of the thoughts that are filtering into my mind. I can't let them out. I have to keep them locked up whatever the cost.

"Hi!" I respond with the best smile I can muster. "How was work?"

Chapter 2

Secrets. Have you ever kept a secret? It's often hard, especially when people ask you directly about it. The longer you keep it, the harder it tries to escape your lips. Eventually, after years of secrecy, it becomes second nature to keep the secret safely stored away. But secrets, no matter how well you think you've buried them, are never far from the surface.

I pull into a parking space at the school bus depot. There's not much there. The parking lot is full of weeds that have ripped their way through the asphalt. The bus depot itself is an old and worn down building, which holds only three double-decker buses. Toward the roadside, a small pub named Jerusalem stands alone. Again, its exterior could do with a good sprucing; in fact, I'm not even sure if it is currently up and running. Standing in his usual place at the corner of the pub I see my best friend, Corwin. His head bobs up and down to the beat of the music blasting in his ears. Turning the car off, I take a deep breath before swinging the door open and facing the world for yet another day. Slowly, I make my way toward Corwin. My feet crunch beneath me on the gravelly ground; I focus on the sound and count my steps. Counting distracts me from my thoughts and calms the fear that has settled in the pit of my stomach. Corwin looks in my direction and a smile spreads across his face.

"Good morning, Brie. How are you?" he asks with probing eyes as I take my usual place beside him.

A small lump forms in my throat. He genuinely cares how I am.

Sometimes I wish I could tell him the truth about the pain I'm in. Instead, I swallow the knot and give him a small grin.

"I'm fine thanks! More importantly, how are you, my friend?"

He nods his head knowingly. He knows I'm lying, but he doesn't push the issue. "I'm good," he grins back. "God really met with me this morning as I played the guitar. His presence is so awesome! I just love Him so much."

He says this with such a joy and exuberance emitting from him, that I know he's serious. His faith is so strong, so steadfast. I'm jealous. I also am a Christian and have chosen to follow Jesus. Well, I did two years ago, thanks to a singing teacher of mine. But recently I've felt as though He's left me and I wander helplessly alone in the dark. Didn't the Bible say He would never leave me? My heart sinks. Of course He'd leave me. I'm not worth sticking around for.

As the rest of the 'bus stop crew' arrives, my smiley mask sets in place. I've been wearing this mask since before I can remember. It seems like an old friend now, one that will protect me. I laugh along with the funny stories told, trying desperately to stay engaged in the conversations. My own laugh sounds empty and I hope no one notices. No one seems to, thankfully. I'm just so weary. I'm losing control, but I can't let my walls down. Corwin offers me one of his gummy bears (this boy never stops eating candy, it seems) and I am reminded that I do have control. At least in some parts of my life. I refuse the candy. My ability to control what I eat gives me a boost of energy. 'You can do this, Brielle,' I silently mantra.

I can feel the sun's warmth, even through my many layers. The cool breeze tosses my curls around my face. I'm sitting on top of the hill overlooking the school. It's lunchtime and people are out playing games and lounging all over the picnic tables. I close my eyes and listen to the sound of the wind pouring over the fields. I begin to relax. The sound of the rushing wind is so familiar; my mind transports me back to New Hampshire, back to my forest.

I step out of the side door and reach up to gently pull the door shut behind me. I walk along the length of the jeep and out through the garage doors. In front of me is a long driveway, wide enough to fit at least two big cars. To my right is a small white picket fence that runs the length of my home.

My mom and I would spend hours tending to the flowers we planted alongside the fence. I never really saw the point — we lived in the middle of nowhere in New Hampshire and no one was going to admire them except us.

In the front yard is a huge beech tree, I run past the tree and up the driveway. Clomp, clomp, clomp. My light up sneakers beat against the asphalt. I don't have long until Dad will be home. The image of his blue pickup truck coming toward me flashes in my mind and I begin to panic. I have to keep it together. I have to make it to my place. I step from the paved driveway to the soft grass, which doesn't have the same satisfactory sound of running feet. As I run toward the edge of the woods, a strong wind whips through the trees, causing birds to fly out and the leaves to scatter. I love that scene; it stops me in my tracks and I observe the beauty of the forest. Then the sound of a low rumble in the distance brings me back to reality. He's back.

The very core of my body begins to quiver in fear. I send that fear to my feet and run into the woods. The trees blur past me and I can hear the occasional sound of snapping twigs as I run, causing my tense body to jump every time.

When I run in the woods it makes me feel like Disney's Pocahontas, except I don't have a cute little raccoon with me. I am used to this route through the forest and feel like I can run through with my eyes closed. But this time my eyes are wide with fear. I pass a large boulder I have named Pride Rock. As I keep running, my breath starts to get more strained and the smell of pine needles fill my nostrils. I am almost there. Ahead of me I can see the light streams flooding through the trees. I slow down.

I can hear the crunch of the fallen leaves of autumns past beneath my feet as I take ten more tentative steps toward the clearing. I stop myself at the edge. Placing my hands on the trees either side of me I proceed to trace the patterns of the bark with my fingertips. The bark is rough and feels like hardened wrinkles. My eyes wander around, absorbing all the beauty I see. The moss that carpets my place feels so soft compared to the leaves and twigs I have just run through. I remove my shoes and sprawl out onto the mossy forest floor. I shut my eyes and absorb the heat that the sun bores down on me. I start to drift out of reality and into my pretend world, a world where I can fly away, far above the trees. How I wish I could fly away. A small tear escapes me and slides down my face into my hair. I hold back the rest. I mustn't cry.

The sound of a cowbell in the distance brings me back to the ground. The sun has begun to set and the shadows of the trees surrounding me have already engulfed my place. I quickly slip on my shoes and, with one fleeting glance at my place, I take off in a run toward home where I have to face whatever he has in store for me. Maybe tonight is going to be okay. Maybe he's too tired to come into my room tonight. Inside my mind, I plead to God that he is too tired. The house begins to emerge from behind the trees. The house, so beautiful but filled with secrets that can never be told. I slow my pace and count my steps into the house...

A distant voice pulls at the edges of my memory. A hand grabs my arm and I instinctively pull my other arm in front of my face.

"Brie! I've been looking for you, what are you doing up here?"

I quickly take my arm out from in front of my face and look up. I'm back on the hill outside my school, thousands of miles away from my past. It felt so real. I chasten myself for being so foolish as to think about the past. Sitting beside me is Corwin. He has a look of concern etched across his features.

What *was* I doing here? Escaping. Resting. "Just chilling," I tell him.

He looks out over the school grounds. "Brie," he says, in a serious tone. My stomach tightens. "I'm concerned about you."

Surprise, surprise! I look at him with an expression of confusion on my face.

"You're not eating."

I open my mouth to spout out some excuse but he cuts me off, leaving my mouth floundering.

"I know, I know. You feel sick, or you ate earlier. They are just excuses, Brie. Anyone with eyes would be able to see that, as much as you try to hide beneath your bulky sweatshirts, you're sick. It's the middle of May and you're bundled up with sweatshirts and even gloves as if it's March!"

"If it were March, I'd be wearing much more than this, I assure you," I retorted.

"Brie, I'm being serious. I'm worried. You've lost so much weight. You need help."

Pft! What does he know? I need much more than help. Besides, my weight is normal, if not heavy. The last time I weighed myself I was one hundred and twenty pounds, a normal weight for someone who is five foot seven. And the week before that I was one hundred and twenty-five pounds. Again, a normal weight. Nothing is wrong with me.

"I think you should see someone."

My knotted stomach drops into a hole. Fragments of my past experience with 'getting help' flash through my mind. There is no way I am going through that again.

"I can't, Corwin. And besides, I don't need help. I'm fine."

"That's what you always say Brie, but you're not fine. This..." he gestures to my body, "...is dangerous. Why can't you just talk to someone? You won't talk to Amanda or me. You need to talk to someone. I can't just watch you starve yourself to death."

"Well, when you put it that way..." I joke. He doesn't look so impressed.

"What's stopping you?"

"They can't find out," I blurt out. My eyes widen with the shock of what just slipped out of my mouth. My mind reels through what to say to take that back.

"They can't find out what?" He looks at me in confusion.

"Uh... you know... that... umm..." I can't get my act together; the cracks in my wall are getting so big now. The secrets are spilling out. Panic rises inside me.

"Brie, you can tell me. I know it hurts, but you have to let it out. Keeping it to yourself will only hurt you more." He sounds like he can read my mind. He can't know, I remind myself. I've never told anyone. Never. I give him a small smile and look away, hoping he'll let it drop.

"Did I ever tell you how I came to live in England?" I ask him, seemingly changing the subject.

"You told me that you moved over here when you were eleven after your mom married an English guy."

"That's only a partial truth." I sigh and look out across the field. I'm so sick of hiding. "You know that my brother and my sister were already married and living here when I moved here, right?"

Corwin nods and remains silent, allowing me to continue.

"Well, after my mother met Charlie and got engaged a couple months later, they decided to come over to England for Christmas and get married shortly afterwards. On Christmas Eve, we were staying with my brother and his family, and I was so happy to be with them that I suggested we stay in England to live. Staying on vacation is every kid's dream, I'm sure." I can feel my throat begin to swell with emotion. "Unlike most other parents, who would not listen to their child's foolish dreams, my mother and Charlie decided that was a great idea. I came over for Christmas vacation and I never left. I never got to say goodbye. And when I said I missed America, or I wanted to go home, they told me it was my own fault that I'm here in England."

"Why?" Corwin asks, his voice just above a whisper.

"Because I was the one who suggested it in the first place. I thought that we'd go back one day. I thought this was just temporary. Now I've been here six years."

"I'm sorry, Brie."

"Me too."

We sit in silence. There's nothing to say. I'm hoping that he's let the 'weight' thing drop.

When will I learn that hoping never gets me anywhere?

Chapter 3

Cracked. A small crack appears in the dam. A small trickle of water leaks out. You quickly plug it up with whatever you can get your hands on and walk away, thinking it will all be okay now. But the crack gets bigger. More and more water is spilling out. You frantically try to plug all the cracks now appearing but it's no use. Water pours and the cracks just continue to get bigger. You can do nothing but watch as your dam breaks and everything you kept so safely behind it falls at your feet.

I think I'm losing it. My entire body trembles as I sit with my head in my hands. My mind is trying to pull me out of reality and back into my past. I focus intently on the floor tiles in between my feet. I slowly count the tiny specs that cover each square. One, two, three...

...The door creaks open, spreading a dim glow across my bedroom...

...four, five, six...

...his silhouette stands in the door frame. I quickly shut my eyes and pretend to be asleep...

...seven, eight, nine...

...my body trembles beneath the covers as my father quietly steps across the room...

...ten, eleven, twelve...

...he sits down at the edge of my bed and slowly pulls back the covers and places his hands on my body. I stop shaking as my mind escapes the reality of what is happening...

...thirteen, fourteen...

"Brie?"

A voice is calling my name, pulling me out of the nightmare I'm in.

"Brie, it's Corwin. You're okay. Do you know where you are? Brie?"

I slowly lift my head from my trembling hands. My eyes swim as I try to focus on Corwin. He's sitting next to me on the bench outside the physics classroom.

"It's okay, Brie. Amanda texted me saying that you ran out of your physics class and asked if I would come check up on you. What happened?" he asks, concern flooding his face.

I turn back to stare at the floor, trying to avoid his eyes that indicate his care for me. I breathe in deeply and shakily release the air.

"I was sitting in physics doing some questions out of the text book. I saw Mr. Dodge walking toward me out of the corner of my eye. Suddenly, the room disappeared and I was…" I shut my mouth. I had already said too much.

"What did you do then?" Corwin asks gently.

"I… I can't remember. All I remember is finding myself here on this bench. Corwin… I think I'm losing my mind."

He stretches his arm out as if to put it around me, but thinks better of it and places his arms on his knees so he is more at my eye level.

"You're not losing your mind, Brie. It's just your mind's way of trying to deal with things you haven't been dealing with for a long time."

Pft… what a bunch of psycho-babble, I think. But he sure does seem to know what's happening in my head.

"And how would you know what I'm having to deal with?" I ask him.

"Brie, I'm not blind. Besides your obvious problems with anorexia," I flinch at the truth of those words, "I can see you are having problems with dissociation and flashbacks. And I've noticed your fear of men and of people touching you."

My eyes widen with shock. What happened to my mask of

'everything is fine'? How could he see all that? I've spent years hiding it. My body begins to shake more violently.

"Brie… it's okay. Brie." Corwin tries to desperately get my attention before my mind slips away again.

"How do you know all that? What else do you know?" I turn toward him, backing away to the far edge of the bench.

"Don't be afraid, Brie. I'm not going to hurt you. I want to help you. And don't worry, I haven't told anyone and people aren't going to make the same conclusions I've made. It's just that in my psychology class we've been studying the effects of childhood abuse—"

I leap up from the bench. My fists are clenched at my side and my mind reels as I try and work out what to do. Nobody was meant to find out. How does he know?

"Brie, don't be afraid. I'm not here to judge you. I'm here to help, to listen."

"How much do you know?" I stand, my jaw locked so tight my muscles begin to ache.

"Nothing more than I just told you. Sit down. Calm down. It's okay," he says gently.

"It's not okay, Corwin. Nothing is okay. I'm losing my mind and I don't know what to do." I sit down and put my head in my hands once again. I can feel my body aching to sob. But I can't. I haven't been able to cry for years. And now I'm afraid that if I start, I will never stop.

"You can trust me, Brie."

I look at him. His eyes are full of sincerity. He knows. Taking several deep breaths, I slowly begin to speak.

"When I was young, before my parents divorced, when my father was around. He would… he would… he… oh God… Corwin, I can't. I can't say it."

"It's okay, deep breaths. I understand."

"I promised myself I would never, EVER, tell anyone. And for years I lied and kept this secret and now it's all coming out and I can't stop it."

"It's time, Brie. You need to deal with this. It's only going to get worse the longer you hold onto it."

"But I can't say it."

"Well, can you write it down?" Corwin asks. He rifles through his backpack and pulls out a small notepad and a pencil and hands them to me. I place the pad in my lap and try to grip the pencil with my shaking hand.

I slowly begin to write:

When I was young. From the time I can remember until I was seven, my father would…

I pause, the pencil poised on the paper, my mind screaming at me to stop. This moment could change everything. This moment could break me free from the secrecy I've carried for years, but it could also be the end of the safety I know behind my mask of secrets.

… sexually abuse me.

I finish the sentence and reread what I just wrote. I gasp in horror of what I just did and frantically try to erase the words, ripping the page as I do so. Corwin gently places his hands on mine and takes the pencil and paper. It's too late. He has seen what was written.

"Brie, calm down." He looks at me and waits for me to look back at him. "It's okay."

He sits with my shaking hands in his for several minutes, dropping his gaze toward the bench. I can't tell what he's thinking, but he probably believes I'm some sort of slut. A shiver runs through me at the thought. Corwin looks back up at me.

"I'm so sorry, Brie." That was all that was said. There wasn't anything to say. I thought that was going to be it. We sat in silence for what seemed eternity.

"I don't want it to be true."

Corwin just nods his head and looks away. I really don't understand his pain.

"What's wrong?" I ask him.

"Wrong? You're asking me what's wrong? Brie, I just found out that my best friend was abused by her father and I feel so helpless."

"I know, I'm sorry. I shouldn't have told you. I understand if you don't want to be friends."

He turns toward me with a baffled look on his face.

"Why would you say that? This wasn't your fault, Brie. How does this change me wanting to be your friend? I just wish there was something more I could do for you."

Now it's my turn to look baffled. I open my mouth to speak, but I don't know what to say.

"So, when did it stop?" Corwin continues.

"My father stopped when he and my mother divorced. I was eight," I say bluntly.

"But the abuse didn't stop there, did it?"

My eyes widen with fear. What did he just say? How can he know? I spin my head around to face him and try to keep my face from showing the fear I feel.

"I don't understand." Which is true, I have no idea where he's getting this.

"There's more to this. I don't know how I know. I just do."

"You can't know." I shake my head and cover my face with my hands. What had I done? I was breaking every rule I had made for myself. Rules that were to keep me and my secrets safe. I'd done so well. I'd obeyed my father and never told a soul. Even when they tried to drag the truth out of me. My father told me that it was just our 'little secret' and if I told someone it would hurt my mother, and I didn't want to hurt my mother. I still don't.

When it all started again four years down the road, just a different place and a different person, I once more decided that I would never tell a soul. Besides, I thought no one would believe me. But today… today I broke my rules and there's no going back.

My muscles ache from the tension in my body. I slump forward. My hands shake and my chest tightens. Air does not seem to be moving into my lungs. Corwin looks at me and must be able to see the panic in my expression because he tries to soothe me.

"It's okay, Brie. Just calm down. It's going to be okay."

I try to escape reality. My eyes find a small crack on the floor in front of me. I focus on the crack, blocking out the rest of the world. In the distance I can faintly hear Corwin speaking, but I continue to stare at the crack.

I feel fingers gently touching the hand that lies trembling in my lap, pulling me out of my trance.

"Brie."

I look up and see Corwin showing such a pained expression that I pull away from him.

"Brie, I can't imagine the pain you're in right now. And how difficult it is to let go of your secrets. But trust me – you're doing the right thing. God will take care of you. He will take you along the road of healing. This is just the beginning, Brie. He will never leave you. You're going to be okay."

What does he know? God has already left me. He left me the first night my father came into my room. He wasn't there during the most painful times of my life. My mother said it was God's will that we moved thousands of miles away from home; she said it was to protect me. Protect me from what? She didn't even know about what my dad did to me. And where did that get me anyway? Into more harm. God doesn't care. He's not with me. I'm alone.

So alone.

Chapter 4

Falling apart. It's like seeing a loose thread on a piece of clothing. You pull at it, thinking that you can get rid of it, but instead the thread gets longer and longer, unraveling more and more. You pull at it more frantically. You have to find the end. Eventually you get to the end, but all you're left with is a large pile of thread which is now so knotted up that it's more of a mess than you could ever imagine. The seemingly fine piece of clothing is completely gone. What's more, there is no way to undo what you just did.

Somehow I made it home. I don't recall any of the journey; my mind had been so far away, thinking through what I had done today. How much I'd messed things up. I turn my car off and place my forehead on the steering wheel. I must get my act together before I go in. Both my mother and Charlie's cars are in the driveway. Even though I've broken my secrecy with one of my friends, my parents can still never know. That rule I will not break. I cannot break. I take a deep breath and put on my 'everything's fine' mask before exiting the car and walking in the back door.

As soon as I open the door to the kitchen, the delicious smell of French toast hits me. My stomach growls in hunger. I think back to what I'd eaten today. I can only come up with the two carrot sticks. Half of me thinks I could have a slice of French toast as long as I don't go overboard on the powdered sugar, but the other half of me is so disgusted with myself that I can't face indulging myself even a little. So, with an ache in my stomach, I pass through the kitchen and into the living room where my parents sit eating their dinner whilst watching

Time Team – a show that *both* my parents can agree to watch. My mother looks up and smiles at me. I try to smile back, but it's like my facial muscles won't work right so I quickly look away to the TV.

"How was your day?" she asks.

"Fine, thanks, how was yours?" I reply as I always do.

"Good, had coffee with Barbara this morning…"

She continues to walk me through her day, but I'm not really listening, I'm just looking at her, nodding my head when I think it appropriate. Can she tell that I feel like I'm dying? That my world is crashing around me? Or is she still as blind as she always has been?

"…Do you want something to eat? There's plenty of French toast in the kitchen."

"I'm okay actually, I had a really late lunch and am still really full. I've got to get upstairs to do some homework." I head upstairs before she can argue with my refusal for food.

Reaching my room at the top of the stairs, I shut the door quietly behind me and flick on the light. I make it two steps into my room before collapsing on the floor. What have I done? A deep pain consumes me and I can't breathe. The room seems to spin around me and flashes of my memories course through my mind. I've unlocked the door. I've opened it up and now the secrets are spilling out into my consciousness. The deep pain erupts into a fire of self-hatred. I once again want to rip myself into a million pieces. I begin to dig my nails into my fists.

The sharpness of my nails brings a moment of clear thinking, like a breath of fresh air. But as the pain in my palm diminishes, the screaming in my mind comes back with a vengeance. I realize that this is the answer. I need physical pain to stifle the pain of my memories that is so much worse. I look around for something that I can use. I spot my arts and crafts box. I rip off the lid, casting it aside whilst searching through the box before I find what I am looking for. My compass. I only used it during ninth grade math to draw circles; my free hand circles were never good enough. Its sharp point is just what I need. I roll up my left sleeve and, with my compass gripped in my shaking right hand, place the point of the compass to the skin on the back of my wrist. The prick of pain already begins to clear my mind. I quickly draw the point across my skin. The pain is so sharp that I suck in my breath. I focus on the pain it brings to my wrist and my body seems to relax a little. I close my eyes and no memories flash through my mind.

Peace. I feel peace. But the sharp pain starts to dull and once again the pain in my mind engulfs me. So once more I pull the compass across my wrist this time going back and forth over the same area. Back and forth. Each time, I push a little harder. Blood begins to seep out of the wound, but I continue to dig. To dig out the pain. Finally, the pain in my wrist causes me to just drop the compass and cradle my wrist.

I can breathe. The room has stopped spinning. I let myself just lay on my bedroom floor as I focus on the pulsing pain in my wrist.

·····•────────◆────────•·····

I jerk awake, drenched in sweat and gasping for air. My heart rate is so rapid that I feel like it's going to escape from my chest. I sit up and remind myself that I'm here in England and I'm alone. I look at the clock. 3:30 am. My whole body continues to shake as I try to block out the memories of my dream. I can still feel him all over my body and I feel disgusting. I want to scrub myself down, but I can't take a shower now without waking my parents. There is no way I'm going back to sleep. I stay still as my heart rate drops to a normal pace. Silently I get out of bed and put on my large fluffy robe and my giant slippers. I slip out of my door and down the stairs, taking each step slowly to try and avoid causing the floor to creak. I go through the living room and dining room into the room that holds my piano. I'm thankful for once that it's electronic because I can simply plug my headphones in and play to my heart's content without disturbing my mother and Charlie. I quickly start playing, trying to escape the pain I feel from the nightmare. The notes to my lullaby penetrate my mind and I slip into a daze full of beautiful chords and notes. Peace.

My eyes are closed and suddenly a face that isn't my father's flashes across my eyes. I open my eyes and look around, sure that he is here. I back away into a chair in the corner of the room and draw my knees to my chest. I'm so tired but I can't sleep. Whether I'm awake or asleep my nightmares haunt me. The silence in the room leaves room for my mind to wander back into my past, but this time into a much more recent past.

He ties my legs to the chair and my hands behind my back. I can't move much now, my mind beginning to race as panic sets in. He squats in front of me, placing his hand on my knee. The game has suddenly turned into a nightmare. A chill runs through my body. He smiles after seeing this.

"You've been bad, haven't you?" he says in a mocking voice.

I keep my head turned away from his face. I can feel him willing me to look at him. His hand moves from my knee up my thigh. Another chill shoots through me. He likes this. 'Stop doing that!' I think to myself. A few moments later, my mind slips away, and I stop shivering.

The sound of a scream brings me back to the chair I'm curled up in. I look around for the source of the scream, and realize it must have been me. I hold my breath, waiting for signs that I woke my parents, but I hear nothing. I bury my head in my hands. Why can't I just forget about these things? Why must I remember? What is it about me that causes people to do this to me? It has to be me. First my father, then four years later it starts again. This time it was my step-cousin, Ted. Two completely different people, two completely different places, one constant factor. Me.

A fresh wave of pain mixed with utter self-hatred washes over me. My wrist still aches from the deep cut but the pain is not enough to keep my emotions at bay now. Instead of going back to get my compass I drop to my knees on the floor and silently cry out.

"God! Why did you bring me here? Why did you bring me to this stupid country? I hate it here!"

I silently sob without crying. Deep down somewhere inside me a voice speaks calmingly, three simple words: **"To save you."**

"Save me?"

Coming to England did nothing but make things worse. Once my dad had left it was just my mother and I and everything was fine. But then once I got here I let it happen all over again. Coming to England did not save me. It's killing me. And now look at what I've done. I've told someone and I don't know what's going to happen. What if my mother finds out? I will not let that happen. I can't hurt her. Besides, my father is right, she'll never believe me. She loves Ted! My whole family does. And he's not all that bad. I can't blame him. There must be something about me that causes them to do this. I didn't stop him.

I stop my inward screaming at myself and just lie in silence on the floor. Too tired to move. Too emotionally drained. I can see the sky outside the window already beginning to lighten as dawn approaches. Despair lies like a heavy blanket on me. How will I make it through another day? As the birds begin to sing I lay listening, imagining myself far away in my woods in New Hampshire. Peace once more fills me, rejuvenating my strength.

One more day, Brie. You can make it. Get up.

And I do. Somehow I keep living.

Chapter 5

Existing. Have you ever felt like your life is spinning out of control? No matter how hard you try to keep your head above water you are constantly pulled under, suffocating in the dark. Those moments of clarity where you can breathe freely are few and far between. How do you survive? The answer: you don't. You simply continue existing.

A tap on my arm pulls me back to reality.

"You were spacing out again," Corwin says.

I just roll my eyes and continue to stare out of the bus window. Several weeks have passed now since I told Corwin about my father. Ted's secret was still locked up in my mind.

What happened to "the truth will set you free"? I felt more overcome with fear than I ever had. I could barely keep my mask on. Countless sleepless nights didn't help either. As if reading my mind Corwin said:

"You look exhausted."

I just shrug, still avoiding looking at him.

"Aren't you sleeping?"

"No," I mumble.

"Why can't you sleep?"

Is he really that stupid? I turn and glare at him.

"Why do you think?" I ask, my voice dripping with sarcasm.

"Nightmares?" he suggests.

"If you want to call them that." To me they were so much more. Nightmares imply bad dreams that kids get about giant squids chasing them or something. This... this was real. This was a memory. I spent my few sleeping hours reliving my past. As if it wasn't bad enough the first time. And my memories were beginning to merge. One second my father would be lying on top of me, and the next second it was Ted and his sadistic grin staring at me. My body gives an involuntary shudder at the thoughts and I try to push them out by focusing on the number of buses that line the bus stop as we pull into the school's driveway.

Corwin sits there, looking helpless. I feel a pang of guilt. I should be trying to be happy so he wouldn't have to be comforting me. But like usual, I ruin everything.

We pull up near the front entrance and the sound of shuffling bags and feet fill the bus as people stand to leave. I remain seated as I wait for the crowd to clear somewhat. I can't handle people bumping into me.

When Corwin stands, I follow and we make our way toward our first class. For him, history; for me, chemistry with Mr. Davis.

Our bus is early for once, so, as I arrive outside the classroom, I peer through the door. The room is empty. I look around and see one of my classmates leaning against the wall of the corridor. Eric, I think that's his name. I take a seat on the nearby bench and try to recall what we were learning about in our last class to keep my mind occupied. A few minutes pass and I can feel my mind beginning to slip in and out of reality as I lose concentration. I can hear footsteps approaching so I look up. It's Mr. Davis walking toward us, but just like that, I'm plunged into my past.

Ted walks toward me, his body filling my field of vision. My hands fumble beneath me, pushing at the carpet, trying to move myself back toward the corner. He's moving toward me now. 'Move Brie, Move!' I scream in my head. But my muscles fail me and I can't move at all. All muscles are tense and ready for the blow.

"*You did, dammit,*" *he says to me.*

I can hear the anger in his voice. I look at his feet, not daring to see the anger in his eyes.

"*I didn't!*" *I plead.* "*I didn't!*"

23

He moves one more step toward me; my back hits the wall as I cower from his fist.

"You did! You idiot!" *he says to me between blows.*

The sound of the classroom door hitting the wall as it's opened brings me back to the corridor. My whole body is violently shaking. Eric gives me a slightly puzzled expression before he turns away and makes his way into the classroom. Mr. Davis looks at me in concern.

"Are you feeling alright, Brie?"

I feel as if I can't breathe. I shake my head. There's a bathroom just around the corner. I'm shaking so much I'm not convinced I can make it.

Mr. Davis seems not to know what to do or say, and simply suggests I get a drink of water. I nod and push myself off of the bench, stumbling towards the bathroom.

Flinging open the first stall door I lean against the cold metal divider. I shut the door and try to keep the room in focus.

Graffiti coats the wall opposite me and I focus on what it says. Things like 'Katie luvs Peter' and 'Jamie's a bitch' are scribbled across it. One catches my attention saying 'You f***ing idiot' and I'm jolted back into the flashback I just had.

"You did! You idiot!" *Ted says and his fists make contact with my arms. Places no one else would see.*

I'm brought back to the bathroom due to the sharp pain of my nails digging into my palms. The slight relief, that small gulp of fresh air that comes with this pain and I know what I must do. I open the front pocket of my backpack and pull out a small rectangular folded piece of paper. I slowly open up the paper and reveal a thin silver razor blade that I had taken out of a disposable shaver. Just at the sight of it, my heart rate begins to drop. I know that the pain inside me will shortly be gone. I roll up my sweatshirt sleeve and with one swift movement I tear a rip in my arm. The pain sends ice through my body, quenching the inner fire and freezing my tormented mind. The blood begins to trickle down my arm, leaving a warm trail behind. My breathing is slow and deep. Peace. For now.

I grab some tissue and wipe up the blood on my arm and wrap

some around the wound to stop it bleeding all over my sweatshirt. My body now full of energy, I wrap my razor back up and store it safely in my bag before rushing back to chemistry class, a smile plastered firmly on my face as I relish a moment of control. A moment of clarity.

I sit on the front row of my chemistry class. I love chemistry. I love how it makes sense. There are no maybes, just right and wrong. Mr. Davis is reviewing what we learned last week about chirality of organic molecules. I feel pretty confident on my understanding of this, but I'm still all eyes and ears. He wraps up his summary and tells us to pair off to work on some questions from the textbook using the model kits to help us. I grab a model kit box from the side bench. Inside there is an array of little colored 'atoms' and various sized gray 'bonds.' I begin to arrange the 'atoms' into color order and the 'bonds' into size order.

"We're meant to be making models with them, not being OCD."

I jump at being spoken to. James Lewis, my lab partner, sits next to me looking a tad impatient. I was wrapped up in my own little world; I completely forgot that we were supposed to be working in pairs. I look around the room at the heads bent over small molecules.

"Sorry, I can't really handle the disorder of the box."

"As I said, OCD." He slides the box toward him.

I leave him to start building the first molecule while I write down the answers to the questions.

"Have you worked out number 2 part A yet?" I ask him.

He looks at me with a sarcastic expression on his face. His eyes are deep brown and his dark brown hair sweeps across his brow. There is about a week's worth of stubble shadowing his cheeks. I suddenly realize I'm just staring at him.

"I guess I'll take that as a no…" I quickly divert my attention back to the questions. I can feel the burn of a blush in my cheeks. What am I doing? Yes, James is attractive, but it's not like I'm ever going to want to date him. He's a guy, remember, Brie? Don't trust a guy. All they want is sex and that is the last thing that you want. I shake my head at my foolishness.

"It's chiral," he says, once again speaking through my thought stream.

"Huh?" I look up, trying to remember what was last said.

He gives a small laugh. One that makes my heart melt. Just a little.

"Question 2 part A…? It's chiral."

"Oh, okay. Thanks," I say, as my cheeks once again burn up in red.

He continues to chuckle to himself and we spend the rest of class talking intermittently while I try to keep my focus away from him and on my work. It's a strange relief to be trying to avoid thinking about something so… normal. Boy issues. How I wish they were the entirety of my issues. But I relish these seemingly mundane problems, where I can pretend at least that my life is normal. For now, anyway.

I pull my car onto the driveway outside my house. I turn the ignition off and release the breath I didn't realize I was holding. A small smile plays at the corners of my mouth as I think about James. Somehow it makes me feel a little lighter and happier. Today had been good. I'd only cut once today. One cut a day wasn't a bad thing. No one would ever notice and it would all be fine. Composing my face so that my mother wouldn't question me on my apparent girly happiness, I get out of my car, grab my bag and head toward the back door.

As I step into the kitchen I can smell ground beef and onions frying on the stovetop. The typical smell of my mother's famous pasta dish, usually only made when guests are coming. My slightly happy demeanour starts to ebb away at the thought of having to wear my mask in front of our guests for several more hours. All I want to do is crawl up in my room and bury myself in a book and pretend that this world doesn't exist.

"Are we having guests over or something?" I ask my mother, who is standing measuring out the pasta into a jug.

"Yeah, a load of the family is coming over."

"How many?"

"Well, there will be eleven of us, in all," she replies.

I rattle off my brother's family, with his two boys and my sister's family with her daughter.

"Who's the extra person? I can only count ten of us."

"Well, Ted is coming too, since his household is away for a few days. I'm sure he'll enjoy being cooked for," she tells me.

But I'm not listening anymore. My muscles are frozen in shock. The breath in my lungs seems to have vanished. My mother notices none of this as she has her back turned toward me, beginning to fish out pots and pans. Thoughts of James are quickly replaced by flashes of Ted's face with his smile plastered across it. 'It will be okay, he's not going to hurt you...' I try to soothe myself silently. 'It will be okay.'

My brother and his family arrive first. I love my brother. We don't talk much. We don't even interact much. But he's fun and always has a way of putting a smile on my face. He's really just a big kid, even though he's nineteen years older than I am.

My sister, her husband and their daughter arrive next. Of course, to my mother, I am nothing compared to my perfect sister. She's in her forties and was already married by the time I was born, so she is more like an aunt to me. However, she treats me more like I'm her daughter than her little sister. I often feel that my mother compares me to my sister. 'Your sister didn't get quite as big as you at this age,' she would say. 'She is great with children; why don't you like them?' Somehow no matter what I do, she does it better. She's bubbly, happy and talkative to everyone. She lives as if nothing ever happened to her, even though I know it did. We have the same dad, after all. I can tell she hides secrets behind her constant smile, but like everything in my family, it's a taboo. We never talk about it. We never even mention the word 'dad'.

We sit around the living room chatting. The conversation isn't interesting enough to hold my attention. I'm focused on the clock. 'Maybe Ted decided not to come,' I think. I hope.

Twenty minutes pass by and my mother calls us up to the table for dinner. We all begin to maneuverer our way around the very close-packed table settings.

As I'm heading to the far end of the table I hear the dreaded sound of the back door swinging open and my mother saying, "Oh, Ted! I'm so glad you could make it. You're just in time, come sit down."

She appears in the doorway with Ted close on her heels. I look down and find a seat in the corner of the room.

"Why don't you go squeeze down there next to Brielle?" she says to Ted.

My heart stops beating. I take a quick glance upward to try and judge his mood tonight. He catches my eye and slowly smiles at me, sending a shudder up my spine.

"Cold?" he asks, as he takes the seat next to me and slyly puts his hand on my thigh.

I stare straight ahead, smile fixed in place. Trying desperately to ignore his hand on my upper leg.

Dinner passes by like molasses. I nibble away at the little helping of pasta I took. Taking many small bites makes it seem I'm eating more than I am and helps avoid any questions. I begin to panic with Ted so close to me, fearing what is to come.

"I talked with Laurie today." My mother says. My ears perk up at the mention of my cousin who lives in Wisconsin. "She and Marshall are wishing they had enough money saved up to come and visit us. But with Alex and Lynn still in school and college, it's not going to work out for a while."

"That's too bad," my sister says, "I was hoping we would see them soon. It's been a long time. I rather miss them."

"Yeah me too. How's the rest of the family over there? Didn't I hear that Andrew is joining the Army?"

Andrew is another of my cousins. When I was growing up in New Hampshire, we would spend most summers over in Wisconsin.

They ended up being like my brothers and sisters. I miss them so much. I try to visit them as often as I can, but it's not enough.

"Air Force." My mother corrects my brother.

Ted's hand squeezes my leg again, reminding me of the reality that I'm in. Just as I think I'm going to lose control right here at the dining room table, my mother directs everyone to the living room and she starts to prepare dessert. This is the time I can excuse myself momentarily. I make a beeline for the stairs and run up, desperate for a chance to be away from him. I go into the bathroom and shut the door, locking it behind me.

I stand with my back pressed against the door, taking in shaky, slow breaths in an attempt to calm myself down. A sharp knock on my door and I jump a foot into the air, my pulse racing.

"Just a minute!" I call out, wishing there was more than one bathroom, especially when we have this many people over.

Another sharp knock. I flush the unused toilet and wash my hands. I unlock the door and whip it open saying: "Alright, alright it's all yo—"

Standing in front of me, leaning on the doorframe, is Ted's large frame. Without another sound from me, he firmly grips my left arm and pushes me back into the bathroom. He shuts the door with a metallic 'click'.

I stand at the side of the bathtub trying to squeeze the bubble bath out of its bottle with my little hands. The bathroom door suddenly opens and my father stands in the doorway. Fear shoots through me and I drop the bottle in the bath. He shuts the door behind him with a 'click' and walks toward me...

Ted's face swims into vision. I'm back in England, but still in my nightmare. I try and gulp down my fear. But it just moves into my hands and legs causing them to tremble uncontrollably. His hand remains firmly gripped on my upper arm. He leans his face inches away from mine.

The smell of cigarette smoke lingers heavy on his breath. A slow smile spreads across his lips, showing his slightly yellowing teeth. A deep laugh emits from him, sending fear shooting down my spine. My trembling stops as I prepare for what is about to happen. He draws the hand not gripping my arm back and I tense my stomach, knowing that it is the most likely place he will aim tonight. As his hand propels forwards I tightly shut my eyes and try to escape what is happening. But, instead of the instantaneous blow I'm expecting, nothing happens. I look down. His fist is a hairs' breadth away from my stomach. He continues to stare at me and begins to laugh even harder now.

"You're not scared, are you?" he says sarcastically.

I say nothing. After several seconds he releases his grip on my arm and I mechanically move out of the bathroom and down the stairs. Fixing my smile in place as if nothing had happened, I join the rest of my family in the conversation about the concert being performed in our church in a few weeks' time. Ted joins us after several minutes and he also pretends that nothing happened. Nothing really did, I guess, although my left arm is sore and I know bruises will appear by tomorrow. But it's not that bad. He didn't really hurt me.

Ted has always been so good at pretending that nothing happened that I often question whether it really did. Maybe I have some sick twisted mind that fantasizes about these things? Or maybe I just think that what he does hurts more than it should? Maybe I'm just weak? Maybe I just bruise easily? Maybe my mom's right and Ted doesn't know his own strength? As I sit there listening to my family chatter away I'm lost in thought about the time, almost four years ago, I almost broke my rule and told someone about Ted...

...My mother was working late that day and she told me to go to Ted's after school so that I wouldn't be home alone. I went, and as usual, he was in the mood to hit me more than touch me. He hit my leg so hard that tears had pricked my eyes, even though I never cry. I was so thankful to hear the car horn outside, indicating my mother had arrived to rescue me from Ted's anger. I got in the car and my mother could see the tears in my eyes.

"What's wrong?" she asked.

I shook my head. I didn't want to tell her. But something stirred in me and instead of saying 'nothing' I found the courage from somewhere. And, ignoring my dad's advice from years ago, I said, "Ted hit my leg. And now I've got a bruise the shape of a hand print."

"Oh! Ted probably didn't mean it. He doesn't know his own strength. You bruise really easily too, remember?" She smiled at me and pulled off toward home.

Anger burned inside me. How could I have been so stupid to think that she would believe me? But what made it worse than her not believing me was that she defended him!

But isn't that what I always do? Defend him? Tell myself that he doesn't really mean it? Or that what he does to me is just normal interactions between family members? Somehow I cast aside the negative thoughts about this all being wrong, because if I thought it was, I don't think I could survive...

...Remembering this, I know that I can't ever tell my mother, much less anyone else. I do bruise easily. It really is nothing. Nothing ever happened.

Chapter 6

Laughter. There are many different types of laughter. They say laughter is good for the soul. But sometimes it is just a cover for a much greater pain beneath the surface.

"Brielle!"

A distant voice calling my name resonates over the most beautiful chord I was holding onto. I take my hands off the piano and look around. There better be a good reason for this disturbance, I think, as I get up and head toward the voice.

"Brielle," my mother says, coming halfway down the stairs with papers in her hand. "What are these?"

I take a closer look at the papers and stop dead in my tracks. In her hands she holds several pages that Corwin printed out for me about sexual abuse. He thought that it would help me to see that my reactions are totally normal. I had taken one look at them and, realizing that I had all of the symptoms, shoved them under my mattress. They don't allow me to live in denial. I hadn't thought about them again. Now here they are in my mother's hands. She's looking at me. I'm lost for words.

"You think you've been abused?" she asks sarcastically.

When I say nothing, she laughs. Her laugh pierces my heart. Even if I were brave enough to tell her, she wouldn't believe me. I shake myself out of my trance and quickly respond, grabbing the papers out of her hand.

"Of course not! They were... Corwin gave them to me to read, he wanted some help on his psychology essay."

I brush past her and run upstairs to change. I need to get out of here before I break down. I quickly dress, grabbing my razor and my car keys as I rush out the back door before my mother can say a word. I hear her call something at me as I close the gate, but it's too late, I don't want to hear anything she has to say right now.

I hastily get in my car and drive off without doing up my seatbelt. My mind is whirring and I can't seem to think straight. I drive toward the countryside where I hope the open space will help clear my head.

A few minutes later I arrive at an area at the side of the road where you are able to park your car while you walk on the nearby trails. I can feel flashbacks on the threshold of my consciousness.

I glance around at my surroundings. In front of me there is a large hill covered with pine trees and I can just about make out the blue triangle on a wooden post near the edge of the forest indicating a public footpath. To my right and left are miles of fields with small towns scattered on the edge. It's no New Hampshire, but it will do for now.

The afternoon sun is high above me as I step out of my car. I turn and lock it, even though there seems to be no sign of human life around for miles. A sudden wave of emotion washes over me, forcing me to lean against my car to stay upright. How could she laugh? Maybe she knows how ridiculous and unbelievable it all sounds. It is unbelievable. Hence it probably didn't happen. But even as I think this, the darkness wins and I'm pulled into my past...

I stand on my tip toes looking out of the window at my mom hanging the washing between the trees in the side yard. The bathroom door opens and I continue to look out the window, pretending I didn't notice. Maybe he doesn't want anything, I foolishly hope. I can smell the wood of the windowsill and I concentrate on the pine scent as my father comes behind me...

I blink away the dryness in my contacts as I take in my surroundings. I'm back in the English countryside but the scent of pine still hangs heavy in the air, making me feel sick to my stomach.

33

I shove my hands into my pockets and feel around for the cool metal blade. Finding it, and just holding it in my fingertips, I feel a sudden break in the pain. I decide to hold off the inevitable a little longer and head toward the woodland trail, counting my steps as I go.

The sound of leaves crunching beneath my feet is a comforting sound. It reminds me of my wanders into the woods of New Hampshire on my way to my place where I could escape the reality of home. I place my hands on the rough bark of the trees, smiling to myself as I think back to when I used to call them 'tree wrinkles.'

But suddenly, a wave of rage sweeps through me. How could I let this happen? How could I let myself be taken away from my forest, my safety, my home? If I hadn't asked to stay here, I would have been fine. More than fine. I was happy. Just me, my mother and my forest. Instead, I was plunged into my nightmares once more. Just a different person in a different place. The same me. Why did I let this happen to me? Why didn't I fight? And if I didn't fight, why not tell someone? I'm so stupid. A stupid slut. I look around the forest I'm in. This is not my forest.

"I hate this country!" I scream into the trees. But no one hears me.

Chapter 7

Masquerade. A ball where everyone dresses up with a mask to cover their face, their identity. In reality, we all live a masquerade. Each of us wears a mask to cover up our true feelings, our wounds, our desires. We try to hide who we really are. We try to be someone we are not.

I step out of the third floor bathroom outside the chemistry classrooms into a busy hallway. I cradle my freshly cut arm to my stomach and smile to myself. See! I can control the pain. I am in control. Taking a deep breath, I head toward the cafeteria, telling myself that I can control myself further and not eat too. As I round the corner I hear my name being called.

"Brie!"

I turn to see a tall and slender girl in a brightly colored dress practically skipping her way toward me. Her face beams with joy. I force myself to smile back at her and drop my cradled arm to my side.

"Hey up, me duck!" Amanda says in her thick British accent. "I'm on my way to the Christian Union meeting, you coming?"

"Umm, actually, I was just heading down to get something to eat."

"I've brought loads of food, you can share. Really, I insist!"

"Uh–"

"Cool, let's go." She decisively links her arm around mine and pulls me off toward the room where the weekly CU meetings are held.

A tremble of panic stirs inside me. How can I go in there and face all of those Christians? They think I am one, but I'm way too messed up to be a Christian. If they all knew the truth, they would kick me out in five seconds flat.

I look around for an empty chair in the corner of the room where I will be hidden the most. About forty people fill the room. Most of them are passionate about God. My heart suddenly swells with emotion as I look around at each of them. I can't believe how many young people there are just in this room who have fully devoted their lives to Christ. I was raised to believe that there were very few Christians, much less young Christians. I begin to inwardly praise and thank God for bringing these people into my life, but suddenly remember He doesn't care. I'm too broken. Useless. Dirty. Pushing these thoughts aside, I beeline for a seat in the very back corner of the room as people begin to take their seats.

Today's speakers are Jo and Joe. Both of them are hilarious and have no trouble holding an audience's attention. I feel a pang of jealousy for how easygoing they are. Across the room I spot Corwin. He sits deep in thought. Thankfully, I don't think he's spotted me. Of all the people in this room, he is the only one who knows what an imposter I am here.

As the talk continues, I struggle to remain focused. I'm trying to remain 'present' in the room and not have flashbacks of my past, which seem to come much more readily when I'm in emotional distress. To keep my mind occupied I begin to name all of the objects in the room. Door. Table. Box. Pencil. Chalk board. Light. Plug socket. Window. Blinds. This method of keeping my mind occupied is surprisingly efficient and the talk is over before I know it.

Jo closes the talk by putting on a song from YouTube. The song is called *All who are Thirsty*. The music begins and I start to name some more objects in the room until the second line stops me.

"All who are weak."

Weak? Christians aren't weak. They are strong in God. They aren't broken. I look at the screen that is showing the words, thinking I must have misheard. I hadn't. I frown as I try to wrap my head around the lyrics of the song.

"...Let the pain and the sorrow, be washed away..."

I suddenly can't breathe. This song is talking about me. I'm weak and pathetic and there is so much pain and sorrow in my life I feel like at any second I'm going to just break apart and no one, not even God, will be able to put me back together. How can this song sing about all that just being 'washed away?' I shake my head and try to block out the words. They can't be true. God can't care about me because if He did… well, I believe God is never changing, so if He cares about me now, then He cared about me back when I was little, back when–

'Don't think about it, Brie!' A small shudder escapes me as the song comes to a close and the sound of shuffling chairs and feet fill the room. I jump out of my seat and make a dash for the door before anyone can stop me.

I emerge into the hallway and stand in confusion. I just have to get out. I finally get my bearings and head down the hall toward the side entrance of the school that leads to my hill. I am practically running as I reach the top. My gaze sweeps across the field in front of me. Everything seems dull and gray and lifeless. Not unusual for June in England. My head is spinning. I just stand there. Suddenly my mind latches onto one train of thought. If God cared about me when my father did those things to me… then why didn't He stop him?

"Where were You?" I cry out.

"Brie?"

I whip around and see Corwin about ten feet away from me with his hands in his pockets and concern etched on his features. Drops of water roll from his hair onto his face. Why is he wet?

"Brie, why are you out here in the rain?" he asks.

Rain? I concentrate on the feel of the exposed skin on my face and begin to feel the pitter patter of raindrops hitting my cheeks. A puzzled look darts across my face.

"I–I didn't realize it was raining," I reply truthfully.

"Are you okay?"

"I was just in that CU meeting."

"I know, I saw you."

I look at him, trying to find the look of judgment for my

participation in the Christian meeting. Instead I find an expression of compassion. How can he not judge me? How can he still be here for me? Look at me, I'm a mess!

I simply nod.

"You looked confused in there. Why?"

"Because... the last song played implied that God cares for those who are weak and messed up. And I realized if God cares about me now, then God cared about me then and... and I don't like that."

Corwin nods as if he understands.

"You don't know why God let it happen to you?"

I slowly nod.

"Brie..." His voice breaks with the sound of pain and I don't understand what I did. "God never desired for those things to happen to you. But that doesn't mean He wasn't there. It doesn't mean He didn't, doesn't, care deeply for you. He loves you, Brie. More than you can imagine."

The sting of tears prick my eyes and I'm suddenly thankful that it's pouring with rain. Is what he says true? Does God really love me? Broken and messed-up me?

Chapter 8

A lie. At first it doesn't seem so bad. A lie here and a lie there. You justify it because it's to protect other people. After a long time of lying you begin to believe it as truth. Lying becomes the only way you can survive. Nothing ever happened.

I must stay awake. It's 4:30 am and the idea of going back to sleep, back into my nightmares is enough to send shivers up my spine. I consider going to play the piano, but instead choose to go look for a book to read thinking it can help me escape my reality.

I silently slip out of my room to the end of the hallway into the spare bedroom. It's a small room where we store things that don't really have any other place to go. To my left, a closet full of Charlie's suits; to my right, two bookshelves with books, papers and boxes of photographs. In front of me is a window with blinds half open, allowing the orange glow from the streetlight outside to cast eerie shadows through the room. I move forward and fumble around the lamp until I find the switch, then light illuminates the bookshelves.

I let my eyes roam over the book titles, searching for one that piques my interest. As I search, the writing on an envelope in a stack of paperwork at the bottom shelf catches my eye. *Police Documents.* I kneel down on the floor and remove the envelope from the shelf. It's white with green trimming. Judging by the weight of it, there are a lot of documents inside. I turn over the envelope and open the unsealed flap. I pull out a wad of papers and place the envelope to the side. The top document is titled *Police Report.*

I frown in confusion. Police report? Is there something about Charlie I don't know? Then two words catch my eye: *sexual abuse.* I feel as if my heart has skipped a beat. My eyes race around the words trying to place them into context.

"She is very quiet and denies any sexual abuse."

I'm suddenly reminded of a day from ten years ago. The day I first decided to lie...

...I stood on my blue steppy-stool leaning over the sink whilst brushing my teeth. My mother entered the bathroom and walked toward me. I spat the toothpaste into the sink, placed my toothbrush back into its cup and stepped down from my stool. My mother was rummaging through the closet until she produced the comb she was looking for.

My heart dropped a little. Combing through my snarly hair was a painful process.

I turned around so she could reach my hair more easily, but instead of beginning the painful act she began to talk to me.

"I want to ask you something," she said.

I turned toward her. I could see the redness surrounding her eyes. They remained wet, a telltale sign that she'd been crying again. I didn't understand why she was so upset. Dad had left about two months before. I couldn't have been happier, but she had become so sad. I'd been trying to cheer her up, reading Bible verses to her from my kid's Bible. I'd been keeping my room really tidy too. But nothing seemed to help.

"I need you to be really honest, okay?" she continued.

Honest. I didn't really know what that word meant but I nodded my head anyway.

"Has anyone ever touched you where they shouldn't?"

I wasn't sure what she meant. She must have seen my blank look because she went onto explain: "I mean, has anyone ever touched you in your private parts. You know, down between your legs?"

My mind recalled all the past times my dad had done just that. Was that wrong? It had hurt, but so did my mother combing my hair.

Were things that hurt me wrong? I suddenly became very scared.

I was going to be in big trouble. I recalled my dad telling me that if I told Mom she would be upset. She was already upset; I didn't want to make it worse. So, I shook my head.

The relief that flooded my mother's face told me I had done the right thing, but it quickly faded away and she looked at me seriously once more.

"You're sure?"

I nodded.

"Okay, you have to tell me if anyone ever does. You shouldn't let people touch your private area, you know that, right?"

I once again nodded.

"Okay, now turn around so I can comb your hair."

I gritted my teeth in preparation for the pain. I now knew the correct answer to the question and it didn't take long until there were more people than just my mother asking me the very same thing.

One week later the police stopped by and sat me at the dining room table along with my mother. The police officer started by talking to her while I focused on the floral pattern of the seat cushion. I didn't like the police coming here and asking all kinds of questions. I wished they would leave us alone. Unfortunately, that night they weren't just going to talk to my mother. The police officer turned to me. I continued to stare at the cushion.

"Has anyone ever touched you inappropriately?" he asked.

I didn't know what inappropriately meant, but I assumed he meant what my mother meant. I shook my head. My mother looked pleased with this. The police officer just nodded. I think I got the question right again.

One week later, the police were back. A woman this time, but the question was the same. And so was my answer.

When the lawyers and the psychologists started asking me similar questions I knew what the right answer was. Even when they showed me pictures of naked people (they didn't look quite the same as my dad) I knew I shouldn't have seen it before so once again I tried to say the right answer. Most of the time I tried to say I didn't want to talk about it. This response seemed reasonable enough to them and they didn't push the issue.

My favorite psychologist was named Judith. She never made me talk about my dad. Instead we always played snakes and ladders.

Eventually the questions stopped and I felt as though I had done well on the test. To make sure I didn't ever mess up I began to repeat to myself over and over again that nothing ever happened. Nothing ever happened...

...I continue to stare at the document. My hands are shaking. I try to push down the fear that is rising up within me. I turn over the page and continue to scan the document.

"He admits to two counts of sexual contact with Brielle." No... Oh, God. No. This can't be. *"One when Brielle was six months of age. He admits to placing his penis to her lips to check her sucking reflex. The second when she was two years old, he admits to touching her clitoris to see if it produced a reaction."*

My mind races. I stop breathing and the room begins to spin. No. This can't be true. I focus on the paper, reading and rereading the lines. I must have read it wrong. It's not true. It can't be.

"Brielle seems intelligent but withdrawn. She denies any further acts of sexual contact with her father."

They knew. My mother knew. My dad admitted to it. No. Please... no. I can't remember these acts. Six months old. Two years old. No! With my shaking hands I jam the papers back into the white and green envelope and shove it back onto the bookshelf. It's not true. It can't be. How can I deny my memories when my father himself admitted to it? Maybe he was lying... but why lie about something like that? I can't hold down the panic any longer. I silently retreat to my room to clear my head with a blade.

The rest of the day seems to pass in a blur. People talk at me, but I can't hear them above the screaming in my head. It was real. The abuse was real. I wasn't just imagining it. My father admitted to it.

Given, he didn't admit to everything, but why admit to anything? No! Brie, it didn't happen. Your father was obviously crazy; he admitted those things, but they weren't true. It wasn't true. It's okay. It's all a lie. Nobody hurt you. And yet my mother acts as if she doesn't know anything, laughing at even the suggestion of such a thing. Is she in denial?

A piece of paper suddenly fills my vision. I snap out of my train of thought. My biology teacher, Miss Shaw, is handing out today's notes on the synaptic cleft and how neurons transmit electrical signals through the body. It's actually one of my favorite parts of biology, the cell, so intricately designed. I don't see how people can't see God in that.

"Are you okay, Brielle?" Miss Shaw asks me. "You seem a little out of it."

You could say that again, I think.

"Oh, I'm fine." Lie. "I just didn't get much sleep last night." Actually true.

"What do you think, Brie?" Iva, my biology lab partner asks me.

"What do I think about what?" I ask.

"Are you sure you're alright? You keep spacing out."

"Yeah, yeah. I'm fine. Really, I just didn't get enough sleep," I say again and fake a yawn to emphasize my point. Gee... what was with people today being extra observant of my lack of focus?

"Stress? I'm totally stressed out these days too. Our final exams are in, like, two weeks and I have to get straight A's in all my classes to get into my first-choice university."

"Ach. Thanks a lot for the reminder," I say, my tone dripping with sarcasm. It's unusual for me to not be fretting about exams, especially when they're this close. But with everything going on in my head, exams seem to be the least of my worries. I also need to get straight A's to get into my first-choice university, Northern. In fact, for me a B is a fail. And for my mother, anything less than top of the class is a fail.

I remember when I received my English grades after my final exams in 11th grade. I had gotten an A in English literature and a B in English language. I was so excited about getting an A in literature because I'm truly awful at English, so an A was nothing short of a miracle. I got home and showed my mother my grades, the rest of which were mainly A's and A★'s, and I pointed out my A in English literature.

"See that, Mom! An A. In English!" I beamed at her. She continued to look at the paper.

"What happened here?" She asked pointing at the B under English language.

"Mom, I got an A in lit."

"So why didn't you do better in language? Did you just not study hard enough for the test or what?"

She was never satisfied. If I wasn't the best, I wasn't good enough…

"Which university did you put as your first choice again?" Iva once again interrupts my thoughts.

"Ummm…" I try to make sense of the bit of the sentence I heard. First choice? Oh, university. "Northern."

"I've heard that's a pretty good university."

"Yeah, not bad."

"Aren't you going to do chemistry there and isn't it, like, ranked third in the country for that or something, only after Oxford and Cambridge."

"Something like that." In fact, she was exactly right. Northern University was very highly ranked for chemistry. But it wasn't really the university I wanted to go to. Corwin was going to Sheffield, along with some of my other friends. I loved Sheffield as a city and their chemistry department seemed really good. I would have put that down as my first choice, but I had been praying about where I should go to university for a long time and I don't know why, but I felt like God was telling me to go to Northern, just as He told me to go to this school. I know it sounds crazy. And I can't even explain how He told me, or why He would talk to me. I just know. This school has been amazing; I've made such good friends, most of them Christian. I'm sure God has plans for me at Northern.

'What are you thinking, Brielle? Why would God have plans for you, you little dirty slut? All you do is lie and God hates liars! God wants nothing to do with you!'

I let out a sigh. I hate myself so much.

"I know... stressful time of year!" Iva says, and I'm thankful she can't hear my internal screaming.

I walk into my green and cream living room, rolling my eyes inwardly. Of course it's green and cream – every room in the house, save my own, is green and cream. The only two colors my parents can agree on. This sort of childish behavior really annoys me sometimes. But I'm past caring about their marriage these days. When they first married, they argued all the time and I was sure they would get divorced quickly. Some nights my mother would get so mad that she would storm out of the house and drive off into the night, leaving me in the house with Charlie whom I barely spoke two words a day to. I would be terrified of her never coming home. But she always did. And they never got divorced, although sometimes I still think they should have never married in the first place. Maybe then I wouldn't be stuck in this ridiculous country.

"How are you?" My mother is sitting in her armchair with her crossword puzzle book on her lap.

How do you think I am? Words written on the documents flash through my mind. She knew. All this time she knew. Can someone just forget that sort of thing? Perhaps she believed me when I said nothing happened. Perhaps that's what she wanted to believe. It was easier than believing her husband was doing such things to his little girl.

"I'm fine," I say, not letting myself speak more in case it all spills out.

"Are you sure, you seem sad?"

Now you care? Now? Anger boils up inside my chest and I struggle to keep my mouth from screaming at her.

"I'm fine," I calmly say, while trying to change the subject so I can prevent myself from exploding. "Just thinking about going to Northern. I really don't want to go, I mean Corwin and everyone seem to be going to Sheffield. But... I feel like this is where God wants me to go." Again I'm filled with a sense of knowing I was right but with a hint of doubt as to why God would be leading *me*.

"Well, I was actually praying about this during my quiet time this morning."

Every morning she studies the Bible along with about fifty different devotionals whilst chomping, very loudly, at her cereal. Maybe it just sounds loud to my very empty stomach.

"I was praying about you going away to university next year and where God wanted you to go. I felt like I got two words from Him: cathedral and city. I had no idea what that meant. I talked to Charlie about it at lunch."

Where *was* Charlie? I was suddenly distracted by his absence.

"...Northern! Crazy, isn't it? I had no idea that that was what Northern is known as. That has got to be God, don't you think?"

What? I think I missed something. "Huh?" is all I manage to get out.

"Northern is also known as Cathedral City."

I look at her in surprise. I feel blown away, suddenly realizing that it wasn't just my imagination, but that God really was directing me. As the shock wears off, I am filled with an overwhelming sense of God's love. Corwin's words slowly filled my mind. Maybe he was right. But the information on the documents upstairs is not far behind. If God cared, where was He then? I stopped that train of thought in its tracks before I could show any sort of emotion in front of my mother.

"Cool. I've got to do some homework." I begin to head up the stairs, but halfway up I remember Charlie. "Where's Charlie?"

"Oh, he's working out of town for a few days, so it's just you and me."

Great... "Oh," I say, and continue to retreat to my room, leaving my mother with her crosswords.

With the door securely shut and my closets checked for people, I sit down on my floor. I have so many thoughts tangled in my mind that I can't seem to find a way toward understanding what I am thinking. Panic sets in and I crawl over to the drawer where I hide my blades. As I reach out for the drawer handle I feel a twinge of guilt. Maybe I shouldn't do this. But it's okay, right? I'm not hurting anyone else; no one's going to care.

Again, a feeling of guilt pinches the back of my mind as I think about God directing me to Northern. No, God can't care about me. I pull open the drawer and slide my hand down the side of it until I find the little piece of paper that wraps around my blade. I unfold the paper and hold the cool metal in my fingertips, but instead of quickly bringing relief to the panic that is beginning to overwhelm my mind, I just stare at the blade. I am mesmerized by the way the light bounces off it in several different angles. Frustrated by this momentary distraction, I rewrap it and put it back safely into the drawer.

Spotting my journal, I take it out. I haven't written in it for a while, but I maybe I can write the thoughts that seem so stuck inside my head. It has worked in the past. I grab a pen and settle myself on the floor, leaning against my bed. It would be much more comfortable on top of my bed, but I try to be in my bed for as little time as possible. Focus, Brie.

I open the journal to a clean page. Pen in hand, I pause. What do I write? The date. That would be good. I glide my hand to the right-hand corner: June 3rd. Okay... now what? Write Brie. Just write.

Chapter 9

Denial. You close your eyes and tell yourself over and over again that nothing happened. Nothing ever happened. Your memories are lies. Denial implies you refuse to believe the truth. But what if it's not denial, what if nothing really ever did happen?

Fourteen, fifteen, sixteen, seventeen—

"Brie?"

I feel my whole body tense and jump as I gasp.

"Brie?"

I look around, trying to get my bearings.

"It's okay, Brie. You're at the bus stop. You're okay."

I nod. I realize I'm sitting on a bench outside the Jerusalem pub. Corwin is sitting next to me. He turns his head away from me and looks toward the fence across the parking lot. I can see his mouth moving slightly.

"Are you saying something?" I ask him.

"I was praying."

"Oh. I thought I'd lost my hearing or something!" I try to make light of the situation.

"You don't have to pretend, Brie. I can tell you're hurting."

"No, I'm not," I respond quickly.

"I know we haven't talked much about it all. I haven't wanted to push you. I've been trying to give you space. But I think you need to talk about it. And I want you to know I'm here to listen."

"I don't know what you're talking about." I knew exactly what he was talking about. Pain is searing through my mind and I want to close my ears, my eyes, everything, just to shut it out. Nothing happened.

Corwin emits a sigh and places his elbows on his lap and looks out toward the road for a few seconds before taking a deep breath and turning toward me.

"Yes you do, Brie. I understand why you don't want it to be true. Denial is a typical reaction for this."

"No, it's not. How would you know?" I say, more angrily than I intended. Here I was trying to convince him that nothing happened and he uses that to turn it around as more proof that it did.

"I've been talking to my mum."

My eyes widen in fear. People can't know this. What if they tell someone? What if my mother finds out?

Seeing the fear plastered across my face, Corwin hurries on.

"I didn't tell her *who* I was talking about, I was just saying I had a friend… She works with this kind of thing in the community groups she runs from our church. I just wanted some advice. I'm finding it hard to know what to say or do."

Huh… I never thought about it being hard for him.

"I'm sorry. I have been really selfish about all this. I didn't think about how you're feeling, I shouldn't ha—"

"Brie. That's not what I meant. I'm fine. I want to help you and I don't know how. I care about you."

I flinch at his words.

"I don't want you to," I say quietly.

"I know. I know. It scares you. The people in your life who have supposedly cared about you have let you down or hurt you. But I don't want to hurt you Brie. I want to help you. I appreciate that you're not going to understand that yet. But one day you will. Brie, please let me help you."

I just sit, shaking my head.

"I can't. I can't. Nothing ever happened—"

"Yes it did, Brie."

"No. Stop. Please. Nothing ever happened. Please!"

"Brie. Yes, it did. And it was horrific."

My hands are shaking so violently. I jump to my feet and place my hands over my ears. Shaking my head back and forth.

"No... no... no... please. Make it go away. Please..."

"Brie..." Corwin stands in front of me, trying to get me to look at him. "Brie, it's okay. It's okay."

"Nothing is okay, Corwin. I found police documents in my house. He admitted it. I didn't even remember those things. He admitted it!" I gasp for air. Panic pounds in my ears. I want to cut. I want to cut it all out, all the pain, all the dirtiness inside me. From the corner of my eye I see two more people from the 'bus stop crew' heading toward us. They call over to Corwin.

"Is Brie okay?"

"Yeah, she's okay," he responds.

They nod and keep their distance. Good. People shouldn't be near me. I am so disgusting. I had my father's penis in my mouth at the age of six months. I was born a slut.

"Who admitted what?" Corwin lowers his voice so as not to be overheard.

"My dad... he admitted things he did to me."

Corwin nods. I guess there really isn't anything to say. We stand outwardly in silence, but inwardly I feel like the world is crashing thunderously around me.

"I forgot something in my car, I'll be right back," I quickly say, as I hurry toward my car, swinging my book bag around carefully, so that no one would see me, I pull out my blade from the front pocket. Once on the other side of my car, where I'm blocked from people's vision, I quickly make two small cuts on my forearm, trying to place the cuts over past scars. The pain rips through me and casts aside all the painful memories and thoughts that were scattering across my mind. I take several deep breaths before opening the car and ducking inside to look as if I was trying to find something whilst pressing some tissues on my wounds.

I hear the rumble of the bus and I quickly shut the car door and lock it before jogging back to the others with a smile firmly in place and my arm carefully positioned against my side. Corwin looks at me with concern stamped across his features. I turn away. His care for me sends a fresh wave of pain through my mind. I take a deep breath and focus on the pain pulsing through my arm.

The bus rumbles behind me and I turn and follow others onboard. I choose my typical seat, facing backward next to the window, and I'm struck how it represents my life right now. I'm constantly looking back on my past. I have no hope for my future. I've turned my back on it. And deep inside me the seed planted weeks ago grows a little more.

"Corwin?"

He has taken the seat facing forward across from me. He turns to me in surprise. I guess I was silent for longer than I thought.

"I need to ask you to do something for me."

"What?"

I pause, trying to decide how to phrase what I'm about to say.

"If anything were to happen to me... I need you to take my journals. You have to take them. My mother can never find them."

"What do you mean?"

"Well, I've been writing in a journal more recently. But I've been writing things that she shouldn't know." Ever know.

"But why – what would happen to you that would make me need to get them?"

"You know... car accident or I get sick or something. Please, Corwin. Just promise you'll get them."

"Brie..."

"Please."

"I'm not promising. I think you need to tell your mother."

"What? No, no, no. I can *never* tell my mother."

Corwin remains silent and I decide to drop the subject before he gets mad at me.

"Are you hurting yourself, Brie?"

I control my facial expressions as cautiously as I can. I guess he isn't going to drop the subject.

"What makes you think that?"

"I know you, Brie."

Panic begins to rise and I focus on the dull ache now in my arm. He can't know me. If he did he wouldn't be sitting here talking to me. I turn away from his probing eyes and look at the houses blurring by the window. How do I answer him? Is it really that bad? I'm not hurting anyone else. Surely that's okay.

"Yes," I finally say.

The corners of his mouth pull down into a frown, but he recovers quickly and nods.

"I understand."

I feel as though my jaw would be on the floor if it were physically possible. I am in shock. I was expecting words of judgment, telling me how stupid I am or how attention seeking it is. But rather, he looks at me with... compassion. It's so much worse. I close my eyes to try and block it out.

"How can you understand?" I say, with my eyes still shut.

"You are in pain, it's obvious. And maybe you think it's the only way to express the pain. My mum said that self-harm and eating disorders are common among people who have been sexually abused."

Stab. Stab. Stab. Stab. His words hit me like a knife. No. My eating issues are nothing to do with anything. I was not sexually abused. I made it all up. I made it all up!

The bus pulls into the stop in front of the school. Rather than waiting for everyone else to get off first, I jump out of my seat, grab my bag and head toward the door before the bus has even completely stopped. Corwin isn't far behind me.

"Brie, you need to talk. Please."

"I have talked, Corwin. I asked you for a favor. I'm begging you. Please. Please take my journals. Please." I stop next to the entrance and turn to face him.

He looks at me doubtfully for several seconds.

"I can't promise, but if something happens... well, nothing *should* happen..."

"Gah… never mind," I say, as I turn and walk away from him. He doesn't follow me this time. He doesn't understand. I need to prepare. I know this now. Something *is* going to happen. Not now, but eventually. I can't survive.

Chapter 10

Choice. We all have it. Small choices are made daily, such as what sweatshirt we should wear today. Or what route we will take to get to our destination. These minor choices often don't have much impact on our lives. However, once in a while, one little choice, seemingly innocent and standard, can impact our lives forever.

Five o'clock. Late enough. I swing my legs out of bed and pad across my room to flick on the light. Last night my dreams were full of my dad and Ted, all taking place at Northern.

This week my thoughts were occupied with facts and figures needed to get me through my exams, which went okay so far. But every now and then I found myself mulling over whether I should even bother going to university. Thinking about the future is hard, when I don't even see myself getting there. What if God doesn't even really want me to go there? Every time I think this, the same uneasiness settles into my stomach. What do I do?

Maybe I should just end it all now. Guilt lays heavy on my shoulders at the thought. I can't do that to everyone. My friends, my family. But how can I keep going? I feel like my world is falling apart. I can't hold it all together. I can't.

As I think through the choices I have, I realize *I* can't hold it all together, but *God* can. Maybe, just maybe, I can get through this if I follow God and His plans for my life. What do I do? Go to Northern.

Just as soon as the thought enters my mind, I feel the weight of unease lift from deep within me. I *know* I am making the correct decision, although I don't know how I know. I just do. The relief I now feel from the making of that decision is instantaneously replaced with an intense hunger.

198 calories consumed yesterday. Pretty good, Brie, pretty good. Isn't it? Why do I do this? Control. I crave control. It's alright, isn't it? I'm not hurting anyone else. Just like my cutting. My stomach gives a little growl as if in response. I roll my eyes and head downstairs.

My mother is already up, sitting at the dining room table behind her mound of books and crunching away on the loudest cereal known to mankind. It is uncommon, but not unheard of, for her to be up at this hour. She doesn't sleep the greatest either. I wonder what her excuse is.

"Morning," I say, as I walk toward her.

A smile spreads across her mouth, which is currently full of cereal and milk. She gulps it down.

"Hi!" she says in drawn out surprise. "Are you going to join me for breakfast?"

I almost say no, but something nudges me inside. Probably my stomach. What if this is damaging me more than I know?

"Okay," I say. I can't believe I'm doing this. I go into the kitchen and pull out a cereal bowl for the first time in what seems forever. I grab a box of Cheerios and pour myself half a bowl before making my way back to the dining room.

I sit down across from my mother at the table. She moves her mound of books out of the way so she can see me. I grab the milk and pour just enough to make the cereal float. I pick up my spoon and dip it in, pulling out a small spoonful with five Cheerios. At this moment, they feel like the biggest Cheerios on earth. I stare at them as my mind screams at me: 'I hate you, Brie! You're so fat already. You can control yourself. Don't eat.' I close my eyes for a moment and try to silence the screaming.

Once again I'm reminded of Corwin's words. "God loves you, Brie." My eyes fling open and I shove the spoon in my mouth. The sweet taste of honey fills my mouth and I dip my spoon in for another bite.

I can feel my mother watching me. I look toward her. She is just smiling at me. I smile back as I plow my way through the cereal. After that small bowl of cereal my stomach feels as if it's going to explode, but the growling has stopped and somehow I'm proud of myself. I did it. I ate.

Today I made a choice. I made a choice to survive.

PART 2

Another wave slams me beneath the surface. The salty water burns my lungs and I breach the surface, gasping for air. I swim on. Keep going, Brie. Land is not much further now. Keep going. I move forward but suddenly another wave batters me underwater. My body is tossed around in the undercurrent like a rag doll. I try to swim toward the surface, but I no longer know where that is. The darkness has swallowed me. Not even the slightest glimmer of light directs my path. My legs kick and my arms thrash to no avail. I want to get out. I'm running out of air. Panic fills my mind and I stop flailing. 'I thought you were helping me, God! Where are you now? I want to get out. Please take me out of here. I can't go on.' The darkness is pressing on my mind, but suddenly I hear my name.

"Brielle! Brielle Joy!"

It is the sound of many people. Many voices chorusing together, cheering my name. Suddenly several hands plunge beneath the waves and pull me up to the water's surface. All around me are the familiar faces of my friends, beaming at me and calling out my name.

"You can do it, Brie!"

"Go Brielle!"

I take a deep refreshing breath of air and continue my swim toward shore.

Chapter 11

Hide and seek. Have you ever found such an amazing hiding place that, when you play hide and seek, no one ever finds you? Unfortunately, reality isn't like that. Somehow, at some point, it always finds you.

My feet pound the cobbles as I run. Flashes of my forest back in New Hampshire whip through my vision. Keep running, Brie. You're almost there. I try to push away the images that are invading my thoughts. Pound, pound, pound. The empty cobbled street resonates as I run past the bookstore, up the hill and toward The Green.

I emerge from the little side street onto a large expanse, which mainly consists of a large area of grass in the middle. I run up the side of the square with the castle on my right. Sounds spill out from the student bar. I turn the corner as I reach the old stone library. The cobbles have now turned to large slabs of concrete, but the clap of my feet hitting the ground continues to echo about the square. A small old-fashioned lamp lights the way as I head toward the cathedral. *Keep running, Brie.* I take a deep breath and focus on the pain that shoots down my arm. It is accompanied by a slow trickle of warmth making its way out of my freshly cut skin. My mind calms somewhat as I concentrate on that pain. The pounding stops as I run off the pavement and onto the grass. I slow down, allowing my breathing rate to ease. After taking ten long strides up a small grass hill I am standing in front of a long stone wall. *My* wall. A peaceful sensation sweeps through me as a gentle breeze sends loose curls around my face.

I step forward and place my hands on top of the wall. My breathing is shaky and I feel as though I'm going to collapse. I turn and allow myself to slide down the wall to the ground. Looking up, I see the cathedral that towers over me. Its gothic architecture is illuminated by lighting, casting it in an eerie glow. Suddenly the image of the cathedral is wiped from my vision and is replaced by images of my father...

"I found you," he tells me.

I hold back the whimper that threatens to escape from my throat. I thought that if I hid and he couldn't find me, all would be okay tonight. When I heard his truck come down the driveway, I decided on hiding beneath the table underneath the window in the living room. It had large leaves that hung on either side and would keep me out of sight. Or so I thought.

He had come in the back door and talked to my mother in the kitchen for a while. I stay as silent as I can, barely daring to breathe. I thought my plan was working until I hear him enter the living room. I watch as his feet walk directly toward where I sit, curled up beneath the table. He stops only two feet away and drops to his knees. His large hand reaches toward me and I pull back as far as I can. He grabs the bottom edge of the table leaf and pulls it up slightly with a high-pitched squeak. I can now see his eyes and they bore into mine. I look down. He found me.

My mind starts to pull away, leaving my body with my dad. Tonight, I am going to fly far above the forest. I am going to be free. I'm vaguely aware of being carried but I try to think of it as flying. My dad lays me on my bed but I imagine lying down on fluffy white clouds. Peace overcomes my mind as I drift through the pale blue sky...

A gentle hand on my shoulder tears through my memory. My whole body is shaking violently. I jerk my head upward and see a large figure towering over me. I duck my head instinctively.

"Brie?"

Relief fills my mind. The person is addressing me by the name of Brie and therefore must not be my Dad or Ted. The figure turns and slides down the wall next to me. From the light bouncing off the cathedral I can now see who it is. Peter.

We met about three weeks ago on my first day attending Northern University...

...I sit on the edge of my bed watching the clock tick by. My new room is large and there is a lot of empty space. The one big window casts shadows about the walls. The ceiling is high and the window is set with its sill at my shoulder's height. Outside the window I can see the battlements that line the castle walls. I stay as silent as I can, looking out of the window at the dawning sky, careful not to wake my roommate, Arin, who lies sound asleep in the bed across from me.

I arrived yesterday afternoon. My mother and Charlie dropped my stuff and me off and, rather reluctantly on my mother's part, left.

I couldn't sleep at all. Sleeping in a new place is always hard for me. But for some reason last night, I got flashback after flashback. I tried to blast music in my ears. I tried to count, to read. But nothing was working. I finally resorted to cutting. It was a habit I was trying to break. I would hate it if people started noticing the scars. I want to make a good impression here. I feel as though Northern is a fresh start for me. I am finally away from Ted. From home. From my past.

I look at my watch. It's now 7:30 am. Finally. Breakfast starts at 7:45 am and I'm sure being a little early won't hurt. I stand up and silently walk across the room and out the door, checking that I have my key before letting the door shut without a sound. I walk down the seventy-five stairs and out into the courtyard. The sun is just up, peeking over the walls of the castle that reach high around me on all sides. I breathe in the cool autumn air as I walk up the stone steps toward the Great Hall. The steps are worn; in fact, most of the castle is worn. But that's not surprising really. The castle was built in the eleventh century. I can't even begin to get my mind around the fact I'm living in a building that was built one thousand years ago... one thousand... nope, not even going to try.

I turn the corner to see the catering staff busying themselves about the kitchen, which, like most of this place, looks really old.

The only thing that reassures me that I've not just walked into the medieval era is that the kitchen is filled with stainless steel modern cookware. I see a small stand with breakfast items at the end of the serving area and I head over, grabbing a bowl and a spoon on my way. I must eat breakfast. I know that if I don't, I'm likely to not eat for the rest of the day.

Ever since I started eating again it has been hard to keep doing it. Every day is a challenge. A challenge I defeat every time I eat breakfast. After grabbing some cornflakes and a splash of milk, I head into the Great Hall.

Each time I step inside, it takes my breath away. I can't believe I live here. The ceiling is so high, I can't make out the detail of the wooden rafters. A stained-glass window rises dramatically at the end of the hall. Eight long tables fill the main floor, each surrounded by many deep red cushioned chairs. On the opposite side of the hall is a balcony that I've been told is a part of the library. Above the balcony are little suits of armor and weaponry hanging in neat rows. It is all so surreal.

The hall is currently empty but I hear the shuffling of feet and the murmur of voices coming from the entrance, so I'm sure others are on their way. Butterflies find their way into my stomach as I think about meeting new people. I must look normal. I set my friendly mask into place and take a seat on the nearest table, facing a huge fireplace that looks unused. Several minutes later two girls approach with cereal bowls in hand and set them across the table from me. I smile and say hi. They return the greeting and we sit in silence for several seconds, which feels like eternity when you have a butterfly farm in your stomach, before a guy walks by and joins us. He's tall, blond and blue-eyed. His smile is so genuine it reminds me of Corwin and I feel a twinge of homesickness, or 'friend-sickness' as I'd rather think of it. The tall guy sits on my right and I give him a smile. I try not to feel nervous. He's just a guy. He's not going to hurt me. I take a mouthful of my cereal. As I do so, I notice a small band on his wrist with the letters WWJD – What Would Jesus Do? My eyes light up and I turn to him.

"I've got a band like that," I tell him, pointing to his wrist. "I'm Brie," I add, realizing I haven't even introduced myself.

"Ah! Great! I thought it would be a good way of finding some other Christians here. I'm Peter," he smiles.

"Nice to meet you."

"So, I guess there are the usual three questions, one of which we've already gotten through," he chuckles softly. "I guess the next question is where are you from? It's obvious it's not anywhere close by, judging by your accent."

Hmmm... I was afraid of this. Once again the questions. I have an extremely strong American accent for someone who has lived in England *almost* half her life. But how do I explain this and not get into detail about the reasons behind moving?

"Well, as you might have guessed, I'm from America originally, but I moved over here a while ago when my mother married an English guy. Obviously, I haven't picked up the accent. What about you?" I am presuming he is from the south judging by his rather posh British accent.

"I see. Very interesting. I have grandparents from America! As for me, I live in Wales, and I'm similar in as much as I haven't picked up the strong Welsh accent. I'm originally from down in Bath."

Baaath. I supress a giggle.

"Very nice. So I guess the third question was going to be, what do you study?"

He nods. "Yep. I'm taking physics and maths. Yourself?"

"Chemistry and math. Core A?"

"Yeah! We'll be in some classes together, it seems." And he appears genuinely happy about this. He seems like a really nice guy. I chastise myself for getting too hopeful. People aren't going to like you, Brie. Just keep smiling and hope people don't hate you.

"I can't believe it's the first day. I arrived yesterday, on my birthday in fact."

"Oh, happy birthday!" I tell him. "It's my birthday today, believe it or not."

"Happy birthday! It seems we're birthday buddies."

I smile at the friend implication. Maybe...

...Peter now sits next to me, quietly speaking into the dark. He's praying. I close my eyes and rather than focus on the words I focus on the rhythmic sound of his hushed voice. The deep and rich tones are calming and I can feel the pain inside me draining away, leaving me emotionally exhausted.

"How long have you been with me?" I ask him while still staring at the cathedral.

"About fifteen minutes. You seemed to be in another world. Are you okay? I came to your room after you texted me, but you weren't there. I know you like this spot so I thought I'd try it and sure enough, here you are."

I nod, not really knowing what to say. I had texted him just before I cut, trying to distract myself. My call for help hadn't worked too well, but I am appreciating his presence now.

We continue to sit in silence for several more minutes until the cool night air starts to get to me and I realize my teeth are chattering pretty violently.

"I-I-I th-think we shhhould get going," I say. "Th-thank yooou s-s-so much for c-coming and s-sitting with me. I'm f-feeling much better now, b-but a little on the ch-chilly s-s-side." I laugh at myself and how ridiculous I must sound, talking between my chattering teeth.

Peter laughs kindly and nods at me in the knowing way that reminds me so much of Corwin. He stands and offers me a hand up, which I ignore as I push myself up from the cold, damp grass. We start heading back across The Green and toward the castle.

"I found out Arin is in our math classes," Peter tells me.

"I guess that's not surprising since we all do math," I say with a hint of sarcasm.

"How is it having a roommate?"

"It's good. Really good. But it's also weird since my siblings are so much older than me. I grew up as an only child so I never had to share things. But it's new and fun. And on top of that Arin is

64

great. It's super cool that we're both Christians and doing chemistry together."

"Is she in your room right now?"

"I don't know, she wasn't when I left, but that was a while ago."

We approach the castle gates, which are large black wooden doors with big bolts of iron across them. In the very bottom left hand corner is a small door cut out of the larger door, which remains open. Stepping through the little door brings us into the courtyard. Directly across from the gate is a roundish tower that sticks out farther than the rest of the castle. On the top of the tower is a clock that is illuminated by the upward yellow light. I don't know what it is with these old buildings and upward lighting, but it sure does give the buildings a creepy glow. Peter and I make our way over to the door tucked away a few steps to our right. I turn to bid him goodnight.

"Thank you again for coming to find me. I really appreciate it. I'm sorry," I say, embarrassed.

"No need to apologize, I'm happy to help in any way I can. I hope the rest of your night goes well. Sleep well, Brie."

Haha... I wish. "Thanks!" I say with a smile before turning around and hurrying up the stone staircase.

Chapter 12

Anger. Have you ever watched water boil? It starts off slow. The heat is full blast but nothing is visible on the surface. Then small bubbles begin to find their way to the surface. Finally, after some time, the surface is churning as the water boils and the steam rises. Anger can be well hidden with an outward appearance of calm; however, one day it will boil over. The question is: when?

The sound of a far-off alarm creeps slowly into my consciousness. I peel open my eyes and fumble around with my hand to stop the alarm from getting too loud. I raise my head a fraction or two and cast my eyes toward Arin's bed. I see the familiar human-shaped lump lying under a mountain of covers a few feet away. 'One, two, three...' I begin to count in my head, and just like clockwork, she begins to stir.

I close my eyes briefly and try not to think about the nightmares that plagued my night. I take a deep breath and try to cast them as far away as I can in my mind before putting my smile firmly in place and flinging off my covers. The cold morning air hits my bare legs and I quickly jump out of bed with the thought that if I get them moving the cold won't be so bad. Arin remains lying down, but I can tell by her breathing that she is awake.

"Morning!" I say, as cheerfully as I can. The slight husk in my morning voice causes it to come out much more whisper-like than I intended. Arin's face peers around from the side of the mountain she is lying under and she gives her usual 'morning sunshine' smile.

Her beautiful features are petite. In fact, the whole of her is petite. She's barely five foot two.

"Good morning!" she replies, much more exuberantly than me. She too pushes off her mound of covers and leaps out of bed. Her long golden hair swishes along after her as she bounds toward her towels that hang on the radiator beneath the window. I wait for her to grab her towel and leave the room for a shower before getting ready myself. We've been roommates for three weeks but I'm still not comfortable changing in front of her. I'm barely comfortable changing in front of myself. I spend as little time naked as I can. Flashes of Ted's grin as he looks at my naked body cause me to fall against the closet door.

"Get out of my head!" I cry out to the empty room. Get out, get out, *get out*! I look around for the bag that holds my razor. I don't have long until Arin gets back. I find a razor wrapped up in a little piece of paper, tucked away in the side pocket. Just holding it calms me, but not enough. Never enough. Two swipes across my arm and I've broken free from the darkness. For now. I hear the bathroom door slam shut down the hall. I quickly put my blade back in my bag, wrap a makeshift bandage around my fresh wounds and pull a sweatshirt over my head before Arin reappears in the room.

She smiles, but her smile quickly fades when she sees me. I'm suddenly aware of how much I'm shaking.

"Are you okay? You look really pale."

"Yeah, I'm fine. I've got problems with low blood pressure, is all. I'll be fine."

"You sure?"

"Yup!" I give her a smile.

"Okay..." She is unconvinced but seems to let it slide. "You coming to breakfast?" she asks as she puts away her shower gear.

"Yes, I'll see you down there, okay?"

"Alright!" She practically skips out the door.

I stand at the sink wishing I could be that happy. I shake myself. It's your own fault you're in this situation. You are just so stupid. First you let it all happen with your dad and Ted and now you are letting it all affect you!

I turn and see my reflection in the mirror that hangs on the wall above the sink. Bushy curls fall around my face. I look into my blue eyes with anger.

"I hate you, Brielle." I suppress the urge to pull the razor back out and tear myself to shreds. Maybe I shouldn't eat. I'm getting so fat. Another thing that is my fault. I shouldn't have started eating again in the first place. Anger. It wells up inside me and I feel as though I'm going to explode. I grit my teeth as I stand in the center of my room trying to decide how not to fall apart. I dig my nails into my hands and focus on the pain.

"Gah!" I growl and storm out of my room, screaming inwardly at myself with every step as I descend toward the courtyard. I walk across the courtyard and head up the stairs into the Great Hall. As I step across the threshold into the dining area I walk straight into Peter. I jump back in surprise. I was more in my own world than I realized. Peter has a grin on his face and I remember to smile.

"Ahoy, Brie!"

I give a little wave, not really sure what to say. What was with today and people being so… cheerful?

"Are you going to Castle CU tonight?"

"Oh… I totally forgot. Uh… Yeah? I guess so. Are you?"

"Yes. Should be good. See you later!" He grins at me as he heads out the door.

I take a deep breath. Great. The fresh cuts across my arm feel weighted with guilt. I know how much Peter and my other Christian friends in the Christian Union would disapprove of me and judge my coping mechanisms if they knew. Apprehension wells up inside me and I try to swallow it back. Thankfully, as I head toward the table that holds all the cereal, Arin comes up to me and starts rattling on about the lab class we have today. Her worries fill my mind, pushing out all of my own. I breathe a little easier, sitting down with her and digging into my cereal to discuss our 'plan of action' for when we get to lab.

I arrange to meet Arin on The Green in ten minutes, leaving me just enough time to run up to my room, grab my bag and brush my teeth before heading to the science building for another stressful day in the lab. As I think of the chemical reactions that will distract me from myself a smile spreads across my face. My schoolwork literally saves me from imploding. I look out on the day with a hint of hope. Maybe, just maybe, I can make it through another day.

The bells chime eight o'clock as I run across the courtyard. The sound of my heeled shoes on the stones echo around the walls. My black gown trails behind me in the wind, and I feel a little like Batman with a cloak. I also feel rather sick with myself after just eating at formal dinner, our university's bi-weekly tradition in which we have to dress up in dresses and black robes and be served our three-course meal by candlelight in the Great Hall. It's a strange but fun tradition, despite the extreme additions to my waistline in the process. But I have no time to let myself feel the full force of my self-hatred. I am heading down to the Norman Chapel for the CU meeting, as I told Peter I would. As I reach the other side of the courtyard I pull open the old wooden door and a wave of heat surrounds me as I step into the dark stone tunnel leading to the underground chapel. As I emerge into the room, I take in the scene. There are large round stone pillars with wooden benches between them. The stone is all a sandy color, illuminated by yellow lighting. Overall it gives a sense of peace and calm, just what I need right now.

On the benches sit eight people, several of whom have obviously just come from the formal dinner like me, evident by their black gown attire. I take a seat next to a girl called Liz, one of the leaders of the Castle CU. She smiles at me warmly and I try to make my smile look as genuine as possible. Rob, her husband and fellow CU leader, begins the meeting.

"Right guys. Tonight, we thought, as we still don't really know each other very well, we'd share our testimonies on how we became a Christian. This would be a great exercise for us to do because it not only encourages one another in the power of God, but also helps us be ready if others ask us how or why we are Christians. Testimonies are an important tool for spreading God's truth. We thought we'd split off into pairs and share."

I angle myself to face Liz. She smiles again and, seeing that I'm not about to talk, begins her testimony. Her voice is soft and her accent is blatantly from the south of Britain.

"Well, I grew up in a Christian home. I had always heard about God and how Jesus died for my sins. None of that was really a revelation to me. It wasn't until I was about eleven years old when I realized the full extent of how much I needed to be saved. I thought by going to church, I was a Christian. But one day I realized that I was also a sinner. The funny thing was, that after I gave my life to Christ, I didn't really notice a huge turnaround, as I was already living in a Christian home, under Christian morals, but something did change in me that day. I can't really explain, but I've never looked back since."

I nodded, slightly lost in thought about my own home life. Yes, my parents were Christians. But if my dad was a Christian, I wanted nothing to do with it. Thankfully, God had other plans.

"That's an amazing testimony, Liz. How beautiful it is to have known God's love your whole life! I was similar, I guess." Flashes of my dad's face come to my mind and I shake my head slightly to try and get rid of the images.

"I grew up in a Christian home as well, but it wasn't until I was fifteen that I found Jesus for myself. I was taking singing lessons with a woman named Mrs. Robinson. She was a singer at my church in Manchester and she was from New Jersey." I think back to what a life-saver those lessons were. An escape from my nightmare.

"She would get me to sing the songs we sang in church. But before I would sing, she would ask me what the song meant. I never really knew for sure, but I wasn't stupid, so I was able to make up something about God's love for us, although I didn't truly understand. I didn't think God could ever love me. Why would He?"

I'm still not sure He does.

I continued, "She would also share with me about the amazing things God had done in her life. She talked to me about His hand on her life while she was a missionary in France. Her life sounded exciting and fun. But more than that, it seemed real. The God in her life was so real. I found myself jealous for what she had. One day I realized – she had Jesus. That was what I was missing. After I gave my heart to Him, I was able to truly understand what I was singing for the first time." I smile, but my mind takes me back, remembering that Jesus saving my soul did not mean He saved me from my past... or my present.

Liz and I continue to talk about how awesome it is to share our testimonies, but a deep sadness takes root in my heart.

"Well guys," Rob says, "I hope you all found that useful and encouraging, I know I have. Shall we end this time with some prayers?"

As people say their requests, panic rises in my mind. What should I say? I can't let people know about the struggles I have. They'll see me as weak, or worse, they'll worry about me. Liz suddenly speaks, dragging me from my panicked thoughts. All eyes are on me.

"Umm... yeah. Uh, just some prayer for my labs... they're um... difficult right now." Everyone nods knowingly and I feel relief. That's a reasonable thing to ask for prayer about. Unfortunately, it's the least of my worries.

Chapter 13

Trapped. Have you ever seen a bird get trapped inside? It flies around searching frantically for a way out. You attempt to aid it by opening every door and window there is. But still the bird cannot escape. How foolish, you think? Why can't it see the way out? How foolish are we sometimes? How blind to the way out of our situations?

Fallen leaves scoot around my ankles as I make my way down the cobbled street toward church. Ahead of me a small girl dressed in a pink dress wobbles along the top of the cathedral wall. Her graying father stands beside her holding her hand. Her face is scrunched in concentration. Suddenly, the father decides she's had enough wall-walking and grabs her around her stomach and holds her to his chest. They walk away from me but over his shoulder the little girl stares at me. I feel as though she's crying out to me, asking for me to help her. I can do nothing. I'm frozen on the sidewalk. Her eyes continue to bore into mine until they disappear around the corner. The air has left my lungs and I grip onto the stone wall for support. My head whirrs in panic. What should I do? Should I help her? She didn't say anything though. It was just a feeling. Not everyone is your father, Brie. Pain whips through my mind for both the little girl and me. I try to take several shaky breaths to calm me down but my mind has another idea.

I wrap my arms around my father's neck. His prickly chin tickles my inner elbow, making me squirm. He holds me with one arm underneath me.

His hand gently strokes my leg. I try to push myself away, but I can't. I'm trapped in his arms. There's nowhere to go. No way out.

"Brie!"

The slap of shoes on the cobbles brings me out of my past. I attempt to regain my composure as Peter comes alongside me.

"Oh, Peter. Hi," I say in a breathless tone. I check myself and try to get my act together before he becomes suspicious.

"Are you heading to Connecting?"

"Yeah."

Peter and I walk toward the student café where the service is being held. He tries to engage me in conversation but the girl's screaming eyes fill my thoughts and I can barely concentrate enough to walk.

"Yeah, fine," I reply, hoping that he was asking a question to which that was a suitable answer. Even if it wasn't, he seems to get the message that I'm not really with it and we continue our walk in silence.

'Get it together, Brie. You're being ridiculous. Her father is probably amazing.'

Small bubbles of self-hatred rise to the surface of my mind. I plunge my hands into my pockets and my fingers find the small wrapped up blade. I let out a sigh of relief – it'll be okay.

As Peter and I enter the building, I excuse myself to go to the bathroom.

My hands shake as I put away my blade and try to make myself look calm and happy. I take one last hateful glance at the mirror before making my way out to the Connecting service.

I enter the café. The tables have been stacked away and the chairs placed in rows. Dim lighting creates a warm atmosphere, but I feel as cold as stone. I skim across the faces until I spot Peter. He smiles at me and I try to smile back but it feels so phony. Hoping he doesn't notice, I take the seat beside him. I can feel my hands still shaking and I stuff them in my pockets to try and hide it. The worship band starts to play as the service begins. I sing the songs, attempting to push all unwanted thoughts out of my head. It seems to be working until we start to sing *Adoration*.

The words come up on the screen and I begin to sing, harmonizing with Peter's deep voice. But as we reach the bridge, I suddenly realize what I am singing.

"Children in our Father's arms…"

The words catch in my throat. God can't be my father. I don't want a father. They only hurt you. Panic and fear suddenly grip my lungs like a vice. I struggle to stay standing and am thankful that as the song ends we are told to take our seats. The service proceeds without me catching a single word.

'God will only hurt you, Brie. He doesn't love you anyway. Who would?' The pain of these truths tears through me and I concentrate on the steady pulsing pain in my arm.

Suddenly, words break into my whirring thoughts. I look up to see their source. They come from a guy called Tim. He stands at the microphone speaking calmly, but his words hit me forcefully.

"I believe that this message is for someone, or more than one person in this room. I have a picture of someone cutting themselves and then a picture of the cross," he begins and my heart races. He's talking about me. My legs suddenly feel like jelly. He continues and I wonder if I should run, then realize my legs will not carry me far.

"I feel like God is saying that by hurting yourself or punishing yourself, you are saying that Jesus's sacrifice, that the blood He shed on the cross for you, wasn't enough. That your sins are too big for even God to forgive."

No. That's not what I think. I try to breathe, to calm my racing heart. But my hands begin to shake more violently. His words keep ringing in my ears. Deep down I know that what he says is true. I believe that I'm so disgusting that even God can't love me. I'm the slut of the family. My heart hardens against Tim's words. What does he know? He doesn't understand. No one can love me. No one can forgive what I have done. Not even God.

The service ends and I rush out the door before even Peter can say a word to me. I can't stop cutting. It is the only thing I can rely on. Pain. How else can I survive? Besides, I'm only cutting every other day. Sometimes I'm even making it three days without! I am fine. Everything is fine.

My phone buzzes in my pocket. I pause, halfway through the entrance of the chemistry department. With one hand on the door, I reach into my pocket and retrieve my phone.

Corwin.

Joy unexpectedly leaps within me. I turn from the entrance and head over to a bench located in front of the library.

"Hello?"

"Brie! So glad you answered. I was hoping you had time to talk for a minute?" The sound of his voice makes me long to be back where we saw each other most days.

"I can talk for a little bit, but then I have to head to class."

"How have you been?" It's a simple question, but I know Corwin is asking so much more.

"Not so good." I say.

"I was thinking about you this morning and I felt I needed to call you and see how things were going. I know that you have a lot to process, especially now that you're not at home."

"What do you mean?"

"Well, in a sense, you no longer have to live the masquerade you were living at home, pretending everything was fine, burying the secrets you've held for so long. You now have the opportunity to let down your walls. That probably comes with additional stress and hence your usual coping mechanisms." He pauses. I know exactly what he's talking about, as much as I'd rather not admit it.

"Yeah... I'm trying to cope in healthy ways, but I can't seem to stop cutting. It's just too hard. I feel like I need it to breathe."

"I know it's hard Brie. You've been through so much. I understand. I'm not going to judge you for it. Rather, I want to be here for you. You could text me before you cut, maybe that would help?"

"I doubt it. I'd feel too ashamed."

"Hmmm. Know that I am here for you if you do need to talk though."

"Yeah. Thanks."

"Have you considered seeing a counselor. The university probably has a free counseling service. Perhaps they can help."

"Corwin, I —"

"I know, I know. You have never wanted to go see them. But they are there to help, and you really can't do this all on your own. Just consider it, will you? I'll be praying for courage and strength for you to do it."

"Hmmm. I'll think about it. I've got to go; class is about to start. Thanks for calling. It was good to hear from you."

"No problem. Talk to you soon. Bye Brie!"

"Bye."

Leave it to Corwin to always butt in right when I need him to.

Chapter 14

Forgiveness. The Bible makes it seem so easy to forgive. Somebody does you wrong, you forgive them. Simple as that. But it's not that simple. The Bible only talks of forgiving others. What if it's not others you can't forgive?

"Ugh! I'm so glad to be out of there!" Arin practically skips down the street away from the chemistry labs.

"Me too," I say unconvincingly, even to my own ears.

"You heading straight back to Castle?" she asks as we pause at the crossroads. One road would lead me across a bridge and back to my room, the other to a place I never want to go.

"No." I take a deep breath, steadying myself for the decision I'm about to make. "I've got an appointment at four thirty." I rush on before she can ask anything more. "I'll be back for dinner though!"

She gives me a quizzical glance, but I barely notice as I leave her and head straight on down the hill toward the language department. As I approach the automatic doors I take another deep breath and step through.

The entranceway is made of dull grays and browns. Posters dating back two years ago of study abroad programs and 'French for beginners!' cover the dingy walls. I try to keep myself moving across the room for fear that if I stop I will turn back and never return.

Why would I want to be in an *arts* building anyway? I'm a scientist. A chemist. I use logic and reasoning. None of this airy-fairy crap. Pft! I almost laugh out loud at my own thoughts. I could be in the middle of the chemistry lab and it wouldn't change the way I feel at this precise moment.

As I slowly step toward the stairwell in front of me, I scan the sign informing the reader where all the rooms are located in the building. I look down the list until my eyes hit the one word that stands out above all the rest. *Counseling Office – 2ⁿᵈ floor.*

What made me think this was a good idea? I lift my now lead feet up the stairs toward the 2ⁿᵈ floor. Arin had suggested it a week ago after she found me staring off into space for the fourth time that day and Corwin had mentioned it again last time he called. I feel like they were working together against me. But maybe it could help. Maybe they will just tell me I'm making it all up and then I'll be free to move on with my life. Maybe.

As I reach my hand up to push open the door leading to the second floor, I realize it's shaking considerably. Maybe they'll just confirm I'm crazy.

The hallway to the right of me seems to stretch out for miles. The little sign at the top of the stairs informs me that the main counseling office is on the right. One, two, three, four, five. I find myself counting my steps without thinking as I pass door after door with PRIVATE written across the top. I know exactly what's going on in there. There's some poor frightened soul being made to spill out all her secrets to someone who just ummm's and ahhh's and finally tells her to take some meds and she'll be fine. A small bubble of anger wells up inside me and I swallow it back down before I turn right into the well-lit office.

The walls are white, but you'd barely notice with the number of things cluttered around the office. In every corner plants seem to drape around everything. The filing cabinet, the coffee table and the desk where a middle-aged woman with glasses on the bridge of her nose sits typing away on her computer. Leaves cover everything. It's like I've stepped into a jungle. And if it's not leaves along the walls, it's various pictures of nature scenes. Meant to *calm* you, I suppose.

The woman looks up as I step a little closer toward her desk. She smiles at me in the way that balances between, *please don't be crazy enough to hurt me* and *I'm sorry for what brought you here.*

"How can I help you?" Her soothing voice pours out like velvet, calming the supposedly crazy person.

I do all I can not to roll my eyes. This is stupid, I think. But I smile back. "I'm here for an appointment at four-thirty."

"Can I take your name?" she says, looking once again at her computer screen through her glasses.

"Umm, yeah." Think. Think. "Brielle!" I say, with too much enthusiasm. Yes. I forget my name. Want to add it to your checklist of crazy?

She looks at me slightly quizzically before passing me a clipboard with a sheet of paper attached and a pen. "Have a seat and fill this out; I'll just let Carol know you're here."

I turn around and notice for the first time the six empty chairs lined up against two walls forming a small alcove where the patients wait for their evaluation by some know-it-all *psychiatrist* who actually knows nothing... I swallow back another burst of anger and take a seat. I can do this. Just one time, *maybe* they can help.

I place my bag on the seat next to me and slide the pen from under the clip of the clipboard. Looking down the blue piece of paper I take a deep breath, steadying myself so I don't put it down and run out of the room. I begin filling out the form, thinking of it more like a little test. I can do tests.

Are you currently taking any medication?

Nope... but I will be soon. My stomach does another lurch. I can't do this. I place the pen back on the clipboard and stand up to hand it back to the receptionist, my hands shaking violently. As I turn back around to pick up my bag I hear footsteps coming down the hall. My heartbeat quickens and I forget how to breathe. I hold the strap of my bag so tight I feel as though my hand will cramp any second. It's too late. Carol is already here.

She steps into the jungle room and the first thing I notice is how old she is. Her hair is white and looks like it has been for quite some time. She wears what all old people seem to wear: sweaters and formal pants with black heels that are small but thick. She has a friendly smile and blue eyes framed by heavy black-rimmed glasses. I stand transfixed to the spot. She looks at me and waits one beat before speaking.

"Brielle? Why don't you follow me?" Her voice sounds like an adult speaking to a small child.

I'm sure there are plenty of reasons why I shouldn't follow her, but nothing comes to mind. All I can do is move numbly after her out of the office and down the hall. We reach the third door on the left. She stops, steps inside and holds the door wide open, allowing me to enter the room as she shuts the door behind me. *Click.*

She studies the information on the clipboard, confirming that all the information I provided is correct and my unease increases.

"So, what brought you to England? You're obviously not from here originally," Carol says, looking at me with an encouraging smile.

I don't meet her gaze. Instead I find my scarf, which is balled on my lap, suddenly very interesting. My fingers find their way to the tassels at the end of it and begin weaving their way through the wool.

My toes just barely reach the floor as I sit on the very edge of the chair. I push my toes hard to the right of one wheel and it causes my whole chair to rotate to the right. I catch another wheel with my toe and do the same to the left.

"So, Brielle." *I don't look up. I just keep moving back and forth.* "Do you know why you are here today?"

You're going to ask me if I want to see my dad again. But I don't speak, afraid that I'll say too much.

"Brielle," *she says, attempting to get my attention. I stop spinning to act as though I'm listening but instead I glance over at the big blue teddy that sits on her leather couch against the far wall.* "Do you want to sit next to it?" *she asks.*

This surprises me and I leap off my chair and slide into the seat next to it without any further encouragement. The blue fur tickles my hand as I stroke the big bear's arm.

The 'loy-er,' as my mother calls her, positions herself so that she's once again facing me. I concentrate on peeling the skin off my left middle finger to avoid looking at her. What if she's a mind reader and can know what I've done? All I want is to be out of this room.

"So," she continues, "my job is to speak for you when your Mommy and Daddy are talking to the judge about visitation. Do you understand what that means?"

I nod. Both my mother and my father want me to be with them. My mother doesn't know how dirty I am, so I know why she wants me. My father wants me — he always does.

"What we need to figure out is what you want and what is best for you."

What I want is to be invisible. But no matter how hard I try, people still see me...

"Brielle?" The soothing voice draws me back into the small room where I'm sitting next to a large window overlooking the river. "Are you okay?"

I smile. "Yes, I'm fine. I'm sorry, can you repeat your question?"

"You've been dissociated for several minutes. Does that happen often?"

Oh boy. Here we go. This road is only going to lead to my placement into a mental institution.

"Sometimes," I mumble. She notes something down on the pad of paper she holds on her lap.

"Hmm... well, I asked how you came to be in England?"

"Oh. Umm." There were two answers to this question. Both true. One much more simple. "My mom married an English guy." Simple it is.

"How long have you been here?"

Too long. "Eight years."

"I see. Does your dad live back in America?"

"Yes."

"Do you go back to visit him often?"

"No." I know what is coming next and I really don't want to talk about it. Not now. Not ever.

"Is that an arrangement you're happy with?"

Living in England or not seeing him? I'm living in England so that I don't see him. Am I happy? No. Would I prefer to see him? I guess not.

"I guess so," I say, with a shrug as if it didn't matter.

"So, what brought you here today?" She sits back a little as if to give me more room to speak. She's expecting too much.

"I don't know. I think it was a mistake. I'm fine, really I am. I just... I don't know."

She doesn't say anything, just continues to look at me with sad eyes.

"I guess, I thought maybe you could tell me I'm not crazy."

"Do you think you're crazy?" she asks, leaning forward slightly.

"Well, sometimes."

"What makes you think this?"

"I struggle sleeping. I get maybe two to four hours of sleep each night."

"How long have you struggled sleeping?"

"A couple years."

"Do you know why you can't sleep?"

Yes. "No, I just can't. Even if I get to sleep I wake up thirty minutes later wide awake and can't get back to sleep for hours."

"Is there anything else that makes you think that you are crazy?"

"I hurt myself."

"Mmhmmm. How do you hurt yourself?"

"I cut myself."

"Where?"

Why is that important? "On my arms, legs, stomach..."

"What makes you feel you need to do this?"

"It hurts so much and I hate myself for it." I clamp my jaw shut. I've said too much. She's found the hook she's been looking for and I know she'll not let it go.

"What hurts?"

My heart begins to pound more heavily in my chest and my breathing speeds up.

"I can't. I can't." I shut my eyes as a stab of searing pain bursts its way through my core.

"You can't tell anyone about our little secret, right Ellie?"

My father's eyes bore into mine, illuminated by my blue night-light. I nod.

"Good girl. I love you."

"Brielle!"

I gasp and look up. Where am I? Window. River. Chair. Carol. She looks at me with a huge amount of concern.

"What just happened Brielle?"

"I... I can't."

"Yes, you can."

"I was just thinking about something."

"What were you thinking about?"

"My father."

"Do you have these sorts of flashbacks often?"

Wait just a minute! I didn't say anything about memories. How the heck does she know? Mind readers... gah! I shrug.

"Brielle, I wonder if you'll try something for me? Picture a memory of your father."

I see his silhouette in my doorframe.

"Now put the memory on a TV screen."

I do so. His shadow begins to move closer to me and I curl my arms protectively around my body.

"Now switch the screen off."

I try to stop the memory. But I can't. He's almost at me now. I can't breathe. I can't move.

"Try switching the channel."

My mind is frozen on the picture in front of me. He's sitting next to me stroking my stomach now.

"Brielle!"

My head snaps up to see Carol looking at me.

"I can't do it." I'm practically gasping for air.

"It takes practice. But I think it may be helpful for you to get control of these flashbacks. I understand that you probably don't feel comfortable enough with me now to tell me what happened. But I hope that over time we can build a relationship. What do you think?"

"I can't."

"Well, just think about it over this week and get back in touch with Sharon in the main office if you want to make another appointment."

I nod and get up, still trying to calm myself down so I can breathe normally. Carol smiles and walks me to the door.

Once out in the corridor I scramble around my bag to find my iPod. I put the earbuds in and press play. Immediately Evanescence screams into my ears, pushing out the memories still lingering. I dig my nails into my palms and head out of the language department back toward my room. 'Five more minutes and you can cut. Only five more minutes.'

The castle door slams behind me and my feet pound up the first set of stairs. I pause at the top long enough to check the in-out board. It is a list of the castle room numbers, next to which a golden bar slides between the words IN and OUT, indicative of the occupation of the room. Next to J31 the golden bar covers the word IN.

A wave of relief sweeps through me and I sprint up the next seventy steps. I slam through the first set of doors and search my pockets frantically for my keys.

You are almost there, Brie. I hear a small jingle in my pocket and the feel of a cool metal key brushes against my fingertips. Aha! I grab the key and shove it hastily into the lock, turning it ninety degrees to the left before leaning my body against the door and flinging it wide open.

Within seconds my bag has been dropped on the bed and my blade removed from the front pocket. My breath is unsteady as I grip the thin razor in my right hand. Pain pulses through my core and my legs can no longer support me. I drop to my knees and place my forehead on the carpet. Dry sobs escape my mouth.

"I hate you, Brie. I hate you. I hate you. I hate you. I HATE YOU!"

The pain tightens my lungs.

I jerk myself up to kneeling and rapidly push my sweatshirt sleeve above my elbow, leaving my right hand poised above my left forearm ready to strike. Now.

The cool blade indents the soft skin under the pressure of my fingertips. All I need to do is swipe it across. I close my eyes.

Buzz buzz. Buzz buzz. My whole body spasms in surprise and my lungs gasp some much-needed air as my cell phone buzzes in my jeans pocket.

What the heck? All I craved at that second was relief from the pain that grasped my mind. Now someone, probably my phone company, had scared me half to death and interrupted what I needed most.

I pull out my cell with my free left hand and look down at the tiny screen.

1 Message from Corwin.

My eyebrows rise in disbelief.

'Brie! How are you? God loves you so much! He thinks you are amazing! You are! You are my favorite Brie!'

Corwin, Corwin, Corwin... Oh, what timing you have! My grasp on my blade loosens and I reread the message. Air begins to fill my lungs easily and my trembling stops. I close my eyes and once again place my forehead on the floor. My chest heaves and sobs break from my lips and resound throughout the empty room.

The God of the universe loves *me*. Me. Disgusting, dirty, stupid, me. How? How can that be true?...

"I love you, Ellie."

"I love you too, Dad."

"No!" I grit my teeth together. I don't want love. I don't need love. Love only hurts me. No, no, no. I can't let God love me. I don't want Him to. "Please, no."

I remain on the floor in silence. A peace like a blanket drapes over my shoulders. I stand up slowly and put away my blade. For now, I remain uncut.

Chapter 15

Dread. The instant you think about it your heart turns to ice. Your insides contract and you desperately want to stop the clock. To not let the day you're dreading come. But there is nothing you can do. Time moves on despite your protest.

"Right. Well, remember that you have exams after the Christmas break, so don't see it as a time to relax."

I feel the room fill with apprehension about the upcoming exams after Professor Gregory's words. My insides twist and I feel every muscle in me tighten. Was it that time already? The end of my first semester was here. I'm not ready. I can't go home. Thankfully, Arin starts to chat away about what they could ask us before my mind can break through my defensive walls.

I make my way out of the lecture hall along with the rest of the chemists, all of whom are talking about what they will be doing for Christmas. Their voices bounce off the walls so that all I hear is a loud hum. I feel my heart begin to pound heavily in my chest, my hands shaking. I've got to get out. I squeeze myself between a few people and out the door. The cold winter air hits me welcomingly. Arin catches up to me and we both turn and head toward the castle.

My mind desperately tries to focus. Arin's voice resounds in my ears, but her words don't make sense. Arin turns towards the Castle library but I barely notice. Memories try to pour their way into my thoughts. I begin to look around trying to keep a grip on the present. Tree. Lamppost. Pub. Sign. Car. Bus. Window. Leaflet. Bridge. *Ted's* smile. Stairs. *My bedroom door swinging open.* No! Cathedral. Grass. Gatehouse. Castle.

As I approach my room I begin to lose focus and grip on the world. Darkness purges my mind as I place my key in the door and push my way through. I'm alone. I race across the room in a scramble for my iPod, hoping that music in my ears will help drown out the memories threatening to break through my thoughts. I get to the bed and sit down with my iPod in hand. But it's too late. The darkness has won.

I sit on my bed with my legs hanging off the edge staring at the computer screen.

'What r u up to 2nite?'

I place my hands on the keyboard to reply. I hear a footstep outside my bedroom door and my body tenses. For a moment, there is silence. Suddenly my bedroom door opens and Ted steps inside. I jump in surprise and my knee hits the bottom of the computer table. I gasp and he looks at me in mild amusement. I try to remain calm but my heart is racing. In an attempt to ignore his presence, I look back at the computer.

"Scare ya?" he says, his tone mocking.

"No," I say indignantly. He merely laughs and sits next to me. I try to ignore him and concentrate on what I was doing before he came in. My friend, Corrine, is waiting for a reply. I set my hands on the keyboard and go to type but am once again interrupted by Ted. He has shifted his body closer to mine, I can feel his eyes boring into me and I try to pretend he doesn't exist. Frozen in fear, my heartbeat races. Don't move, Brielle. Maybe he'll go away. Maybe it'll be okay. Those thoughts are shattered in seconds. His hand reaches up and gropes my breast. I gasp and Ted smiles.

"I'm busy, Ted," I try to say with force. But my voice sounds weak. I am weak.

He stands up, ignoring my comment, and starts to undo his jeans. I look back at the screen. Corrine has replied.

'Fine. Ignore me then.'

I glance at Ted and see him moving closer to me. I can smell the semen. I look past Ted and stare at the picture on the wall. It's a painting of a small boy with a straw hat standing on a wall next to the sea. Beside him is a small black and white Collie. I try to picture myself there. I try to hear the ocean waves crashing on the sand instead of Ted's heavy breathing. I try to feel the ocean spray on my face instead of the wetness between my legs.

I jolt back to my room in the castle. Pain, fiery pain, rips through my core. I'm sitting on my bed. My body violently shakes. How long have I been sitting here? I look out my window and the dusky shades of pink shock me. I glance at the clock. 6:00 pm. I got home at around 4:30 pm. I can't have been here for an hour and a half! I feel like I just sat down. I look down at my shaking hands and curl them into a ball. I feel the sharp pain of my nails digging into my flesh. 'Breathe, Brie. Breathe.' I focus on the pain but I can't stop the truth from creeping into my thoughts.

My own body has betrayed me.

I make one final sweep around the room with my eyes, making sure I haven't forgotten anything. Arin's side of the room is already empty, leaving a huge void. My bags are all packed and lined up next to the door, ready for when my parents get here. As if on cue, I feel the buzzing of my phone in my pocket.

"Hello?"

"Hi! We're just parking in the castle courtyard. You all packed and ready?"

"Yep," I say, "I'll be right down."

I take one deep breath before emerging out onto the courtyard and facing my mother. She turns around and beams as she hears the door slam behind me. I waddle over toward her, laden with my luggage. Charlie swiftly takes away the bags and begins to load them into the back of the car as my mother promptly grabs me into a hug. I feel my body stiffen at the contact, but I allow it.

Over the years my mother has moved from the reserved, non-hug type to being rather warm and friendly. I'm just not sure I've caught up. She draws back from the hug and gives me a once over.

"You've put on some weight! You're getting quite chunky."

Hello to you too. A fierce burst of anger swipes through me and I dig my nails into my palm and pull away from her.

"Yes. Yes, I have. Getting quite fat really!" My eyes sting with unshed tears. Don't let her get to you, Brie. I turn to head back toward my room to retrieve more bags, leaving my mother standing alone, unsure of how she's offended me.

"I don't mean it like that!" she calls across the courtyard. "I was just saying... you know... you have put on weight over this semester! That's all I'm saying."

She's already said enough. There was no "Hello." No "I've missed you." No "How are you?" Just my mother and her obscene bluntness.

I ignore her and dash up the stairs two at a time, slamming into my room in record time.

"Gah!" Two seconds with her and I already can't wait to be away. She just doesn't see. She doesn't see how much I already hate myself. I need no more reasons to, but she insists on pointing them out.

I hastily grab my book bag and the box lying next to it with anger still pulsing through my veins. I look around the room. Empty. I stomp down the stairs, causing my box to rattle in my hands. I don't even remember what is in here. But I don't care if I break everything I own right now.

I stop just before rounding the final corner to recompose myself.

"Shake it off, Brie. Shake it off," I whisper to myself. And I do. I give my body a little shake, stand tall and walk out to greet the next four weeks of my life with the best fake smile I can muster.

Chapter 16

Desensitized. Have you ever noticed how after about ten minutes of wearing your perfume you can no longer smell it? Or how after a prolonged period of hearing an alarm go off you no longer notice it? There are only so many punches you can take before you no longer feel them. There are only a certain number of times you can hear your bedroom door open in the middle of the night before you no longer hear it. You're numb.

I sit on the edge of my bed. My bedroom walls surround me but I feel as vulnerable as I would in an open field. My arms are folded tightly over my stomach as if to guard it from attack. But it's not my body I need to protect. My mind is suffering an onslaught of memories. Flash after flash. My breathing is shallow and shaky. Pain holds me firmly. Shivers run though me despite the warmth of the room.

My skin cries out for the blade, but my mind stops me from getting it. I'm paralyzed. I deserve this pain. I don't deserve freedom from it, however temporary it might be. Disgust wells up within me and I feel as if I'm about to vomit. I fall onto my knees on the floor, doubled over.

"God! Help me!" I cry out over the screaming in my mind. And just like that the shivers cease as the warmth of the room wraps around me and reaches into my core. I remain on the floor just soaking in the atmosphere. Peace. That's what it is. Total peace. My memories silenced, my pain erased, peace. Tears of joy begin to roll down my cheeks.

"How can You care for me, God? I'm disgusting. I'm covered in scars. I'm ugly. I'm nothing You would want anything to do with!" Instantly a vision fills my mind.

A large boulder sits in the middle of the vision. It's got lots of moss on it and huge chunks missing. Grooves like scars cover it on all sides. It's an ugly boulder. But next to it is a man. He is a sculptor. He circles the boulder, admiring it. You can see the complete delight in his eyes. He dances and leaps around joyously. He loves this boulder. At first I can't see why, but as if someone spoke the reason, I suddenly understand. He loves this boulder despite its scars because he can see what it *will* be, how beautiful it will be once he has finished carving it. He knows that it will take time and a lot of painful work to remove the chunks and moss and to smooth away the scars. But he is a master sculptor and nothing is too difficult for him to do.

Tears now flow readily onto the carpet. God knows what I will be one day. He loves me despite my scars.

I'm suddenly filled with a great desire to play the piano. I jump up from the floor and head downstairs. Thankfully, my parents are out shopping right now and shouldn't be back for some time.

Once at the piano, I sit but do nothing. I remain like that for several moments just basking in this new revelation of God's love. And just like that, it comes to me. The chords, the music and the words all at once. I grab a sheet of scrap paper and jot it down.

"Unloveable, broken and bruised. Unbeautiful, shamed and abused. That's what I see in the mirror staring back at me.

"Unvaluable, timid and scarred. Unforgiveable, guilty and marred. That's what I feel, when the pain of this world seems so real."

"Oh, help me to see through Your eyes. I am beautiful. I am redeemed. Your body broken. Your blood set me free. When You look into my eyes, You see loveable, a child of God, love unending, grace undefined. Show me what You see in me. You see beautiful."

The words are not from me, but for me. Joy fills me for what seems the first time in years. I am ecstatic. I feel like nothing can ever bring me down again.

How wrong I can be...

◆————◆————◆

Numbness chills me to the bone. I feel nothing. The darkness has swallowed me whole and my mind feels empty. I am void of emotion. It is like my body and my mind have shut down.

If someone were here talking to me, I'm not sure I would notice. If my surroundings were on fire, I don't think I would flinch. How did I get here? I try to take back control of my mind but I stop immediately. I try to move but I have no strength. Fear begins to wrap its way around my throat, cutting off my air supply. I can do nothing to stop it.

I try to once again figure out how I got here. Where am I? I glance up. Darkness. I glance to my right. A faint light casts a glow onto the wooden floor beneath me. Focus on it, Brie. Little by little I begin to feel again.

I'm leaning against a cold stone wall with my knees tucked up next to my chest. My arms are wrapped around my knees. To my left is another wall. An inch above my head is the underside of a counter. I'm hiding. But from what? I can't remember. What if they are here? Who, Brie? Flashes of my dad searching for me come to my mind, sending instant chills through me. I slam my eyes shut and pull my hands to my ears as if to block it all out.

"He's not here. It's okay, Ellie. It's okay. He's not here," I whisper to myself. I feel my hands begin to tremble. I hear footsteps on the stairs. I catch a cry in my throat. "He's not here. It's okay."

I have to get out of here. Move, Brie! I roll to my knees and stand up. I realize that I'm in the castle at Northern in a small alcove off one of the castle corridors. I think I am one floor above my room. With shaky limbs, I begin to move. I am constantly glancing behind me, making sure he's not there. I reach the stairs and carefully begin to descend them. Footsteps again echo on the walls. I look down and see a figure move beneath me. With a gasp, I slam myself into the wall of the staircase. The figure continues to round the stairs.

92

I can now see them. It's not him. My breath releases. It's Arin, my roommate. She sees me and smiles.

"Brie!" Her smile fades rapidly as she continues to look at me. "Are you okay?" She is paused at our door. I am five feet away.

I nod and look back up the stairs, just in case. I look back at her and force myself to smile. She doesn't seem impressed.

"Come on, Brie, I'm making some coffee. I know you want some!" With one last glance up the stairs I follow her into our room. She places her book bag on her bed and I take a seat at my desk chair, feeling stiff with fear.

Casting another glance at me, Arin begins to gather the fixings for coffee. My eyes keep flickering to the door, praying it won't open. I don't feel safe.

"So, what's up Brie? You seem really scared. It looked like you had seen a ghost in the castle. I know there are rumors of them." She laughs and tries to lighten the mood, but I know she is concerned.

I look out of the window at the dark sky, illuminated by the full moon.

"I'm fine," I begin to say, but then realize there is no point in lying. "Actually, I'm not."

I slump forward in my seat and rest my head in my hands.

"I don't know what is wrong with me. One minute I am here in my room and the next thing I know I am 'waking up' somewhere else, having no idea how I got there. It's terrifying."

"I imagine it would be. Were you thinking of anything in particular when you were here in your room? Or do you not remember?"

Arin looks sad, but as always, she remains calm and strong. Just what I need. I'd be freaked out if my friend were having time gaps, but she takes it as if it's normal.

"I don't remember." I release a large sigh. I am exhausted.

"Have you thought any more about going to the counselor again?"

"No. I... I just can't."

"I understand. Do you want to push down the coffee press? I know you love to," she smiles.

"You know me so well."

I grin back at her, pushing the recent events away from my mind. But as we continue to talk into the night with coffee in hands, the fear remains so that as Arin says goodnight, my eyes remain wide open. I cannot sleep because every time I close my eyes, my father's figure standing in my bedroom door flashes across my mind, causing my eyes to fling open and search frantically around the room for him.

'He's not here, Brie.' I can hear Arin's steady breathing. I lay back down. What happened to the joy I possessed only days ago? It's like I take one step forward and two back. I thought I was healed. God, I thought I had gotten over it all! But now I'm more of a mess than before. In fact, now I feel like I really am going crazy. I can't go to an insane asylum. I just have to hide this and hide it well.

Chapter 17

Escape. We have fire exits when we need to escape from a fire. We have thoughts on how we will escape from an awkward social situation, maybe a fake phone call, bathroom trip, etc. But what happens when you need to escape your past? No matter how hard you try, you're trapped.

The sun sets behind the row of houses across the valley from my wall outside the cathedral. Shades of pink and purple streak across the sky – a beauty I cannot appreciate because I feel as if darkness has once again swallowed me.

In the Connecting service this evening I learned that it is not pain that defines us, but the love of our heavenly Father. I can hear the words and understand them with my mind, but my heart remains cold and cut off from accepting them.

God's love. I cannot see it as a good thing. Yet at the same time, I look to the cross. God loved the world, *me*, so much He sent His son to die on the cross so that *I* might have eternal life. And I am so thankful for that. But still the confusion of love remains. I hear about love all the time, on the radio, on TV and in church, but I can't get the way my father loved me out of my head.

Arin tells me that that is not real love, but how can you say that your father doesn't love you? Are they not meant to? Am I not a part of him? But if my father loved me, why did he hurt me?

I stuff my fingers in my pocket and with very little thought, I grab my blade and swipe it across the side of my leg. The numerous scars on my arms are becoming too obvious. I watch the blood trickle down my leg. My thoughts continue to spill over.

Why is it that only pain relieves pain? That sharp stabbing pain as the edge of the blade digs into my skin relieves all the pain I feel inside. But only briefly. Time passes and I sink back down. Down to feeling sorry for myself. I have life very good compared to most. Who am I to complain? But the pain is so intense I just want to end it. I want to die. To jump off a bridge and feel the rush of freedom through my body before I plunge into the icy water below. My insides scream but my mouth stays silent. I cry inside but my eyes remain dry. I have learned over time to bottle all of my emotions. That's all I am. A bottle full of pain, anger and sadness. Lord, please help me know what to do.

I look down at my feet hanging over the edge of the wall. I know I won't jump but in the back of my mind I want to. I don't remember when I started thinking about dying. I guess I knew that eventually that would be the only way out. The pain I can cause myself is so temporary, I'm starting to not feel its effects at all. I need more.

The sudden strike of the cathedral bells causes me to jump out of my train of thought. It's 8 pm and the sky is already a dark shade of blue. I swing my legs back over the wall and jump down, turning my back on the cathedral as I head toward the castle while the bells resound around me.

If anyone knew what I was planning, they would send me to an asylum for sure. But by the time I've climbed the stairs to my room I have made up my mind on what I must do. Smile in place. No one can know. I must continue as normal. No one can know.

The bedroom door slams behind me as I dump my book bag on my bed. I dig out my homework and grab the relevant textbook from my bookcase before dropping them onto my desk and planting myself down on the desk chair. I open the textbook to page eight hundred and sixty and begin to read about cycloadditions. I read and reread the first sentence three times, not taking in a single word.

"Gah, focus Brie!" I yell at myself. But it's no use. Work seems impossible right now. My thoughts drift back to last night…

I had gone into my room with a smile firmly in place. Arin looked up from her pile of papers on her desk and smiled back. I took a seat at my desk and logged into Facebook. There was no point in trying to work while in that mindset. I just needed a distraction. My message inbox indicated that I had one new message. I clicked on it and the message opened. I froze instantly. Staring back at me from the screen was an image that has haunted me for years. It was my father. His smile looked genuine. He was wearing his typical gray suit. I felt as if the floor beneath me was shifting. I could hear the blood humming in my ears. This couldn't be happening. I broke my eyes away from the screen but I could still see him.

Arin glanced up at me.

"Are you okay?" she asked.

"Yeah," I barely whispered, placing another smile on my face. I forced myself to look back at the message.

'Hi Ellie,

My, what a beautiful young woman you have become! I have seen on the news that tuition fees for college have gone up a lot over there in England. I just wanted you to know if you need any help, I'm always here for you.

Love, your earthly father'

Earthly father? I couldn't get my head around what I just read. I couldn't work out what was the most significant piece of information. He knows I'm in England. I'm not sure if I expected him to or not. I suppose I did. But he knows I'm at college. And earthly father? What is that all about? Was he now trying to be all Christian? As if!

He was that way when I was a kid. And now he's trying to be there for me. After all he did.

A part of me felt good about this. My dad cares about me. But I reread the first line. "Beautiful young woman..." Yeah, all he cares about is getting more pleasure from my body. I shuddered involuntarily and quickly shut my laptop. I grabbed my headphones and pushed music in my ears to drown out the thoughts and memories that began to flood into my mind...

I stare at my textbook, lost in thought. Anger and fear pulse through me. How could he? How dare he? He has no right to contact me after ten years! I don't think I heard a single word today in lectures. Normally I use my work to distract me from the rest of my life. But this is too strong. I must focus. I grab the blade from my pocket. 'No, Brie!'

"Ahhhhh!" My scream fills the empty room. I know cutting is not the answer. God is. But I can't seem to turn to Him right now. I grab my phone. Distraction. I need a distraction. Peter pops into my mind. He is a great distraction. I quickly give him a text asking if I can come over.

My phone buzzes with his reply. He's free, so I grab my coat, scarf and keys and head out. His house is a thirty-minute walk uphill from the castle. I begin to pound my feet into the ground, counting every step. My breath begins to become more labored as I climb the last stretch of the hill. Finally, I reach his house and ring the doorbell.

I hear Peter's rapid footsteps descend the stairs moments later and the door swings open. My muscles once again tense up.

"Hey, Brie! How are you?"

"Oh, I'm good, thanks. How are you?" Good is my new word for fine and I think he knows it.

"I'm really great," Peter replies in his usual cheerful manner.

Sometimes Peter reminds me so much of Corwin. They both follow Jesus, they both are caring and compassionate and they both have a very joyous outlook on life.

"You want some cookies?" he asks brightly.

I follow him inside and sit down in the corner of the kitchen on the other side of the table. A little distance makes me feel much more safe.

"You know me too well!" I laugh, and it actually sounds genuine for once. I feel myself loosen up a little. Not everything is bad right now.

Peter sets a plate of cookies down on the table in front of me. I feel guilty for eating them and self-hatred bubbles to the surface. I shove it down and begin to nibble at one of them. Chocolate chip, my favorite. Peter continues to move around the kitchen, cleaning up dishes and putting away food items that had been abandoned on countertops. He chats about physics and our math classes, making small talk to put me at ease.

It works. I feel comfortable here, talking with him about nothing too important. Peter seems to know exactly what I need. A friend. A distraction.

A door slams upstairs. I jump in my seat, causing my leg to bang on the table, which in turn makes me realize that my legs are trapped. My lungs squeeze and I can't take another breath.

I can hear Peter calling my name, but it sounds so distant. The kitchen fades and an image of my father reaching for my hand fills my vision. I try to pull away but I whack the wall with my elbow, pulling the kitchen back into focus. Peter's face radiates concern as he reaches across the table toward my hands that grip the edge of the table.

"It's okay, Brie. You're safe. Breathe." His voice is calm and reassuring.

His words make me realize I'm not breathing. I take a deep lungful of air and let it go in a shaky exhalation. My limbs are trembling from the flashback.

"What happened?" Peter asks, his face still filled with care and concern for me.

Ugh! "Nothing. I just realized I couldn't move. I'm claustrophobic, that's all," I smile, in attempt to ease his concern.

"Do you want a glass of water?" he asks, getting up with one last glance toward me. I give another grin and he turns to retrieve a glass from the cupboard.

"Sure!" Phew! I thought he wasn't going to drop what just happened. But it seems he's let it go.

He sits down and hands me a glass. I take a sip, letting the coolness trickle down my throat, grounding me into the present. I grab a second cookie and begin to nibble at it. After a few minutes of silence my muscles become less tense and my mind also begins to relax.

"Shall we move into the living room?" Peter asks, interrupting the quiet.

I glance at the plate of cookies. Following my gaze, he adds, "and we can take the cookies with us…"

I give him a sheepish smile and he laughs, taking the plate of cookies into the living room. I follow him in and take a seat that is slightly angled toward his in the alcove of the window. The orange glow from the streetlight below casts strange shadows against the frosty windows.

I clutch my water and cross my legs away from Peter. He just looks at me for a while before helping himself to a cookie. I feel another ripple of fear creep inside my stomach. I look to the door we came through. Could I make it to the door in time if Peter tries to hurt me?

Don't think that way, Brie! Peter is a good guy. He's not going to hurt you. I glance at him suspiciously, not sure I can believe that. He has a look of genuine care on his face. I relax a little. There is no hint of him wanting me, for now at least. I continue to sip my water.

"Why are you afraid?" Peter asks.

I try to speak before fully swallowing and begin to choke on my water, gasping for air between coughs. Peter stands as if to help me, but I place my hand up to stop him.

"I'm… ok…" I manage to squeeze out of my burning throat. He sits back down.

"What did you say?" I whisper, trying not to cough. I'm sure I didn't hear him right.

"You're scared. I see fear in you a lot."

I look at the cookie in my hand, not sure of what to say.

"What are you scared of, Brie?"

For some reason, when people use my name I feel so much more vulnerable. It's like they know me.

"You," I say, in barely a whisper.

"Me?" he says in surprise. "I'm not a scary person."

I look away, to the floor, to the couch, to the door. Anywhere but at him. I can't believe we are talking about this.

"It's not just you. It's all men," I say, still not looking at him.

Peter says nothing, but nods as if he understands. I think back to my earlier thoughts and question whether to tell him. Maybe he can help me. Maybe he can help me know what to do.

"I often think about dying," I say, diving in head first.

Peter's eyes widen a little in surprise but he says nothing, allowing me to continue.

I take another small bite of my cookie and glance out the window.

"It's the only option I can find sometimes. The pain is so unbearable. So deep. I can't do anything about it. I try to cut it out, but that doesn't work for long. If I was dead... it wouldn't hurt anymore." I speak slowly, almost as if to myself.

"What causes all this pain?" Peter asks, quietly and gently.

I close my eyes, not wanting to speak.

"When I was younger," I take a deep breath before rushing through the next sentence, "my dad sexually abused me and then when I moved to England another member of my family did, until I came here to university." I end the sentence with a slight laugh and a shrug of my shoulders. I chance a glance at Peter. He looks distraught. I bite my bottom lip in an attempt to stop the laughter from leaking out.

"I know you know some of my past. I just... I just hate myself so much for letting it all happen. For even sometimes wanting it." Disgust fills my stomach.

"What do you mean?" Peter asks gently with no hint of judgement.

"I didn't want the sex… but I wanted my dad to love me. I sometimes enjoyed the hugs and cuddles. They just didn't always end there."

"I'm so sorry, Brie."

I shrug my shoulders again. "No big deal. I'm just scared now. That's all."

"It is a big deal, Brie. Don't try to minimize it."

"I'm not!" I retort.

"Yes, you are," he says firmly.

I sit expecting the waves of guilt to come crashing down on me for saying too much. But they don't come. In fact, I feel a little lighter, as if a small weight has been lifted.

Peter takes a deep breath and lets out a sigh.

"I don't know what else I can do for you except to pray."

"There is nothing you can do. It's a fact of life. It happens."

"But it shouldn't."

I shrug and eat the last bite of my cookie. My hands tremble slightly.

"You know it's not your fault," Peter states. He tries to get me to look at him by angling himself more toward me.

I feel my body back into the opposite side of the chair.

"Brie!"

I look up at him, shocked by the force of his voice.

"It's not your fault."

A shiver runs through me.

"I have to go." I stand and place my glass on the table between us. "Thank you for the cookies."

Peter looks as if he's about to argue, but eventually sighs and stands up to walk me to the door. We tramp back down the stairs and he opens the door, letting the chilly night air wrap around us in the hallway.

"I know you think that death is the only option for you, but it's not. I'll be praying for you. God can get you through this, He can heal your wounds," he says.

I nod, thank him once again, and make my descent down the

hill toward the castle. Tears begin to roll down my cheeks and I feel as though I'm going to fall apart right here on the sidewalk. With a shake of my head I continue to walk down the hill, wiping my tears away with the back of my hand.

I can't handle the way people care. The looks of concern and pain on their faces. It makes me feel as though this is something more serious than it is. And that makes it hurt all the more.

I hear footsteps behind me and the hairs on the back of my neck stand on end. Northern is in a relatively safe city, especially in the area I'm in. But my irrational emotions take over my rational thoughts and I speed up my steps, turning my head often to check that the person walking behind me isn't gaining on me.

I make it to the castle and run up the stairs, I feel worn out from the battle of emotions this evening, but I know I won't sleep, for as soon as I close my eyes the nightmares will invade. It seems my days and nights are filled with flashbacks of my past that I can never escape.

Chapter 18

Control. There are parts of our lives that we have control over. We can control where we go, who we befriend, where we will live. But there are also those parts where, no matter how hard we fight, we have no control. Things like getting sick or when a loved one dies. This forces us to turn the pain and the anger inward and expel our control more forcefully into other areas.

Both Arin and I forgot to shut the curtains last night. The cloudless night sky allows the moon to shine brightly into the room. Everything seems so still. So calm. Yet I know that all over the world at this very second thousands of young girls are being sexually abused. My heart aches with the thought of their pain. I feel warm tears roll across my face and onto my pillow. There is nothing I can do for them. My chest heaves and I push my face into my pillow to silence the sobs so as to not wake Arin. 'Why, God? Why let this happen? They are just children! They don't deserve it.'

A sob catches in my throat. So was I. I was a child. A very young child. I didn't deserve it. I didn't deserve it! Suddenly the anger toward myself is redirected toward my father. I burn in anger at him, tears pour onto my hot cheeks. He did this to me! Pain and anger beat heavily in my chest.

'Why did you do this? Why? I was your child. You loved me!' my mind screams at him. But he did love me. He would give me hugs too. The good and the hurt mixed so well together. How can I be mad at him? I am the one who made this happen. Just like it

was my fault the second time. I cannot be angry with my father…
or Ted. It's not their fault. It is only mine.

I pull the anger back inside me. I deserved everything I got. My
eyes dry up and I let the anger comfort me. This was all my fault. I
let it happen. I didn't stop it. I was in control.

As these thoughts fill my mind, I close my eyes and feel myself
succumb to the much-needed sleep.

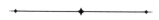

I stare at the brown gunk sticking to the sides of my round
bottom flask. This can't be right. Dread fills my stomach. What if
I did it wrong? What if I fail? I look frantically over my lab script.

– Grind caraway seeds

I did that.

– Add 150 mL of ethyl ether

– Heat vigorously for 2 h collecting the distilled fraction

Check, check.

– Slowly add H_2O via a dropping funnel during distillation

I did all this! I look back to my experiment. Nothing has distilled
yet. The flask at the end of my condenser remains empty. I'm such a
failure, I can't do anything right.

"Hey Brie!"

"Gah!" I jump into the side of the fume hood, causing me to
whack my arm on the taps that line the wall. I turn to see Arin
standing there with a smirk on her face. "Geesh! Don't creep up on
me like that!"

"Sorry. I know you're jumpy so I can't resist!"

"Ha. Ha," I breathe out sarcastically. "I'm already on edge from
stress. My experiment isn't working."

"Why not?"

"If I knew that, I would be doing something to fix it!"

"Hmmm…true…" she says slowly. "You can't always be perfect,
Brie."

'I sure can try,' I think, while rolling my eyes.

I have always strived to be perfect. In fact, I never had a single detention in my life. However, there was one time my English teacher kept me behind after class, which is a horror for any goody-two-shoes. I never get kept behind...

The class filed out and I was still packing my bag. I was dreading the end of school that day. My mom was working so I was going straight to Ted's. My body did an involuntary shudder as I tried to stop my thoughts in their tracks.

"Brielle, can I have a word please?" Ms. Brooke said as she sat awkwardly in her desk chair. She was at least eight months pregnant and was huge.

I looked to the door at Corrine who was waiting for me. She shrugged and left. I felt my stomach squeeze with worry. What had I done? Was I in trouble? My mother was going to kill me.

Ms. Brooke stood up and waddled toward my desk where I stood waiting impatiently to leave. She perched a hip on the side of my desk and looked right at me. I focused just over her right ear out of the window. Direct eye-contact made me uncomfortable.

"You seem to be very aggressive lately."

Aggressive? What was she talking about? I wasn't aggressive. Perhaps I hit the occasional boy for looking at me, but I wasn't mean to her.

"Is everything alright at home, Brielle?" Her voice was gentle and quiet.

My stomach dropped. She knew. She couldn't know. Thoughts of what Ted had done just a couple days ago flashed through my head. No, she can't know. No one knew.

I looked down at my bag and spoke in a voice as steady as I could muster.

"Everything is fine at home," I said with a small smile and a quick shrug, attempting to ease her mind and make her drop it.

"Okay... I'm always here if you need to talk to someone, Brielle. Remember that."

"Thanks, I will. Was there anything else?"

"Nope, that's all. You can go."

I grabbed my bag and rushed out the door without a second's hesitation, letting out a big sigh as I hurried to catch up to Corrine who had just rounded the corner at the end of the hall. That had been close. Too close...

"Earth to Brie!"

"Huh?" I say, shaking myself out of my own little world.

"I said, are you going home for all five weeks on Friday?" Arin says with a note of impatience threading her words.

My stomach tightens further. Home. The semester had flown by. It was time for the study break. I would spend two weeks in the USA visiting my family in Wisconsin. Alex, Lynn, Andrew... My mind rests with ease at the thought of spending time with them. They don't criticize my weight or make me feel threatened in any way. They are what I imagine family should be like. However, I'll be spending the other three weeks at home. The hand holding my lab script begins to shake. I set it down on the edge of the fume hood and stare at my failing reaction.

"Yeah... I am," I reply, after a minute or so.

"Looking forward to it?"

"Oh, sure!" Sarcasm colors my tone. 'Can't wait to hear my mother complain of how fat I've gotten.' I say silently.

She gives me a 'I'm sorry' kind of look. She knows how my mother can be.

"Hope it goes better than you expect!" she leaves me and meanders back to the fume hood she was working in.

I turn back to my experiment. I'm going 'home' in a few days. Back to America. Hope stirs deep inside me. Things are going to be okay. Maybe I won't have to come back! I feel my mouth pull into a smile despite my failing experiment.

A small movement in the condenser catches my eye. I watch a small drop of yellow liquid slowly roll down the condenser and make a small 'plop' into my empty flask. Product at last. My smile stretches further across my face. Things really are going to be okay.

A loud voice blaring through the speakers interrupts my concentration on the book I'm reading, one of Jodi Picoult's latest. I glance over the edge of the book. People sit scattered around the waiting area at gate twenty-three. Some are reading as I was, others are sitting staring at their laptop screens, and a lot are trying to take in a few Z's before the next leg of their journey.

I push myself up on my seat a little more and set my book down onto the empty seat beside me, quickly checking that all of my bags are there and nothing is out of place. Travelling on my own seems to cause me to be a little more paranoid and hyper-vigilant. Both bags remain seemingly untouched next to me. I lean back against the chair once more, but my muscles remain tight. I feel that the art of relaxing is something I'll never master.

An orange glow cast across the waiting area draws my attention to the large window on the other side, next to the boarding gate. A beautiful sunset embraces the concrete jungle of Boston, MA, casting long shadows as the last rays of sun hit the numerous planes covering the tarmac.

A sense of loss grips me, causing a lump to form uncomfortably in my throat. I wish I had never had to leave this place.

New Hampshire is only a couple hours' drive from here. I'm so close to home. But I can't go there. Pain of this realization twists in my stomach. I am just on a transfer flight to Chicago, where my cousins will be picking me up and taking me to Wisconsin, the place the rest of my mother's family resides. I'm excited to see them, of course. With them I can be myself. I'm not the 'American girl,' or the 'crazy person,' or the 'depressed person.' I'm just me.

Another crackle echoes around the departure gate.

"We will now begin boarding flight DL5560 to Chicago."

I grab my passport out of the front of my book bag and head over to gate twenty-three, wheeling my little suitcase behind me. I get in line behind a tall man in a business suit. I feel my body tense up more with the close proximity. I position my suitcase between us, acting as a small protector. As small as it may be, it makes me feel better.

The line moves forward and the man standing ahead of me moves to the desk on the right, leaving me to see the attendant on my left. No longer feeling trapped, I move forward with a smile to hand the permanently smiling woman my passport and boarding pass.

"Have a great flight," the attendant says to me, handing back my passport and boarding pass.

"You too," I say automatically, and then, catching my error, I smile apologetically and head through the gray doors down the little ramp to the plane.

At the plane door, there is a gap between the plane and the ramp, large enough for me to see the shadow of the land outside. My chest tightens with emotion.

"I *will* be back."

As I step away from the crowd I look up and see him standing there with my polka dot suitcase already in hand. I can't help but let a huge grin spread across my face as I see Alex, my cousin, not only lifting the weight of my suitcase, but lifting my worries and fears from my mind as well. Without hesitation I let go of my little suitcase and make three long quick strides toward him and fling my arms around his neck, which is about half a foot above my head. A childish giggle escapes my lips. I release him and he just looks at me with a small grin.

"Hi," I say, still giggling. He's now huge compared to the last time I saw him. I can't believe it's been so long.

"Hello!" he says.

And that is that. I go grab my abandoned case and we head out of the airport side by side. I'm practically bouncing, I feel so happy, so free... so safe. For some reason that's the way Alex makes me feel. Like no harm will come to me while I'm with him. Like the world could explode and he'd still stop me from being hurt.

Alex is a guy of few words and he just smiles as I tell him all about the movies I watched on the plane and the funny moments I had traveling on my own. Unwanted thoughts don't even cross my mind as I sit in the passenger seat and he drives us out of Chicago and North toward home.

"It's good to have you home, Mei Mei."

I smile at this nickname, meaning little sister in Chinese.

"It's good to be home, Ge Ge Da." My 'brother big.'

Wisconsin was never my home. But since I left New Hampshire it is the only place I feel that I actually belong. It's one of the only places I can let my walls down. It's one of the few places I feel safe.

Chapter 19

Fate. Some people believe the events in our lives are a result of fate, that we don't in fact have free rein in our lives. Others believe life is a completely random set of events. Few can doubt, however, that when certain things happen, it's more than just a coincidence.

My eyes open and squint into the sunlight that now streams through the blinds. It takes a moment or two to remember where I am. I was so exhausted yesterday that I'm not sure if I really made it to Wisconsin, or if it was just a dream. I look around the room and realize I'm really here in America with family I love. A surge of joy flows through me, causing me to fling myself out of bed and throw on some clean clothes from my suitcase that magically appeared in my room.

I open my door and walk down into the living room, shoving my hair into a ponytail as I go. *Bang.* The noise of a cupboard door slamming shut causes my feet to fly a foot off the ground and my heart to hammer heavily in my chest. Alex appears from around the corner and takes in my terrified look.

"Scare ya?" he says with a mischievous grin.

"Just a little." I force a small laugh.

"Well, I wasn't sure if you were ever going to emerge. But I thought it would be good for you to try to get onto the right time zone, so I let you sleep."

"How considerate of you." I try to let my muscles relax.

"Andrew is picking you up from here shortly. Did you hear he's got a girlfriend?"

"No… when did this happen?"

Andrew is another cousin of mine. He's very athletic and one of the most caring and sincere people I know. I'm not surprised at all that he's got a girlfriend. I just hope she's good enough for him, something I'm not sure is possible.

"Maybe around a year ago."

"Wow. That long? Isn't he joining the Air Force?" My lack of communication, much less visitation, with them stings.

"Yes, but not for another year or so."

The rumble of an engine causes my muscles to tense up once again, while Alex peers out the window.

"He's here! I'm sure you can stop on the way to wherever you're going and get some breakfast in you!"

I grab a jacket and my bag and rush out the door. Andrew steps out of his truck and I practically fall into his arms from the top step of the porch. His arms wrap tightly around me and I feel tension trickle out of me. I know, as I knew with Alex, that I'm safe.

Andrew puts me down and gives me a huge grin.

"Welcome *back* to the states!"

"Yeah, yeah. Don't remind me!" I say, with a grin mirroring his.

I turn to get into the passenger side of his truck. I feel a twinge in my mind, as if it's trying to run away. I shake away the feeling, pull open the door and swing myself onto the bench seat. Andrew starts the engine and I reach back and pull my door shut. The door makes a loud squeak as it slams against the old rusting metal frame and the twinge in my mind becomes a jolt into my past.

"Where are we going, Daddy?" I ask, swinging my legs beneath me as I perch on the blue bench seat of my dad's blue pickup truck.

"We're going to the dump," he replies, looking over at me for a few seconds before turning his attention back to the truck. He starts the engine with a loud roar and makes his way down our long driveway.

"Do you want to help Daddy drive, Ellie?"

"Okay."

"Come over here and sit on my lap. I'll push the peddles and you can steer."

I scoot myself over and crawl onto his lap.

"That's it." He positions me in the center of his lap and I grab the steering wheel with both hands and stare out at the dirt road with tufts of green poking out in the middle.

"Good girl, Ellie," my dad mumbles as he shifts beneath me so that his hand is now underneath me, stroking me on top of my underwear beneath my sunflower dress. "That's it, keep it straight."

I continue to stare at the road as he slips a finger under my underwear and moves it around. I continue to concentrate on being a good girl and keep the truck going along the dirt road.

A sharp poke on my arm brings the interior of an old gray truck into focus.

"Are you okay, Brielle?"

I turn and see Andrew with his brow furrowed.

"You were spacing out. I couldn't get your attention. What's wrong?"

I take a deep breath and quickly release it, trying to expel the fear that grips my chest.

"Oh, I'm just tired, I guess. Still not adjusted to the time change." I give him my best fake smile.

He doesn't seem so convinced, but proceeds to put the truck in reverse. I need to change the subject fast.

"So," I flash a quick grin at him, "what's new?"

He catches the meaning.

"I'm sure Alex has already told you everything about Jade," he says with a smile.

"Jade, is it?" I feign surprise. "Alex mentioned you were dating someone, but he didn't get a chance to tell me much more. So... do spill, I'm not in the mood for digging."

Andrew chuckles softly and shakes his head.

"I don't know what you want to know. I met her at my school. She's amazing, beautiful, talented... we're going to meet her now. I need to do some work on my truck at my grandpa's old barn. I'm sure you'll like her."

"I don't doubt it!" I can tell that he more than likes her. He adores

113

her. I feel a pang of jealousy. I will never find someone to feel that way about me.

"So, tell me about what you're doing now, Miss Brainiac!" Andrew flashes a grin back at me. Banter is something I love with this part of my family. We can joke, but I know that they care and will protect me.

"Hey now. Just because I love chemistry, doesn't mean I'm smart."

"Love and chemistry should never be in the same sentence," he begins to laugh. "Admit it! You're a geek!"

"Ha. Ha. Very funny. I like to work. If that makes me a geek, then so be it!" I can't help the smile that pulls at the corners of my mouth.

We continue to talk and I watch fields of corn and various other crops, not yet in season, fly by outside, with small interruptions for old red barns or tractors. The openness makes me feel at home compared to the cramped conditions of England.

Andrew slows down and pulls onto a dirt path next to an old wooden barn. Andrew parks the truck next to a small black car and gives me a quick smile before jumping out to meet the girl standing in the path. I get out of the truck and follow him.

She wears faded jeans and a baggy hooded shirt. Her blonde hair is pulled back into a neat ponytail. Her stance is somehow protective of herself and I feel a jolt of familiarity. Andrew bounds over to her and gives her a quick hug before turning to me.

"Jade, I'd like you to meet my cousin, Brielle."

"Brie," I correct and flash a smile.

"Hi, Brie, it's nice to meet you," she says, stepping closer and taking my hand in a firm handshake. Her smile is friendly, but as I look at her I can see her eyes are guarded. Again, familiarity emits from her. But I've never met her before, I tell myself.

"It's nice to meet you too," I reply.

"Well, while you two get to know each other, I've got to go rummage around the barn for the spare parts and tools I need."

"Let me know if you need any help," Jade calls over to Andrew who's already making his way into the barn. "I'm actually pretty good with car mechanics," she says to me with a shrug.

I can't shake away the feeling that, although I've never met her before, I have seen her every day. She looks at me, her eyes level with mine. And in that second I understand. The reason she seems so familiar is because I look at those guarded eyes every day. I recognize that stance as if it was my own, because it is. She reminds me of myself. I see her pain, her past, in that brief moment of eye contact. I feel my heart ache for her. What can I do?

"Do you want to sit in my car and wait for Andrew to finish his truck? It's kinda cold out here," she offers.

"Sure." I follow her and get in the passenger side. The warm air inside the car feels good on my already frozen cheeks.

"That's better," Jade says, with a smile. "So, Andrew tells me you're a chemist too. I will be starting a chemical engineering course in the fall. I really like chemistry and also enjoy the 'hands on' part of engineering."

"That's awesome. Yes, I'm a chemist. I'm studying it back in England."

"Yeah, he mentioned you're living over there. What made you move there?"

A very simple question with a very complicated answer. I debate momentarily on whether to go for the simple, 'my mom married an English guy,' but instead go for more truth. I feel myself opening up to her, this girl I just met. It's more like I have known her all my life.

"That's actually a tricky question and quite a long story," I hesitate.

"Well," she glances outside the window at Andrew with his head buried in the hood of his truck, "I'd say we've got time." She gives me an encouraging smile. Does she too sense the connection we have?

I take a deep breath, not sure of what I'm going to say. I look out the window and into the nearby cornfield before turning back to Jade.

"My mom and dad got divorced when I was eight. Well, they started to. The custody battle lasted years. I saw police, lawyers and psychologists on a weekly basis." I pause again, not knowing how much to share. Jade is attentive, so I continue.

"My mom remarried when I was eleven. We went to England to announce the wedding to family over there, my brother and sister were already living there, after marrying English people themselves. On Christmas Eve, my mother told me we were going to stay and live in England. Her and my stepdad, Charlie, went back to New Hampshire to pack up everything, leaving me in England with my brother."

"Whilst she was in New Hampshire, the police turned up on her doorstep, informing her that she was disobeying court orders by not having me in counseling." I glance up at Jade who is now showing signs of concern, but she gives me a small smile of encouragement. "Well, it turns out there's not much they can do if you're in a different country. So, until I was eighteen, I wasn't allowed to go back to New Hampshire."

"I hate England. It became like a prison for me. I never got to say goodbye to anyone and I was never able to go back." I feel tears prick my eyes. I didn't realize how much those wounds still hurt me. "But my mom was happy, and I guess that's what is important."

"I'm sorry," Jade says. "My parents are also divorced. They divorced when I was about eight. Why did your parents split up, if you don't mind me asking?"

Normally I tell people that it was because of an affair my father was having, which is true but not the whole truth, especially from what I read in the police documents a while ago. The suspected abuse was a major factor. I don't know how much to tell Jade, but something makes me feel like telling her the truth, so I do. "My father... well, he wasn't a nice man. In fact, he is one of the reasons I hate men so much now."

"I hate men too," Jade says quietly, as if to herself.

I continue, "He abused me." I feel Jade's eyes on me. "In a loving way, if you get what I mean." I turn to see her eyes boring into mine.

"I know *exactly* what you mean," she says. "Mine was too."

A knock on my window causes us both to jump and a small

scream to escape from my lips. Andrew puts his face up to the glass. It's red from the cold. I open the door a crack.

"I'm about done with my truck. You girls having fun talking in the nice, warm car?" he asks sarcastically. I glance over at Jade; she catches my eye and smiles.

"Yes! In fact, so much so that we want more time to talk. Do you think I could kidnap her for the night?" She looks at me. "Would you like to have a sleepover at my house?"

I can't help but smile. "Yes, that would be great!"

Andrew stands, looking slightly rejected.

"Don't worry, Andrew, I'm not going to steal away your girlfriend! And trust me, we won't talk about you!" I say, with a laugh.

"Alright. Well, if you're sure…"

"We are," Jade and I say in sync and laugh. I close the door, leaving a bemused Andrew standing outside his truck watching us leave.

———————◆———————

I stare at the dark shadows that spread across the ceiling above the bed I'm lying on.

"I know this sounds strange, but I have a fear of opening doors."

I turn on my side to see Jade's reaction. She turns on her side and faces me with a small smile.

"I have the same fear. Sometimes I don't know whether to close a door or not. I fear that if I close the door it will open, but if I don't, I'm inviting people in."

"I know! Me too." We both fall silent for a moment. It had been a long night already. The last time I had checked the time it had been 3 am. My voice was getting tired, but I was still very alert. I couldn't believe what was happening.

All these years I had felt alone. Alone in my shame. Alone in my fear. Alone in my past. But today I found someone. Someone who knows *exactly* how I feel; not only sympathizes, but empathizes too. Her past is uncannily similar to mine. She too has been abused by her father, and then later in her teenage years by her mom's boyfriend. I worry that that specific abuse may not have stopped.

We share our deepest darkest secrets; things no one else knows. I find out that Jade has never told anyone about any of it before. I feel honored that she would tell me. I can't believe what a bond we are sharing. Our reactions, our fears, our shame – all exactly the same.

I feel an odd combination of emotions. I am sad this has happened to her, but happy to have met someone who can actually understand me.

"Do you think you'll tell Andrew?" I ask her.

She remains silent for a few moments before speaking.

"I hadn't thought to tell him before. But sometimes I freak out and he doesn't understand. I feel bad because I know it's not his fault. But I'm scared he'll see me as the disgusting person I am and he'll not want to be with me," she tapers off.

"I understand," I say simply. How can I tell her that she isn't a disgusting person, that it wasn't her fault, when I don't believe that for myself? "But I think you should tell him. Andrew is one of the most caring people in the world. He wouldn't reject you. It would help him understand you better, I'm sure."

"You're probably right." We once again go quiet, lost in our own thoughts.

"Do you believe in God?" I ask her.

"Yes. But I've not been to church in a while." I twinge at that reaction. So many people believe that going to church is all there is to being a Christian, when in fact there's so much more. "Do you?"

"Yes. He's the only thing keeping me alive in many ways, but I'm referring to the strength He gives me not to give up. Sometimes the pain and fear become so much I just want to end it."

"No, don't do that—"

"I know, I know. It's not smart, but I'm not thinking straight when I'm trapped inside my head, trapped in my past. There have been times where I've wanted to end it and I've cried out to God and right there and then I feel His presence engulf me," I say with a smile.

"I wish I could have as strong a faith as you."

"But you can! I'm not as strong as it sounds. I often doubt God. I question where He was when it was all happening. I question how He could let this happen, and how my father, who professed to love Him, could do all of that."

"Does He answer?"

"He hasn't yet. But He's put people in my life to guide me and to encourage me along the journey." Jade falls silent again. I decide to finish my 'sermon' there and not push the subject.

I hear her open her mouth as if to say something, and then close it again. I feel like she wants to say something but is scared to.

"I'm sure I'll understand whatever you are wanting to say. We're pretty similar, you and I."

She laughs quietly.

"Yeah, we really are. We're like twins. I was going to ask… well, I was going to say…" She fumbles for words. I know exactly how that feels. "Did you ever want it to happen?" She turns and looks at me.

I check my emotions quickly so as not to offend her or make her feel worse.

"Yes… and no," I say quietly. "I enjoyed parts of it. My father would tell me he loved me, and he would hug me and hold me, tell me I was special and a good girl. I liked the attention. My mother always seemed so distant, not really showing affection to me like that. But I didn't like the rest. While I didn't know it was wrong at the time, it still hurt."

"Hmmm. Yeah, I get you. But did you ever… you know… feel pleasure?"

I hear the disgust in her voice.

"Yes," I say simply. "And I hate that I did. It makes it so much more complicated. When Ted would hit me, it hurt and I didn't like it. I didn't want him to do that, so I never felt dirty about it. But when he would… touch me, I would feel pleasure sometimes and I felt so disgusted with myself. I still do."

"Me too," she says. I look at her and give her a sad smile. "Do you think we'll ever get over it?"

I hesitate; the phrase 'get over it' had once been said to me by my friend Corrine in high school. Just before I went to university I had told her about my dad. I didn't dare tell her about Ted, she thought he was 'hot' and I felt ashamed of what was happening. Her response was, 'well it's been a long time now, can't you just get over it?' Her words had hurt more than I let her know.

"I don't think we'll ever 'get over it' per se, but I feel that we will grow and learn from this, and maybe one day it won't haunt us the way it does now."

"I hope so," she says wistfully.

"Me too… me too."

Chapter 20

Doubt. Like a seed, doubt is planted into a hopeful mind. The seed then begins to grow and multiply, its roots plunging deep into your thoughts. Soon it takes over and kills belief. Your hope is gone.

It's a day of tears. I left Alex, Andrew and Jade at Chicago's O'Hare airport eight hours ago. Jade presented me with a beautiful handmade bracelet. It was then that the tears began to leak out. I'm going to miss her so much. I can't believe how similar we are. We have matching scars, figuratively at least. I hugged them all goodbye, hoping that it wouldn't be long before I saw them again.

The day after Jade and I had talked all night, she told Andrew about her past. He handled it well, she said. I can see that he loves her so much; I think he will be a strong support for her to heal. I wish I had an Andrew. Or an Alex. They are both amazing guys. Yes, a man that is good! Shocking.

A movement out of the corner of my eye causes me to jump. I look up from my journal to see that it was just the passenger next to me re-crossing her legs. She's an older woman with dyed auburn hair, worn in a giant poof around her head. Thankfully, she's a good person to sit next to for nine hours since she keeps to herself and has been sleeping for the past three hours.

My heart rate settles and I look out the window next to me. All I can see are the top of the snow-white clouds that cover all the land and water below. We should be landing shortly, I think. I glance at my watch. 10 am England time. Yep, I'll be landing in about twenty minutes. I return my attention to the sea of clouds outside the window. As if on cue, I feel the plane begin the descent. We dip beneath the top layer of clouds with a flash of white against the window. As we emerge on the other side I feel a sudden rush of emotion.

Puffy white clouds drift quietly past fields, streams and roads, which, when compared to Wisconsin roads, seem like a child has drawn them with a crayon. The twists and turns have seemingly little direction or purpose.

That's how I feel. I feel like my life is just a mix of turns, heartbreaks and fears, which seem to have no purpose or direction. However, I also know that these twisty, turny roads lead me home. My life is in God's hands, the best place it could be. I feel the elation of hope deep inside. Things are looking up.

◆

"Look at how skinny I was!" my mother says, pointing to a picture of her in a photo album we are looking through at the dining room table.

I clench my teeth, afraid that if I open my mouth I'll end up screaming at her. I know I don't take after her in body figure. I realize I'm fat. I know that a guy will never like me. But maybe that's a good thing. I hope I don't take after my mother in any area of life. She and Charlie have argued every day since I got back here a week ago from my trip to Wisconsin. I hate it. Every time I hear them begin to raise their voices I put on my headphones and pound Evanescence into my ears.

When I first moved to England, my mother and Charlie would argue and eventually my mother would state that she had 'had enough' and slam the back door on her way out. She would get into the car and drive off into the night. I would watch her leave from my bedroom window, not sure if she was going to come back for me, but sure that she was going to get a divorce and afraid that I would be left with Charlie.

After years of this continuing, I stopped believing that they would ever separate and we would move back to America, but I still find myself feeling anxious each time they argue.

My mother has noticed no change in my mood as she continues to flip through the photo album. I push my chair back and head upstairs.

"Where are you going?" my mother asks, finally noticing me.

"I've got some homework to do," I say, my typical excuse.

"Oh, okay." She sounds almost disappointed. I ignore it and continue up the stairs.

By the time I reach my room I am in a full-blown panic. I don't even know why, but I know I must do something. My hands shake as I search through my purse for my comfort. Pain, inconsolable pain, rips through my core. I grit my teeth once more. My fingertips clutch the small blade wrapped in a piece of paper. I quickly unwrap it and feel the cool of the metal on my skin. I feel slightly calmer already, anticipating the relief I will feel momentarily.

I roll up my left sleeve and look up into the long mirror standing in front of me. My curvy body, covered up with bulky sweatshirts and baggy jeans, stands there as an obvious object of my hatred. I hate you, Brie. And with that final thought I swipe the cool metal across my heated skin.

I watch as the deep red blood finds its way out of my open wound. I wish escaping from myself was that easy. I wish that I could just cut myself open and escape the nightmare of being me.

I turn away from my ugly image in the mirror and see the piano that my parents have moved into my bedroom beneath the window. I pull out the bench, push on the power button and put on the headphones so I don't alert my mother to the fact that I'm not doing my non-existent homework.

My fingers find their way over the keys. The rage I feel inside blasts through the headphones as discords clash violently up and down the octaves. It builds and builds until I finish abruptly, allowing the surge of notes to continue to ring out. I feel broken. I feel no hope. I feel only pain.

'God! Why don't you love me? Why weren't you there for me? Why did you bring me here, to this stupid country I despise? Why did you even allow me to be born?' My questions blast through the silence in my headphones. I close my eyes and allow my fingers to once more flutter across the keys in front of me. This time a gentle melody resounds and without hesitation I begin to sing along with this unknown tune.

"Here I am heartbroken. I'm scarred by this world so cruel. And there You are, arms open. Waiting for me. Waiting for me.

So here I kneel before You, for You to come fill up my life. Oh...

Joy of heaven's peace. Come fill my life again, I want to know You, I want to know You, Lord."

The music sounds beautiful. The words resound deep within me. I quickly grab a scrap piece of paper and write out the words and music roughly. I feel the pain start to ebb away, and a peace settle around me as I write it down. It's like God is answering my cry.

I look down at my arm and see the streaks of blood staining my pale skin. It's like a slap from reality. God can't love me. God doesn't care. I turn off the piano and go into the bathroom to clean and bandage my cut.

I wash the dried blood from my arm, turning the flowing water bright red. I see that the blood is still trickling at a fast rate out of the open wound. It doesn't usually take this long to slow down bleeding. I wipe away the blood with a tissue and look more closely at the wound. It's deep. I see a lot of exposed flesh. I've never cut this deep before. A ripple of fear races down my spine. What have I done? It's got to stop bleeding or else I might have to get stiches, then people will know and I'll have to go to a mental institution and my mother will find out. My mother can't find out. What do I do?

My thoughts run into each other in a sheer terror until I put on the brakes and calm my swirling mind. Nothing. I'll do nothing. I'm sure it will be fine. I take a long strip of bandage and wrap my arm several times. It'll stop. It has to.

I watch as the clock ticks over to 8 am. Finally, a reasonable time to get up. It feels as though I've been watching the clock for hours. In fact, I have. I didn't sleep at all last night. I couldn't. Every time I closed my eyes my father's image would be right there. It would feel as though he was on top of me, breathing heavily in my ear. My chest constricted and I thought I'd suffocate. Eventually I snapped out of the nightmare and lay silent in the moonlit room, waiting for the dawn to come.

I carefully slip out of bed, trying not to make a sound as I make my way to the bathroom, silently locking the door behind me. I don't want to face my parents yet, but I don't want to lay in my bed a second longer. I look down at my bandaged arm. A violent red streak of blood has seeped all the way through the multiple layers. Slowly I unravel the bandage. The skin around the wound is red; the wound itself is still a pool of fresh blood. A wave of nausea washes over me. I place my hands on either side of the sink to try and keep the room in focus. Blood starts to spill down my arm once more.

Oh crap. It won't stop. I turn on the cold tap and begin to wash the blood away. The wound looks very pale and fleshy beneath the blood. Another wave of nausea crashes over me and I quickly look away. I'll just ignore it. It will be okay. I shakily place a fresh bandage around my arm and retreat to my room. It's time to start getting ready for church.

I emerge from my room twenty minutes later, dressed in my typical baggy jeans and dark sweatshirt, purposefully picked to hide any blood seepage that may occur. I take a deep breath to calm my hands that still tremble at my side and head down the stairs.

Downstairs, a quick "good morning" is exchanged with my mother. Charlie is hastily ironing his shirt in the dining room. His bare chest makes me cringe and I quickly redirect my attention to finding something for breakfast. I can feel the tension between them. They must be arguing again. At least it's not verbal today.

Finally, I hear him unplug the iron and my mother stands and walks toward the back door with an icy silence. At least I don't have to pretend to be cheerful this morning. I follow her out the door and wait at the car for Charlie to catch up.

"Are you okay, Mom?" I ask tentatively. I'd rather not have to address her, but I do care.

"I'm just fed up." She begins her typical 'I can't stand Charlie' rant. "He just doesn't listen. I've told him over and over again…"

I'm sorry I asked. She continues to speak while I tune her out and stare at my warped reflection on the side of the car. What if this is the true image and everything else we see is warped? Thoughts of what reality is defined by whizz through my head until I hear the gate slam shut and Charlie's hurried footsteps clomp down the alleyway. My mother stops mid-rant and gets into the car. Once Charlie's in, with a slam of the car door, he whips out of the driveway. We are, as per usual, already late. They can never be on time, I swear. Another 'quality' I'm glad I didn't inherit.

My mother begins to speak, or rather continues her rant, toward Charlie this time. He stops her short with a huff and a suppressed yell, telling her to 'just drop it.' Again, I ignore it to the best of my ability and stare into my dead eyes reflecting in the window.

I might be dying. If the bleeding doesn't stop, I'll die. This will all be over. I won't feel any more pain. The thought doesn't scare me, which, in turn, surprises me. Instead, I feel a peace with the idea. I don't have to live like this. I don't have to live.

As we pull into the church parking lot, a quiver of fear slithers down my spine and I shake it off. There's no reason to be scared, it's just church. I hop out of the car and head into church without my bickering parents. Maybe I can sit with my brother.

As I enter the foyer a man stands there with a hymnbook in one hand and the other hand outstretched to welcome me. I tense my shoulders and grit my teeth as I take his hand, preparing for any flashbacks that dare to infiltrate my consciousness. Nothing happens and I let out a small sigh as I take the hymnbook and slip into the back of the church.

The service has already started. Music blares and a couple hundred people are standing up around the room, most of whom have their hands raised in praise to God. I'm reminded of the song God gave me last night and another rush of peace settles around me. I spot my brother in the front row. At least there are no other men near him. I go and stand next to him. He notices my appearance and gives me a genuine grin. I look up at my big brother. I'll miss him when I'm gone. The thought comes forcefully, with the realization that I've made the decision already. I'm going to die; I just don't know when yet. It may be soon. I push away the thoughts and try to concentrate on the music and the words that resound around me. But all I hear is noise.

The noise builds, drumming in my ears. My pulse quickens and I feel my breath become uneven and shallow. The room begins to blur out of focus and I can feel the thumping pulse beneath my bandaged arm. I raise my shaking hands and place them on either side of my face and over my ears, a gesture I've found that helps calm me. It's as if I could just shut my eyes and cover my ears to all the bad in the world.

"Help me please! Oh God! I'm scared," I cry out in my head.

And there, just like that, His peace pours over me, relieving me of my burden of pain. My ears open to the words of the song that are being sung:

"T'was Grace that taught my heart to fear, and Grace, my fears relieved. How precious did that Grace appear, the hour I first believed."

Amazing Grace. A song that rings so true in my life. I can't help but smile and join in with the next verses. It's like my pain has been replaced with joy. I feel on top of the world. Once the song is finished, I take my seat and John, the pastor, gets up to preach on the topic of 'Jesus, the *Compassionate* King' from *Mark 6:30-56*.

For most of the sermon I struggle to concentrate and don't take anything in, except for a certain point toward the end of the message. That is:

"Being a follower of Jesus Christ means we are never in doubt. Nothing can stop His love toward us. *Do not fear*, but *trust* Him."

I realize I have both doubt and fear. And I cannot trust. I know that, while I feel full of joy at the moment, it will not last. The farther

I rise, the farther I have to fall. I once more try to push away these thoughts, but they cover me like a heavy dark cloud. Doubt has taken my peace again.

We stand to sing the closing hymn. My brother's elbow accidentally nudges my shoulder. It's not much, but it's enough for my mind to try and pull away from the present. I feel my past on the very edge of my consciousness. Flashes of my father standing next to me in church with his elbow-patched suit whip across my vision. I try to back away from him but end up backing against my chair, pulling me back into the present with my brother. He turns and looks at me as I regain my balance. I force a smile and a shrug, making out that it's no big deal. He smiles back and then turns to continue singing. I can't live like this. I must escape.

Chapter 21

Dead. Have you ever thought you'd be better off dead? It's a rare but fleeting thought to most of us. Our curiosity of the unknown can sometimes lead to such morbid thoughts. As Christians, we believe that life after death is wonderful; beyond what we can even imagine. Others believe there is nothing. We simply cease to exist. Sometimes death is more than a fleeting thought. Sometimes we feel it is our only option.

The sound of my rhythmic breathing is the only noise to reach my ears. The stillness of the dark engulfs me as I lay staring at the ceiling of my bedroom. I feel nothing. I can't even form a thought. I'm once again numb.

The bleeding of my cut finally stopped two days ago. I've been too afraid to cut again since. I don't want to die here at home. I won't put my mother through that. However, the urge to feel again is becoming harder and harder to resist.

The sound of a squeaking floorboard alerts me that I'm not the only one awake at 2 am. I remain frozen with my eyes trained on the small shadows that flicker above me. My parents' door squeaks open and I feel my body tense. I glance toward the door. The hallway light flicks on, pouring light in under my door. I hear my mother's footsteps pause outside my door. She slowly pushes down on my door handle and I watch as the door swings open, spilling more light in and onto my face. I don't have time to pretend I'm asleep. She steps into my room and I squint to see her.

"You're awake. Good." She takes a seat on my piano bench. "I wanted to speak with you about your behavior recently."

I can feel my face register shock and confusion. Why is she telling me this in the middle of the night? I stare at her without response, allowing her to continue what she has to say.

"You've been very withdrawn recently…" Oh, now you notice. "…and I'm really quite concerned. You've been treating Charlie and me not very nicely. You don't speak to either of us and when you're with us it seems like you'd rather be anywhere else." At least my message is getting through clearly.

"Now, I don't know whether it's just stress from school, or what. But I don't appreciate being treated with such coldness. Have I done something to offend you?" I don't respond, rather I just continue to stare at her. "Ever since you've been back for your study break it's like you're not even here. You stay up here in your room all day. If you do speak to me it's only to criticize." Of course my mother would feel as if all I do is criticize her. She always thinks that. I force myself not to roll my eyes or smile.

I have nothing to say so I just sit there staring at her until she's finished. I pick up words like 'unloved' and 'criticized' and I know she's feeling sorry for herself. She doesn't even realize the pain I'm in or the amount I hate myself. She can't hate me more than I do.

I glance at the clock. 4 am. I again stop myself rolling my eyes. She's been yelling at me for two hours. I tune back into what she's saying, hoping there will be a sign that she is almost through.

"If you have not changed your attitude by Saturday I am kicking you out of here and you will not be allowed your car either," she says firmly. Shock ripples through me. I feel my jaw slacken.

She's kicking me out? This is an extreme measure for her. She's never even hinted at this before. And taking my car? How can I get anywhere? I have another week until I go back to university. How will I get there? What will I do once summer comes? My head fills with questions but I remain outwardly unfazed. She looks at me and says, "I'm being serious. I can't stand it anymore."

I swing my legs over the side of my bed and grab my towels from the closet. Without acknowledging her I pass by her and out into the hallway. She follows closely behind me. I step into the bathroom and turn to shut the door. She stares at me. "It's like you're dead," she finally says as I slam the door in her face.

———————◆———————

I am dead. I might as well be. My mother's words from the previous night reverberate in my head as I walk through the damp and dingy alleyway. Rain drenches my clothes and hair. Freezing raindrops roll down my cheeks like tears. If only I had some. If only I could feel something. But I can't. I'm numb. How am I to show feelings toward my mother, positive or negative, when I don't feel any in the first place? I stuff my fists further into my sweatshirt pocket and clench my jaw. I don't know where I'm walking. I'm just walking.

If I'm to be kicked out in a few days, I'd better start making plans. Maybe I could stay with Corwin? Or maybe even somehow get to Arin's and go back to university with her. I can't believe it's gone this far. I know I'm not exactly interacting with them, but that's not uncommon. I guess my outward mask isn't as tightly sealed as I'd like. However, I feel like my problem is all the result of what I let happen. It's no good feeling sorry for myself when I am the one who got myself into this mess.

The sound of footsteps alerts me to my surroundings. I look around and see a man about forty feet away, walking toward me. I feel my heart begin to race and my breathing become shallow. My hands quiver in my pocket. He comes closer and closer. He's about six feet tall with a heavy beige coat on. His head is bent down, keeping the rain off his face. Thump, thump, thump. The sound of his large shoes hitting the pavement match my heart drumming in my chest. I feel my mind try to pull away. Flashes of my father dressed in his heavy coat walking with me in the woods come across my vision. Thump, thump, thump. The footsteps are close.

My father looks down at me and smiles.

Wham! My arm slams against something cold and hard. I blink and the woods have disappeared. A concrete fence lining the alleyway stares back at me. The footsteps are fading into the distance. The man has gone. I feel a burst of pain erupt in my stomach. My hands are shaking violently now. I snap my hairband around my wrist. The small sting gives me no relief. I try over and over again as panic rises inside my chest. It's no use. I slouch against the cold wet concrete and reach inside my jeans pocket to where I keep my blade. I know I'm trying to stop, but I can't. I have to stop the pain before it engulfs me.

I unwrap the blade as quickly as my trembling hands allow me to. I take a quick glance up and down the alley to make sure no one is around. The coast is clear. I roll up my sleeve and make a quick swipe before I even have a chance to think about it. The pain comes swiftly and sweetly. Calm sweeps through my veins, allowing my breathing to slow and my heart to relax in my chest. I watch as the blood trickles out of the wound.

I think of what I've just done and shame washes over me. Why do I cut? I have no reason to whatsoever. There are plenty of people with actual reasons. I'm just pathetic. I can't do anything right. My life is great. I pull my sleeve over the shameful scars and open wound and begin my journey back to my home. At least for now.

My mother is sitting in her chair in front of the window, waiting, as I step in the back door. Her eyes are red and puffy. An obvious sign that tears have been shed. Maybe she and Charlie had another fight. It wouldn't surprise me in the slightest. My hair continues to drip over the carpet. I must look like a drowned rat. But at least I'm a calm drowned rat! I inwardly giggle at my unspoken joke. My mother just looks at me. I slyly glance down to make sure no blood is seeping through my sweatshirt sleeve. I'm good. I look back at my mother. She seems to be inwardly debating on what she's going to say. I wait.

"I was worried. I didn't know where you'd gone or when you'd be back." A strange worry for someone who's kicking me out. "I've been thinking and praying all morning. Brielle, I'm sorry. I'm so sorry. I know I shouldn't have said all I said last night. I was upset and everything just got on top of me. I overreacted. Can you forgive me?"

I feel a wave of shock hit me. I'm off the hook? I'm not going to be kicked out? I can go back to university in a few days?

I feel a huge weight lift from my already rather burdened shoulders. I have no words, so I just nod. I know I've been let off easy. I've not been nice to her. I am as she says. I am dead.

She smiles and stands up, giving me a hug. A rare occurrence for her at one point in time. Over the past few years, her hugs and signs of affection have exponentially increased. I relish the human touch for a moment, knowing I am safe and that it may be one of my last hugs from her. The time is drawing near.

Chapter 22

Time. There is a time for everything, and a season for every activity under the heavens: a time to be born and a time to die, a time to plant and a time to uproot, a time to kill and a time to heal, a time to tear down and a time to build, a time to weep and a time to laugh, a time to mourn and a time to dance..."
Ecclesiastes 3:1-4

Another day. The darkness is constantly there now. It is there when I wake. It is there when I lay down. It is there in my nightmares. It is always there. No matter how hard I try, I can't find a way out. I feel out of control. My façade is becoming harder and harder to keep up. I'm tired. I've tried cutting down my meal portions to give me some sense of control, but it doesn't work.

I've been back at university for a week now. The last few days with my parents were difficult, but I put a lot of effort into being as kind as possible, knowing it was probably the last time they'd see me. I know they will miss me, but with the rest of the family near them, I'm sure they will be okay one day. I'm making sure I don't die around them. They can't be the ones to find me.

Now all I need to figure out is how it's going to happen. I could cut myself so deep I bleed to death, but somehow I feel that someone would notice before it gets that far. I could jump off the bridge into the river. Either the fall or the drowning would work and I'd get the feeling of being free at last. However, I feel that my best plan is to go out as a chemist. Chemical poisoning.

It's strange to think of the way I'm going to die with such ease.

But I don't fear death. In fact, I believe it will be a wonderful release from the pain I'm in now.

My mind thinks through the chemicals we use in lab. Many of them, if ingested, would be fatal, but I don't think I want to take the chance that I survive but am severely injured. Maybe more of a toxin, that isn't quite as corrosive. I remember a CSI show where the victim was suspected of having killed themselves by taking a whole bottle of painkillers. That's what I need, something to kill the pain.

Arin stirs in her bed. I startle, forgetting she is here. I'm so wrapped up in the darkness.

"Good morning, Brie-Brie!"

I smile weakly. That's about all the energy I have. A frown forms on her face.

"What's wrong, Brie?"

"Nothing," I say, shaking my head.

"Something is. You've been so down for so long. I'm worried about you."

Great, just what I need. People to care. "I'm fine, really."

"Liar."

Her voice is so blunt that I look up in surprise. I am lying, of course, but I prefer people to believe me. I shrug. What do I say? I want to die? I'll be sent to a psycho ward for sure.

"I think you should go see someone. Maybe a therapist can help?"

I continue to look at her as if she's out of her mind, but maybe she's right. Maybe I do need help. But I know I don't deserve any. What I need is a way out.

"Can you believe exams are just a few weeks away? I'm not ready. I don't know anything!" Arin continues her worried rant as we sit in the great hall eating our dinner. Or at least *she's* eating. Between her long, seemingly unending chatter, I move my food around my plate without picking it up and eating.

"I know. It's soon," I say, allowing her to take a mouthful of shepherd's pie. My mind, however, is so far from exams that I have very few worries about them. Maybe it's because I know I won't be around to take them. I still study, of course. It's the only thing that keeps my mind occupied.

Rain pitter-patters against the old stained glass windows, echoing the dark and dismal feelings inside me.

"Are you okay, Brie?"

I look up to see that Arin has stopped her monologue and is looking at me with a furrow in her brow of concern.

"Oh, yeah! I'm good. Just tired and stressed about exams. It's been a long day." I try to appease her by giving her my best smile.

My mind drifts back to my thoughts earlier this morning. Do I want to die? Yes. Every day. More than that, I think that I'd be better off having never been born. A rip of pain courses through me, thrusting my body slightly forward. I hug my arms around my stomach trying to hold myself together.

"Are you sure you're okay? You don't look so great."

"I think I just ate something bad. I dunno. I'm going to go to bed."

"Remember I'm not in tonight? I'm heading to Leeds to visit my friend from school."

"Oh, that's right. I forgot about that. See you Monday. Hopefully, if I feel better by then."

I take a deep breath as I stand and clear my plate. Just make it to your room, Brie.

I focus on every step as my feet echo across the great hall, across the courtyard and up the seventy-five stairs to my empty room. The door slams behind me and I'm thrown back in time.

The bathroom door slams shut behind him. I hear the 'click' of the lock button being pushed. My naked body tenses in the bathtub. I stop splashing the water with the palm of my hand. Maybe he heard me and I'm in trouble.

"Hi Ellie. You almost done?" he asks in his deep but sweet voice. It cracks just a little.

I nod my head. Maybe he didn't hear me splashing. Maybe he's just going to get me out and cuddle me.

I go to stand up but my father's arm comes in and pushes my shoulder back down so I can't.

"Wait Ellie. Did you wash yourself really good?"

"Yes," I say. I did.

"Are you sure? Did you wash your privates well?"

I pause and think. I don't remember.

"Let's just do it again to be sure." I hold very still until he finishes.

"Good girl," he says, with a smile on his face.

A door slams somewhere nearby. I find myself curled up on the floor. Tears stream down my face. Have I been crying? I look around the room, not sure how I got here or how long I've been here. Is my father still here? Was he ever here? I feel confusion and fear build up rapidly inside me. I frantically look around the room, making sure no one is here. My chest rises and falls and a wave of dizziness washes over me.

"I can't. I can't," I say to no one, slowly rocking myself back and forth on the floor. "I can't do this!"

My hands tremble as I grab my bag. I need the pain to go away. I need to get it out. I need to get him out! I'm gulping for air as I pull out the blade and swipe it across my arm. One, two, three times. It's not working!

"Ahhh!" I scream. I can't handle the pain. It pushes to take over me completely. I can't fight any more. I can't fight. I see the small bottle of wine sitting on my shelf. I got it at some point and hadn't opened it yet. I also see the two boxes of pain killers on my desk. I was preparing for my menstrual cramps and I decided to get two. I'm not sure why. However, the two objects put together stops my racing mind for just a moment. I can stop this pain for good. Right now.

Without further thinking I get up and within two strides I reach my desk and grab the wine from my shelf. I then quickly proceed to rip the packets of pills out of their boxes. I pop each pill out onto my desk. I have thirty-two in total. That should be enough. I look at the pills scattered across my desk. I open the bottle of wine with my trembling hands.

Now, Brie! This can all be over. Now! I pick up one of the pills and place it in my mouth and chase it down with a sip of wine. Again! I repeat two more times. It becomes easier and easier as the fourth and fifth slide down. My panic has stopped. I won't feel anything soon. As I reach for the sixth pill I accidently hit the Bible that lies on my desk. A twinge of something stirs inside me. Maybe I shouldn't do this.

"But I can't keep going!" I cry out to God this time. "I can't do it! It hurts too much!"

Tears flow fast down my cheeks. My breaths come in short gasps.

"I hate myself so much! Look at what I've done. It was all my fault! I can't. I can't do this!"

I pick up the sixth pill and go to place it in my mouth. As it reaches my lips I'm suddenly hit with the words 'I am with you,' said gently, yet forcefully in my mind. I remain frozen, waiting for more, but no more sound comes. Yet now all I can think about is Isaiah 43. Isaiah 43, Isaiah 43, Isaiah 43. The words swirl around in my mind. I glance at the Bible now half hanging off my desk and glance back at the scattered pills. Isaiah 43! I put down the pill and the bottle of wine and pick up my Bible. Quickly turning to Isaiah, I flip through the pages and find the section. I begin to read:

"But now, this is what the LORD says— he who created you, Jacob, he who formed you, Israel: "Do not fear, for I have redeemed you; I have summoned you by name; you are mine. When you pass through the waters, I will be with you; and when you pass through the rivers, they will not sweep over you. When you walk through the fire, you will not be burned; the flames will not set you ablaze. For I am the LORD your God, the Holy One of Israel, your Savior...Since you are precious and honored in my sight, and because I love you...Do not be afraid, for I am with you."

Words jump out at me from the page. My tears spill over and drop onto my lap. I can't control my sobbing.

He loves me. He is with me. I am loved. These are the only thoughts that whirl around my head.

My whole body shakes as I fall to my knees on the floor. I am loved by my creator! He has saved me! He won't let me drown! Joy bubbles up and pours out of me and I begin to sing an old hymn I know: *Amazing Grace.*

This is not a time to die. This is a time to survive!

PART 3

Somehow, I made it. I can feel the sand beneath my feet. After all those years of swimming out in the endless ocean, finally I have made it to shore. For a moment, all I can see is the sand and I relax in the rays of the sun. But the moment passes. I look around. Fear grips me once more. I cannot go back into the sea. I will not.

I jump up from the warmth of the sand and begin to gather supplies to build my future right here on the sand. I can't go back. I must stay here. Here, where it is warm and beautiful and my weary limbs can rest. I can't believe I made it!

I begin to sing as I make my little house on the beach, but what I do not see is the rising tide. It comes closer and closer, threatening to destroy all that God has brought me to. If anyone were to look down upon my house they would think, 'What a silly place to build a house! Why, if they climb up these cliffs there are marvelous pastures flowing with beauty!' But I do not see. I focus on building my life here, happy in my own little world. I cannot see the danger inching its way closer and closer to me.

Chapter 23

Dream. Have you ever had a dream that you never shared with anyone? You keep it tightly locked away inside you. It's like your little personal bubble of hope, and you're afraid that if you tell someone, they will burst the bubble; afraid that if you speak it, it might not come true.

Nightmare. The opposite of a dream. It invades your sleep. Haunts your thoughts. You also keep it tightly locked away inside you. Not because you are afraid that if you speak it, it might not come true. Just the opposite. You fear if you speak your nightmare, one day it will come to pass.

A scream startles me awake. My eyes open to a darkened room. All I can hear are the muffled sounds coming from the TV downstairs. I quickly slip out of bed and throw on my sweatshirt, which I had discarded in the middle of my bedroom floor. I open the door as silently as I can. Perhaps the scream was just my mother and Charlie having another fight, in which case I would prefer not to disturb them. I slowly creep out into the hallway and make my way down the stairs one at a time, avoiding the creaky parts of the stairs. I pause halfway and crouch down so I can see the living room between the banister railings.

The thing that strikes me as odd is my mother's expression. Normally she is either asleep or fully engrossed in the TV. Right now, however, she is staring toward the dining room with a look of shock frozen on her face. I lean forward to try and see what she sees. And that's when I see him.

He is wearing a black coat and blue jeans. Large work boots

silently thud in the carpet as he steps closer toward my mother. A long sword is clasped in his hands and held out in front of him. Ready to strike.

I feel frozen. I can't make my muscles move. I just sit in shock watching him creep closer and closer to my mother. Within three seconds he has reached her and swung the sword across her throat causing a mass of blood to spurt across the TV and living room walls.

Screaming reaches my ears. The man has frozen. He turns and looks at me. I suddenly realize the screaming is coming from my own lips. A surge of adrenaline pulses through my body. My heart beats wildly. For a split-second I stare into the cold eyes of my father before sprinting up the stairs and into my room where I slam the door behind me and pull a chair over to barricade the door. It won't hold long, I know.

I look around my room frantically, my head spinning from what I just saw. My window is cracked open to let some fresh summer air in. The conservatory is right beneath my window… maybe I can escape that way. I dash to my piano bench and climb over my piano and onto the windowsill. Pushing open the window further I swing my legs out into the cool night air. Bang! My father grunts as he tries to break in the door. I take a deep breath and push myself from the window, landing on the conservatory with a thunk…

My eyes open to a darkened room. A dull throb emits from my knee, from where I just whacked it against the bed. My heart beats fast inside my chest. My breathing sounds as if I've just run a marathon. I pull out my cell phone to check the time. 12:30 am. I only got into bed thirty minutes ago!

I close my eyes and see images of my mother's head being chopped off. It's a nightmare that has frequently visited me over the past ten years. In fact, nightmares have been a part of my life for as long as I can remember. Not only the realistic ones, but ones like this, where my father is murdering my mother. I remember when I was eight years old, I would often wake up in the middle of the night and run into my mother's room to make sure she was still alive. I still do it from time to time.

I shake my head to pull me out of my thoughts. I could really use a 'head clearing' right now… 'No Brie. Don't do this. You are here to have a good time.' I take a deep breath and slowly release it. I let my eyes close but the image of my father once again flashes across my mind. 'Fine! I won't sleep.'

I sit up and lean over the bed railing to the bunk bed below me. My roommate, Sally, a girl from Hill church who is also a chemist, breathes heavily below, tucked away beneath several layers of blankets. I quietly shuffle myself to the end of the bed and climb down the ladder. Each rung makes slight squeaking sounds, but it doesn't disturb Sally's deep sleep.

I grab the sweatshirt that is draped over my small suitcase on the floor, rummage through my purse for my iPod and slip my shoes on before silently sneaking out the door.

The long corridor is fully lit. The white walls blind me momentarily as I walk down the green carpet toward the gym at the other end of the building. Through the small windowpane, I can see that the gym is empty and dark. I could try to find a light switch, but I'd prefer no one know I'm here.

We're currently somewhere on the Scottish border. Every year, just after Christmas vacation, my church does a retreat for three days. They are good fun. Lots of games, teachings and hanging out with people. Last year this combination was my perfect nightmare – I couldn't relax with so many people around.

This year, I feel different. I'm able to talk to people without battling the thoughts that want to take me away from the conversation. I'm able to make it over a week without cutting. And I no longer think about dying either. It's amazing how much has changed in just six months. Peter being here also helps, knowing I can talk to him if I need to.

Six months and three days from the day God saved my life. I still struggle to comprehend how amazing He is and how thankful I am for what He did. However, life has not become bliss. I thought that maybe I was totally healed. Ha! Little did I know. The past six months have not passed without my fair share of battles.

Battles with the ever-present darkness, lingering on the edges of my consciousness, battles with my self-harm addiction, battles with my fear of men, battles with my hatred toward myself, battles with my annoyance of my mother. The list seems endless. I feel as though I just swam across the ocean and now I must climb a mountain. The problem is, I don't think I can.

My footsteps echo around the gym as I pace back and forth from one basketball net to the other. Faint lights spill in from the corridors on either side of the gym. I reach into my sweatshirt pocket and pull out my iPod. I scroll through until I find Shinedown's album. I put the earbuds in my ears and click play. The music pounds in my head, pushing all unwanted thoughts away. I shove the iPod back into my pocket and begin to jog from one end of the gym to the other in time with the beat. If I'm going to be up all night, I might as well lose some weight while I'm at it.

"Brie? Brie?"

A voice drifts into my mind. He was on top of me. He was just here. I feel the panic trapped inside me. I can't tell where I am. The voice comes again.

"Brie? Are you okay?"

I try to find its source but flashes of different images fly across my vision. I feel confused and scared. Where am I? I take a deep breath and close my eyes for two seconds before reopening them. I'm sitting cross-legged in the middle of a gym, staring at a glossy wooden floor. I look up.

Peter stands above me with a worried look on his face. I've done it again. I don't know how long I've been here like this. I feel the heat of embarrassment creep over my cheeks.

"Hi, Peter," I say casually. "What's up?"

"Uh." My casualness obviously catches him off guard. "I was just on my way into breakfast and I saw someone sitting here in the middle of the floor. Are you sure you're alright?"

"Yeah. Yeah. I'm fine," I smile enthusiastically. "Just having some alone time. Is it time for breakfast? I'll join you!" I spring up from the ground to try and confirm my 'alright-ness,' but it has the opposite effect. The room spins and begins to go dark. I topple to the side and fall into a crouched position with my head between my legs in an attempt not to pass out.

"Head rush," I mumble to Peter before he calls an ambulance or something.

He laughs and waits patiently for me to get the blood back to my head. Finally, the room comes back into focus and I stand, slowly, and head out to the dining hall with Peter.

Lots of people are already scattered around the tables with steaming porridge in brightly colored bowls. Everyone seems to be having animated conversations. I feel isolated. Even with Peter standing right beside me. How can I ever relate to people on a normal level when I'm crazy? I'm so messed up. The cloud of darkness moves in a little closer. I focus my thoughts on getting breakfast.

I grab a blue bowl of porridge from an extra smiley girl, whose name I don't know. She's sweet and cheerful. Everything I'm not. Spotting Peter's physics friends at a nearby table, I head in that direction, knowing I won't be good company for him. I sit with the wall on one side of me, Peter on the other and no one across. Perfect. I say good morning to the group and then concentrate on spooning the thick goop into my mouth as the guys talk about the speakers we'll be having today.

"There are three separate ones at the same time. We can obviously only go to one," the tall blond guy says. I've met him before, but I'm atrocious with names.

"What are they?" Peter asks.

"Well, I could be wrong, but I think one's on knowing your gifts, another on hearing from God and a third on how to read the Bible."

"They all sound a little strange. I dunno which one I'll go to. Maybe knowing my gifts. I have no idea what mine are," Mark says in his Irish accent.

"Yeah, I also feel it will be a challenge to decide," Peter pauses as if in thought. "What about you?"

Silence follows and I glance up to see all eyes on me. Oh! That question was for me. Crap. "Umm…I think listening to God, or whatever that was."

"Hearing from God. Yeah, I think I'll probably join you on that one!" Peter grins at me.

I go back to eating my porridge. Last night was really tough. The images of my nightmare had not left me for most of the night. I drifted in and out of flashbacks, having little sense of reality. I'm exhausted this morning. I don't want to talk to anyone or hear from anyone. But maybe I'll hear what God was thinking when He created me, because I'm pretty sure it was a mistake.

Rosie, the youth pastor, gets up and begins the talk on 'Hearing from God.' Her strong voice fills the room where twenty or so of us sit on the most uncomfortable chairs known to mankind. I try desperately to listen to what she's saying, but all I can see are her lips moving. My mind is so preoccupied with the nightmares I had.

I remember when I was fifteen, and my mother's conversation with me after discovering that I still often checked on her in the middle of the night to make sure she was still alive…

"You have done that for so long. Do you know why you do that, Brielle?" she had asked me while we were eating Chinese take-out. Charlie was out of town, hence it was girls' night in, which always involved Chinese.

I shrugged and adjusted my chopsticks to a more comfortable position before attempting to pick up the rather large piece of deep fried chicken.

"It was after your dad left that it started."

I paused with the piece of chicken halfway to my mouth. Did she just say the 'D' word? He came up so rarely. Like never. I glanced up at her and then continued to shove the piece of chicken in my mouth.

"Well," she continued, "after the divorce he was threatening to kill me to get to you. In fact, he tried once, a long while before we divorced." Her face flashed with a haunted look I saw so often in my reflection. I hid my surprise and proceeded to move my food around the plate since my appetite had suddenly vanished. "He was also a prime suspect in the murder of several women in the area who had disappeared." I could no longer hide my shock. I just stared at her like she had three heads. My mind flashed to the woods. The hundreds of acres surrounding our house... perfect place to hide a body, or several...

A nudge on my right arm brings me back to the Scottish border. I turn to see Peter getting up, along with everyone else. What's going on?

Peter gives me a look that indicates he knows I have no idea what's happening, but not to worry. I smile slightly. I'm so glad to have Peter around.

"How about us three in a group?" he asks.

I turn to see Tim, a guy from my church who, on more than one occasion, had shared a prophetic message relating exactly to my situation during my first year at Northern... great.

"Yeah, works for me," Tim replies, giving me a smile. I gulp.

"So..." I begin. Peter picks up the hint.

"We are going to spend time now listening to God for what He wants to say to us. Focusing on one person at a time. Is that right?" He glances up at Tim.

"Yep! Believe that's what we're doing. Who wants to go first?"

I feel my legs begin to shake and I'm glad I'm sitting down. Definitely not me. If I'm lucky we'll run out of time before I get a go.

"I'll go first," Tim volunteers.

We turn our chairs so we form a tiny circle. I position myself so I'm not touching either of them, or in any danger of doing so. Tim and Peter bow their heads and I do the same. I try to clear the clatter out of my head and listen for anything that might be trying to get in.

Silence. 'God, do you have something you want me to say to

Tim?' Silence. 'What am I doing? Why would you talk to me? Why would you use me? I'm useless.' Silence.

Peter begins to speak in a hushed tone. "I feel like God wants you to know that He is pleased with you. You are struggling, but keep going. He is with you."

Wow! He heard all that? He must be totally in tune with God. Silence. Silence. Finally, Tim speaks.

"Thank you, Peter, for hearing that and telling me, it means a lot." He smiles. "It's amazing how much He cares for us, isn't it?"

Tell me about it... I should be dead right now.

"I'll go next, shall I?" Peter says.

I nod and we once more bow our heads in prayer. Silence. Silence. Then suddenly a voice, as clear as if it were Tim or Peter resounds in my head.

"I love you. I love you. I love you."

The words swirl and build in my head, but they are not my own. My heart beats faster. My hands shake.

"I love you."

I swallow my fear and open my mouth.

"Peter, I believe God wants to say to you: I love you." I sneak a peek up at him. His shoulders drop and I see his mouth stretch into a grin. He begins to praise God quietly. I feel a rush of awe. God just spoke through me!

Tim also speaks to Peter about how he feels God wants to challenge him to step up and do what he was called to do. I'm lost in wonder at what just happened.

"Your turn, Brie."

My world, which is floating high in the sky, crashes with force. 'Crap. Me?' It apparently wasn't a question because both guys bow their heads and the silence continues.

'God, I don't think You'll have anything You want to say to me. I'm not really deserving of Your love or anything. I know none of us are, but I'm especially not.' Peter begins to speak, interrupting my thoughts.

"I have a picture of you in my mind as a little girl swinging on a tire swing. You are full of joy with a huge smile on your face. You are laughing. That's how God wants you to be again."

His words stun me. They pierce my heart. My eyes begin to fill with tears and they readily spill down my cheeks. I can see the image clearly. 'Brielle *Joy*. That's who You created me to be.' Before I can continue to revel in the love I feel, Tim begins to speak.

"This may seem like an odd question, Brie, but do you struggle with nightmares?"

My head snaps up and I see Tim looking at me with a peaceful look on his face. How can he know that? No one knows that, much less Tim who knows nothing about me. I nod my head, realizing Tim is still waiting for an answer.

"Yes, I have nightmares almost every night. Because of them I struggle with insomnia and have done so for years."

Tim nods knowingly. How can he know?

"Well, I truly believe God wants to heal your nightmares right now. Right here. Can I pray for you?"

I nod and my crying becomes sobbing. I place my elbows on my knees and my head in my hands. Tim gently places his hand on my back and begins to pray. I'm so overcome with emotion I don't even care that he's touching me. I don't hear what he's praying, I just fall at the feet of Jesus and sob. My heart aches with pain and love both filling it up. I can't stop the tears flowing. They splash at my feet.

I realize Tim no longer has his hand on my back but I'm still wrapped up in such amazing love. My world has been moved. I feel different. I feel just that little bit freer. A smile spreads across my face through the tears. I glance at my watch. 10 pm. I'm suddenly filled with excitement and apprehension. What will happen? Will I sleep? Will I have a nightmare? I believe God's healed me, but what if He hasn't...? 'Don't doubt, Brie. Believe.'

My anticipation grows as my feet pad down the carpeted hallway. I creak open my temporary dormitory and note that Sally is still down in the other room, probably playing a game or something. Good. I need to be alone for a little while.

Thoughts are still whirring around my head. I can't believe what just happened. It's so surreal that I can't even describe it to myself. All I know is something has changed. How much it's changed I do not know yet. I quickly put on my pajamas and climb the rickety ladder into the top bunk. I crawl beneath the blankets and snuggle in thinking of Arin's 'happy wiggle' as she delights in being buried beneath the puffy blankets.

I lay on my back looking up at the darkness, the ceiling texture just barely visible. Somehow the darkness feels less… dark, my fear just that little less intense.

My thoughts begin to slow as my previous sleepless night takes its toll. I feel my eyelids become heavy as my breathing becomes more steady. What's going to happen? Will I be plunged into my nightly terrors? Has God really taken them away? 'God… I pray that You will give me a nightmare-free night. I believe You have the power to eradicate my nightmares for good. Please do. Amen.' My eyelids finally shut and I'm overcome by complete darkness.

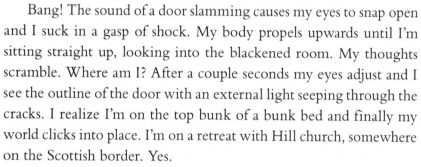

Bang! The sound of a door slamming causes my eyes to snap open and I suck in a gasp of shock. My body propels upwards until I'm sitting straight up, looking into the blackened room. My thoughts scramble. Where am I? After a couple seconds my eyes adjust and I see the outline of the door with an external light seeping through the cracks. I realize I'm on the top bunk of a bunk bed and finally my world clicks into place. I'm on a retreat with Hill church, somewhere on the Scottish border. Yes.

I relax slightly and begin to lie back down. Wait! My body freezes in an awkward pose. What time is it? I assume I've been asleep no more than thirty minutes. I grab my phone from under the pillow and click the center button. My phone clock illuminates: 8:30 am. 8:30… for a few seconds my head does not register what my eyes see. It's 8:30 in the morning. I've slept the whole night. I didn't have a nightmare. I slept. All night! My thoughts begin to escalate in joy. This is amazing. I don't remember the last time I slept through a night without being disturbed by haunting memories or plagued by gruesome nightmares.

I fling the covers back and scramble down the ladder, deciding halfway down to skip the last three rungs and just jump. I land with a thud, expecting to see Sally's face in shock at my jubilant entrance, but her bed is stripped and the covers folded neatly at the end. She must have gone to breakfast already.

I quickly grab my sweatshirt and wrench open the door, stuffing my arms in the sleeves as I bound down the hallway toward the dining hall. I'm almost at the gym when a door next to me flies open and Tim steps out, almost knocking into me. I startle and jump into the opposite wall. Pain shoots up my arm at the same time as I roll my eyes at my stupidity. I *hate* being jumpy.

"Oh, I'm sorry, Brie," Tim says, his voice thick with concern. "Are you alright?"

"Alright?" I almost squeak with emotion. "I'm more than alright, I'm brilliant. Incredible!" I look at Tim who has a quizzical look, as if trying to be happy for me, but not sure why. I continue, "I slept! I slept the *whole* night. I didn't have a single nightmare, which is the first time this has happened in years. God is amazing. Thank you for praying with me last night. Ah!" My words fly together at high speed and I make a small leap in the air. I don't feel like I can quite keep my feet on the floor.

"That's brill! Oh, I'm so glad. Praise God!" Tim's smile is genuine. "Can I join you for breakfast?"

"Certainly." I say, not even hesitating despite his XY chromosome pair.

Tim struggles to keep up with my long, almost leaping, strides as we walk across the dining room, packed with people, to pick up our bowl of fruit. The same smiley girl from yesterday is handing out the bowls again. This time I feel like I can match her grin.

"Thank you!" I say brightly and turn on my heel before bounding over to the table where Peter and his physics buddies sit roaring with laughter. I'm eager to join in. Tim follows and sits across from me.

Again, I don't mind. I'm on cloud nine. No male is going to ruin this for me.

"Hey Brie," Peter smiles as I approach. "How's it going?"

"Stupendous," I squeak.

"Oh really? How come?" he asks.

"I slept, Peter, I slept! No nightmares, nothing."

"That's incredible, Brie," he says.

"I know," I make a small shrug, grin and dig into my bowl lined with peaches, banana, apple and other unidentifiable pieces of fruit.

What if it doesn't last? What if I still have nightmares? Doubt begins to fill my mind as I continue to eat. I have seen God heal me from things in the past. The fact that I'm eating now is proof of that. Come on Brie, where is your faith?

Tim, Peter and I go to pack the rest of our things before leaving. I get on the bus minutes later, knowing this is the beginning of another journey. Knowing it's not going to be easy, but God is with me. And if God is with me, all things are possible. Right?

Chapter 24

Safety. Therapists tell you to go to your safe place. A place where your memories can't hurt you. Others give you an object to 'ground' you, reminding you you're safe. But what if there is nowhere safe? What if your grounding object is taken away from you?

I stare into the void that is my eyes reflecting back at me in the train window. The steady thu-thump-thu-thump of the train's motion has set me into some sort of trance. It's as if I'm there, but not really. I can feel the presence of people all around me, the buzzing of their chatter, but I also feel the presence of people who aren't.

My past still haunts me. No longer in my dreams, mind you. That part has been amazing. I think back over my past week in Northern. Arin and I often talk whilst lying in bed and I no longer dread her falling asleep, leaving me to face my nightmares alone. Instead I welcome the peaceful nights where I know I will wake fully rested. Although I am beginning to wonder how people manage to get so much done and still sleep this long? There aren't enough hours in the day.

I shake myself from that train of thought. Be content. Although my nightmares are gone, my past continues to haunt my waking hours. Even now, I feel its darkness like a cloak around me, threatening to steal the little hope I have hidden inside. I try to snap away from my trance, but I can't. My cold eyes continue to stare back at me. I can just about make out the fields and trees that blur by behind my reflection. It will be another hour or so before I arrive at my destination.

I feel a twinge in my stomach. I can't identify the feelings I have. Fear? Excitement? I should be ecstatic! I'm going to see Corwin at his university in Sheffield. It has been so long since I saw him last and I can't wait. I look forward to telling him all that has happened. Yet I worry what he'll say if he catches a glimpse of my freshly cut arm. A wave of shame crashes around me.

I can't stop. It's the only way I can feel. My fingernails dig in sharply to my palms. The train judders to a stop. The sign at the train station indicates that we have arrived in Leeds. A young woman catches my eye. She is sat on the metal bench with a very worn duffle bag next to her. Her slim shoulders are hunched and her arms crossed protectively across her stomach. Her body is lent slightly forwards over her worn out jeans. Stringy black hair falls haphazardly across her pale face. But none of this is what draws my attention to her.

It's her eyes. Dark brown and large. As if sensing that I'm looking at her, she looks up. For what seems forever we stare at each other and I feel it. I feel the intensity of her pain, so sharp it's like a knife to my heart. She has no hope left. The men in her life have used her and discarded her. Her family has rejected her, her friends abandoned her. She has no one to turn to. Nowhere to go. The train rumbles to life and the steady thu-thump begins again. I hold her gaze as we pull out of the station. She blinks and turns away. I'm once again met with my reflection draped across the bleak scenery.

Tears run down my face. I can barely breathe. My heart throbs in pain for this woman I don't even know. All I know is there is One who can heal her pain. One to whom she can turn to. But how can I find her to tell her? It's too late. Maybe I should have gotten off the train. Maybe I should turn around, go back and... and what? It's hopeless. I can't do anything.

The tears continue to flow. I'm vaguely aware that an older woman has sat down in the empty seat next to me, but I don't care. I can't get the image of the girl out of my head. I can't shake her pain from me. It sticks to me like my own. It's like what happened with Jade in Wisconsin all over again. But at least I could talk to her. Tell her of the hope I have within me. We still often write to one another. This woman on the other hand… I can do nothing for her. *Jesus. Please give her the hope You gave me. Please help her find You. Heal her wounds, Lord. Please.*

I look down at my hands. They are covered in small nail indents, making it look like I've been attacked repeatedly by a cat or something. I didn't realize I was doing it. The lady next to me glances at my hands and I self-consciously tuck them under the table in front of us and return my gaze to the countryside that flashes by. Pain wells up inside me, so strong I can barely continue breathing. I take deep soothing breaths, but they do little to calm me. I have to cut. I think of my blade wrapped up in my right pocket. Just one cut… even the thought of it calms me slightly. Patience. Once I'm with Corwin I can find a bathroom or something. Just wait.

The rest of the journey proceeds swiftly. I find myself in and out of conscious thought. I conclude that I must be dissociating frequently. I'm left with a constant confusion of where and who I am. My muscles ache from unrelenting fear. Rain has begun to streak across the train window as the rest of my tears have dried.

A break in the horizon from the endless dreary fields catches my eye. The tops of sky-riser apartments pierce the low-lying clouds ahead. Sheffield. I scoot across to the now-vacant seat next to me to retrieve my bag from the shelf above. I don't recall the lady leaving. It scares me how much I miss in my episodes of dissociation. Even more scary is that I could have been doing this for years. What if there are things that have happened to me that I still haven't remembered? Could it get worse?

My legs stiff and sore, I stand and begin to make my way down the narrow aisle to the exit door. I brace myself for the train to stop as flashes of the station whip by the small window. It's from there I see him.

A mop of fluffy brown hair bobbing back and forth to music presumably playing in his ears as always. He hasn't seen me yet but, knowing this is my train, he removes his earbuds and begins to sweep his eyes over the train windows hoping to see me.

After what seems an eternity the external train door slides open allowing the biting cold to nip at the exposed skin around my neck and face. He sees me. His face lights up and I feel mine mirror his. I leap gracefully off the train and sprint over to where he stands.

"Brie!" he exclaims as he comes forwards to meet me in a huge hug. My bag slips off my shoulders and I can feel people bustling around me but I ignore them. I soak up the moment in my best friend's embrace.

"Corwin! Oh, how I've missed you." I feel the pinprick of tears sting my eyes. Joy. I feel complete joy at seeing his face. We stand beaming at each other for several moments, allowing the world to continue spinning around us.

"Ready?" he finally asks.

"Yes." My cheeks have begun to ache. I stoop down and grab my fallen bag as I follow Corwin out of the station. As we exit, I prepare myself for the onslaught of freezing rain. But none comes. Instead I'm met with brilliant sunlight, which warms my frozen nose and fingers. The light reflects off the large metal fountain just outside. I skim my fingers through the water that flows down the sides of the metal wall. A giggle bubbles out of my lips. Corwin joins me and laughs his typical laugh.

It feels so good to be here with him again. To hear his laugh.

"So, how are you Brie?"

He turns his head toward me as we walk down the bricked roads that twist through the shopping district. And just like always, I feel the genuine care behind his words. I'm caught off guard and find myself in a small panic, thinking he can read my mind. He waits patiently as I fly though my thoughts and come up with an answer.

My grin diminishes to a small smile as I think of the journey here. "I'm better now that I'm here," I say.

He seems to ponder this, looking down at the ground as he nods his head. I try to distract him from thinking too much about my short answer.

"How are *you*, Corwin?"

It works. He looks up and smiles at me, which instantly reflects on my face. "I'm great," he exclaims. "Now that you're here," he adds.

I turn away and smile to myself. Ah… Corwin. I shake away the thoughts of the woman outside the window and do a small skip, trying to lift the mood once more. "So… what are we going to do whilst I'm here?"

"Anything you want," he says.

"Anything?"

"Anything."

"Hmmm… it's dangerous to give me free reign," I laugh and skip further up the hill we're currently climbing. Sheffield, like Northern, is full of hills. "How about… a walk in the park?" I suggest.

He nods and rubs his chin, looking up into the sky as if for inspiration.

"I think that might be possible. It's just up ahead, not far. Do you want to drop off your bag first?"

"Nah. It's light enough."

"Alright. This way." He makes a right down a small alleyway. I follow him closely. The darkness and close quarters put me abruptly on edge. We eventually emerge into a green park, sparkling in the sunlight from an earlier dousing of rain. My building fears release their grip on me in the peaceful calm of nature. Birds flutter here and there, trying to retrieve worms from the moist ground. Squirrels chase each other through the bare branches of the trees that are dotted around.

The beauty surrounding me captures my attention so much that I don't notice that Corwin has stopped walking, allowing me to wander down the graveled path alone. I turn sharply back to look at him, with my hands on my hips.

"Hey!" I smile at him. "Get your butt on up here and join me for a stroll, my fine fellow!" I change my tone halfway through, ending in my best British accent. Rather poor, even at its best.

He smiles and does a little jog toward me with his hands stuffed into his jacket pockets, causing his hair to flop from side to side. He lands in front of me with a leap. I laugh and turn back to meandering down the path.

One of the many things I love about Corwin, is the need for few spoken words between us. We can talk a lot, but often it is in the silence that we communicate the best.

Our strides match and our shoes crunch on the gravel beneath us. I allow the sun's rays to soak into my exposed skin.

"I have some great news, Corwin." I say with a small smile on my face.

"Yeah? What's that?"

"While I was on the retreat with my church a few weeks ago, a guy prayed over me for my nightmares to be gone."

Corwin slows his pace and looks up at me expectantly.

"God healed me. I was able to sleep through the night for the first time in ages!"

"Wow. Wow!" Corwin grins and shakes his head in amazement. "That's fantastic. Praise God!"

"Yeah... God is good. Sometimes I wish I wasn't so broken so I could help others. You remember me telling you about Jade from America? People like her. Talking with her made me feel like everything I went through was worth it. All the pain was worth going through just so I could completely understand hers."

Corwin nods and remains silent for a moment then takes out a small Bible from his pocket. I say nothing and merely continue to walk slowly beside him as he flips through the pages.

"Aha! Second Corinthians one, verse three: 'praise be to the God and Father of our Lord Jesus Christ, the Father of compassion and the God of all comfort, who comforts us in all our troubles, so that we can comfort those in any trouble with the comfort we ourselves have received from God.' Brie, I don't think God is wanting you to wait until you are completely healed to begin helping others like yourself. He already has been using you."

I let his words sink in as we continue on the path in silence. Maybe God can use me to comfort others. I tuck the thought away inside my heart.

Corwin begins to tell me about his part-time job at his church, all his leadership opportunities and his new music discoveries. Being around him is so normal, it's like we've never been apart.

I look up at the few clouds drifting silently by in the bright blue sky. For a moment, I forget everything. I forget my pain, my past. I forget that I resort to cutting myself to feel. For a moment, I am free and happy.

The moment passes too quickly.

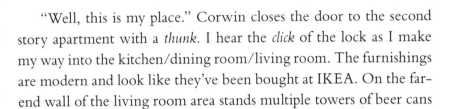

"Well, this is my place." Corwin closes the door to the second story apartment with a *thunk*. I hear the *click* of the lock as I make my way into the kitchen/dining room/living room. The furnishings are modern and look like they've been bought at IKEA. On the far-end wall of the living room area stands multiple towers of beer cans stacked from floor to ceiling.

"My roommates' project." Corwin fills me in, seeing what I'm looking at. "They hope to fill the whole wall by the end of the year."

"Hm. I figured it wasn't yours seeing as you don't drink. Or not that I'm aware of, at least."

"Yeah. Not mine," he laughs again. I feel that we've done nothing but laugh since he met me at the train station a couple hours ago. "Would you like a drink? Water, squash, pop?"

My phone begins to vibrate in my jeans pocket. I pull it out and see 'MOM' written across the screen. I groan inwardly.

"Water, please. I've got to take this," I say to Corwin.

I move over to the French sliding doors that look out onto a small duck pond outside and press the green answer button.

"Hello?" I say, as cheerfully as I can muster. Maybe if I start off happy I won't be as miserable when I'm finished.

"Hello."

My mother's voice stirs a deep anger inside me.

"I'm just calling to see how you are. Did you make it to Corwin's already? That was this weekend, right?"

I feel resentment toward her sudden interest in my life now that I'm away from home. *Now* she cares. Where was she all those nights—

"Yeah. I'm here," I say curtly, cutting myself off from that train of thought.

"Where are you staying?"

"Here."

"At Corwin's?"

"Yeah..." I'm slightly baffled at this line of inquiry.

"Oh, I'm just wondering. Where will you be sleeping?"

"Here."

"In his room?"

"Yeah..." Where is she going with this? A few seconds of silence follow.

"Well... I don't want you to do anything you'll regret. You know..."

It finally dawns on me what the heck she is talking about and the anger bubbles violently up inside my chest. If I could breathe fire, I would be right now.

"Mother. We are just friends," I say as frankly as I can.

"Alright, alright. I'm just making sure."

"Goodbye, mother."

"I'm sor—" I hang up the phone before she has a chance to apologize.

How dare she? She thinks I'm sleeping with him? Ugh. Even the thought repulses me. Not just Corwin, but anyone. I shudder involuntarily. If my mother knew anything about me, she would know that suggesting such things would be absurd. Maybe we should have had this talk when I was three.

"Everything okay?"

I jump at the sound of his voice.

"Yeah. I'm fine." I try to be as convincing as I can. But this is Corwin. He's not going to fall for it. "That was my mother. You could probably guess from my tone."

"Yeah. You don't particularly like talking to your mother."

"You've got that right. She wanted to warn me not to sleep with you. Bah! She's crazy. She doesn't know me at all!"

"You're right. She doesn't know you. You don't talk to her. She doesn't know about anything that's happened, save what your dad said in those documents and she thinks you don't remember those things."

"I know, I know. I should talk to her. You've been telling me that for years. But it's never going to happen. Never."

"I did mean to ask you if you're okay sleeping in my room with me? You can have the bed; I've got an air mattress for the floor."

"That's fine, Corwin. I'm not afraid of you. I know you won't hurt me." I smile to try to lighten the mood.

"So how are you, Brie?"

He takes a seat on the couch and hands me my glass of water. I take the seat next to him and curl my legs beneath me. I look at the wall of cans for a few moments before replying.

"I'm okay," I continue before he can argue. "I thought that after God healed me from my nightmares that I'd no longer have flashbacks or anything. But that's not been the case. I'm still afraid. I'm still in pain."

"Do you still cut?"

I turn back to the cans and nod. We both sit in silence for a while.

"When was the last time you cut?" Corwin breaks the silence.

I think back. "Two days ago," I conclude.

"That's progress, Brie. Two days. Before you could barely go six hours. Healing isn't going to take place that fast. It takes time and work. Praise God for how far you've come already! I've seen such a transformation in your life just over the few years I've known you and it's so encouraging to me to see how God is moving in your life."

"I don't think I can stop cutting, though. I can't go anywhere without my blade. Just the thought panics me."

"Hmmm." Another few moments pass in silence. "Do you think you'd be up for trying something this weekend?"

"That depends," I say hesitantly. "What have you got in mind?"

"Where is your blade now?"

I eye him suspiciously. "In my pocket."

"Do you think you would be able to give me the blade?"

I immediately pull away from him. "Not forever."

He interjects before I freak out completely. "Just for a little while. If you really need it, I will give it to you. Do you think you can trust me?"

I look at his sincere face, pondering this. Could I part with it knowing it won't be far away? Won't I feel the shame before I even cut by asking for the blade? Maybe this is what he wants me to feel so I'd be able to live without it. I take a deep breath and slowly dig into my pocket and retrieve the thin blade wrapped in a small piece of paper. I clutch onto it for a moment, not sure if I can actually give it to him. My hands tremble, but I reach out and place it in his open palm.

"I'm going to put this in my wallet, which stays in my pocket. You'll be able to have it at any time. You can even wake me up in the middle of the night for it. But now I guess since you're sleeping, it won't be necessary," he smiles.

I try to return the smile, but the panic has risen inside my chest. I can't do this.

"You can do this, Brie," he says, as if reading my mind. "I know you're scared. But it will be okay. I'm here for you. God's with you always. You're being so brave. I'm really proud of you."

I make a half-hearted smile and stare at the floor, not sure what to say. I definitely don't feel brave. I feel pathetic.

"So, what do you want to do tomorrow? I have a few ideas," Corwin says, trying to lighten the mood.

I shrug, still unable to fully disengage from my panic.

"Well, I was thinking about a day trip to the Peak District for a hike? The weather is meant to be nice again. What do you think? We could take the bus. It's only a few pounds for a round trip. We could pack a lunch…"

"Sounds good," I say in a small voice and try to smile. It does. I look forward to being out in nature again, but at this moment I'm locked in my thoughts, locked in my fear. The sound of a key turning in a lock echoes from down the hall…

"Brie? Brie!" A hand grabs my shoulder and gently shakes me. I quickly pull away from Ted's grasp then realize it's not Ted. Corwin. I look around at an unfamiliar room. Where am I?

"Brie, it's okay. You're safe," Corwin says soothingly to me.

My eyes continue to flit around the room, trying to make sense of everything. Eventually it all starts coming back. I'm in Sheffield, with Corwin. This is his apartment. I was just talking to him here on the couch. "What happened?" I ask and realize my voice sounds like that of a child's.

"You spaced out. My roommate came in the door and you went. You kept saying, 'He's coming. He's coming.' I couldn't get you to snap out of it." A look of pain remains on his face.

"Oh." I don't know what else to say. "I'm sorry."

"It's not your fault, Brie. Remember that. It's not your fault. They did this to you. Not you."

I nod, to appease him, not believing a word. My core throbs in pain from my unknown flashbacks. Sometimes I remember, sometimes I don't. Either way, I feel the pain from them. I wish I hadn't given Corwin my blade now. I could use a cut to clear my head.

I look down and realize I'm holding a glass of water. My fingers are white from the tight grip I have on it. I loosen my fingers slightly and watch as the blood returns speedily into them.

"Are you okay?"

I jump in my seat and spill some water down my sweatshirt. I guess I had begun to dissociate again.

Annoyance at my own ridiculous stupidity boils up within me. "I'm so stupid and jumpy," I growl at myself.

"You're not stupid, Brie. These reactions are normal for someone who has gone through the things you have."

"I need my blade," I say out loud. My whole body rocks back and forth.

"What's wrong, Brie? Talk to me."

"I can't. I have to. I have to…" My breathing begins to waver. My heart rate increases. My head feels like it's spinning.

"Brie!" Corwin's tone is firm. I look at him. "Brie. Focus. Breathe in slowly. And out slowly."

I follow his voice and try to slow my breathing. It doesn't work.

My hands begin to shake violently and I put down the cup to avoid spilling any more water on myself.

"You can do this, Brie. You're safe. You're safe. He's not here. Just talk me through what you're thinking."

"I need to cut."

"Why?"

"I'm… I'm in pain."

"What is causing the pain, Brie?"

"I am! It's all my fault. It's all my fault. I'm the constant in all this. My father, then Ted. The only constant thing is me!"

"It wasn't your fault, Brie. What your father and Ted did was wrong. It was their fault. You weren't old enough to initiate that kind of thing, it wasn't your fault."

I shake my head and cover my face with my trembling hands.

Corwin gets up and sits next to me. He places his hand on my arm gently and begins to pray.

"Father. You see the pain Brie is in right now. I pray that You will come and comfort Your daughter whom You love so very much. Please come and take her pain away for You are the great comforter. Come give her peace. In Jesus' name I pray. Amen."

And like a cloak, peace and warmth settles down all around me. I feel myself relax under its weight. My fearful thoughts are muted. Tears prick my eyes and begin to flow down my cheeks as His presence surrounds me.

We sit side by side in silence for a long time, both of us in awe of God and His love toward us.

My eyes open to an unfamiliar room. I feel my whole body tense as I try to work out my surroundings. A small rustle next to me causes me to bolt upright in surprise. A human shape lies tucked away in a sleeping bag on an air mattress next to the bed I'm in.

Corwin. I can see a tuft of his brown hair poking out of the other end onto his checkered pillow. Sunlight streams in through his blinds, splaying stripes all down him. I have no idea what time it is, but I don't really care. I slept well after finally getting to sleep last night.

Corwin and I stayed up into the 'wee' hours talking about pretty much everything. From the stresses of classes and how to talk to your friends about Jesus to Corwin's recent music discoveries. I find that I like most of the music he does and often expand my music library through him.

My movements must have disturbed his sleep, because he was now turning over and blinking in the daylight that shone in his face. He takes a few seconds then looks over toward where I sit cross-legged gazing back at him. A smile instantly appears on his face.

"Good morning, Brie! Did you sleep alright?"

"I did. Very well, thank you," I reply politely and grin back at him.

"Are you hungry?" he asks.

I think of yesterday morning and putting on my freshly washed jeans, which fit snugly around my hips. A sudden spurt of anger swells up at myself for how fat I am. Since I began to eat again I have gained about twenty pounds. I feel hideous and I do not want to eat. I do not want to eat ever again.

"I'll have some breakfast," I say simply. I can't go back. I can't.

A few minutes later we wander down the hall into the kitchen area of his common room. As soon as we cross the threshold of the kitchen door I'm struck by the smell of cinnamon.

"Here, do you want to put some cinnamon and sugar on this pie crust for me?"

My mother stands at the kitchen counter and carefully cuts off the excess pie dough from the top of the freshly made apple pie. She then rolls it together in a ball and squishes it into the metal pan before sliding it over to me. I can just about see over the counter. I stand on my tippy toes and stretch my arm out to reach the little shaker that I know contains the cinnamon and sugar.

A bang of a door and the rattle of the china cabinet signal the arrival of Dad. I freeze. I hadn't heard his truck pull in. I'm not ready. He opens the dining room door and steps through, wearing his blue jeans and bulky coat.

"Hi, honey," he says, stepping over to kiss my mother on the cheek.

"Hello, Ellie." He comes over to me and gives me a hug, gently squeezing my upper leg under the table as he does. He pulls away and his hand brushes against my chest.

"I'm just baking some apple pie. It should be ready in forty-five minutes or so. And Ellie's made her own pie crust, didn't you, Ellie?"

I nod, no longer hungry.

"Brie!" A hand touches my arm. "Are you okay, Brie?"

I don't respond. I can't. I'm trapped in pain. Afraid to speak in case I can't stop screaming. Afraid to cry in case I can't stop crying. The pain pulses through me, tightening my lungs and my muscles. I feel myself back into a wall and slowly slide down it until I can bury my head in my knees.

Corwin stoops down next to me and carefully places his hand on my back. "Brie, it's okay. You're safe."

I look up at Corwin whose face is unreadable. I see a flicker of pain cross his eyes as he looks into mine. Am I that disgusting?

"I'm sorry," I mumble as I shimmy up the wall and climb to my feet.

I look around the kitchen for the culprit of this fiasco. I hear the oven fan on and I peek through the glass window and see what looks like an apple crumble. Of course. Another burst of anger wells up inside me and I long to take it out with a blade. If only I hadn't given it to him. Stupid. You're so stupid, Brie.

"There's nothing to be sorry about. It's not your fault." He stares so intensely into my eyes that I must look away so he doesn't see the disbelief that emanates from mine. He has no idea how much it was all my fault.

He backs away and grabs a few slices of bread, popping them in the toaster. I take a seat on a bar stool and he hands me a glass of water. The cool smooth texture reminds me of the blade and I long to smash the glass so I can cut myself with a shard of it.

"You can do this, Brie. I know it's difficult. But I'm here, and more importantly, God's here." He leans on his elbows across the counter from me. What is he, a mind reader or something?

I take an exaggerated breath then let it all out at once in a huff. "I know. But neither your presence, nor His, takes away this pain."

He nods his head in apparent understanding. But how can he? No one understands. I'm reminded of the woman I saw yesterday at the train stop. Her eyes that revealed all. I understood her pain and even then, I couldn't do anything about it. Another wave of guilt and pain pours over me and I grip the glass even more tightly, willing it to break in my hands.

"Brie. Talk to me," Corwin pleads.

"I can't. I just... can't." I hear the crack in my voice.

"What are you thinking about?"

"A woman. Yesterday I saw a woman at one of the train stops on the way here. I saw her and knew all the pain of her past." I rush on, "I know that sounds crazy, but I just knew. Like remember when I told you about Jade and how I also just knew? It was like that. Except this time there was nothing I could do to help her and it broke my heart. It's like God reveals these things to me only to hurt me more. It makes me feel so guilty for getting upset over my comparatively good past when they have it so much worse. How can I be so self-centered?"

"Brie. Brie," he says slowly, waiting for me to look him in the eye, which I do begrudgingly. "You are listening to lies. Your reactions to your past are normal, expected even. Don't downplay what happened to you. It won't do anyone any good. And I'm sorry for the burden you carry when you see these people. But remember, they are not your burdens to carry. Give them back to God and believe in His sovereignty. Pray for them. That's the best thing you can do right now."

The toast pops up and Corwin grabs it and divides the three pieces between two plates. One for me, two for him. He then digs out some blackberry jam from the fridge and hands me a knife to spread it on my perfectly browned toast. I do so sparingly to minimize my caloric intake. I'm still eating, I tell myself. There's no harm in watching how much you eat.

"So..." His change of tone signals that he's going to let this drop for now. "Do you fancy a walk in the Peak district today? It's only a short bus ride from here and I picked up a trail map yesterday on my way to meet you at the train station."

"Sounds good." I push forward my happy smile and bite into my toast, trying to scatter minimal crumbs.

"Great! We can pack a lunch. I can carry it in one of my rucksacks. Let me just go get that." He rushes off down the hall to his room, while I stare into the oven that I can see over the countertop and feel the simmer of self-hatred beneath my skin.

A forty-five-minute bus-ride later and we arrive at our destination. I follow Corwin off the bus and thank the conductor as I step out into the brilliant sunshine.

The bus stop is merely a signpost that stands in front of an old sandstone house. Ivy clings to the sides of the house, leaving gaps for the windows. A quaint patch of garden sits in the front behind a waist high stonewall. Bright colored flowers and bushes bask in the sunlight, catching in every drop.

I turn and let my gaze wander down the small street. It appears to be the main street of the little village. A red post box stands about six feet away next to a small convenience store with a rack of postcards sitting next to the door. I look further down the street and can just make out a small sign indicating that a Methodist church is behind the large hedges.

Corwin and I are the only ones to get off the bus and the street seems strangely deserted for such a sunny day. Corwin takes out a map and I stand, taking in all the quaint English scenes.

"Alright, ready?" Corwin stuffs the map back in his bag with the lunches.

"Ready," I say.

Corwin leads the way along the 'path.' Really, it's just flattened grass at the side of a huge field of grass. The first fifty yards are steep. We climb a hill that seems unending after a winter of being cooped up. But boy, is it worth it. We reach the top of the hill next to an old tree. We look out on the scenery around us. It's breathtaking. I stand in silence at God's magnificent beauty.

The rolling hills flow out in front of us, all of them laced with wildflowers in shades of yellow, purple and blue. Down at the bottom of the first hill, which is covered in yellow buttercups, is a stream that weaves its way through the lowest parts of the moors.

Trees line the banks of the life-giving river providing a stark contrast from the open fields. A gust of wind rustles the leaves and causes the flowers and grass to bow down as if in worship. In the distance, I can see little white puffs of sheep, like clouds on the hillside. Sunlight plays melodies with wind in the movement of shadows making it look like the hills are really flowing.

I turn to Corwin and grin. "It's beautiful," I say, rather lost for words.

"I know. He sure is," he replies.

I lie back against a large rock. The sun's warmth has soaked into it, causing it to warm my back. I close my eyes and feel the wisps of wind play around my neck and face. I let out a satisfied sigh.

"I could stay here forever," I say to Corwin.

"Yeah. It's pretty special," he replies, rummaging through his backpack for a chocolate bar he packed for after lunch. I already refused his offer to pack me one. "Aha! I got it." He tears it open, disturbing the peaceful ambience and lies down next to me, chewing loudly.

I let out a giggle.

"What?" he says with his mouth half full.

"Nothing… you're just funny," I tell him.

We lay in silence for a little while longer. I can feel a conversation mounting from him. It's as if he's just working out the best way to say what he wants to say. My fears increase proportionally to the time that passes.

"How are you finding not having your blade on you?" he eventually asks.

I freeze. For a moment, just a moment, I was far away above my life, soaring in the sunlight. Free. His words are like a slap of reality. I'm not okay. I compose myself silently before answering.

"It's difficult. Sometimes I feel in a panic because I don't have it. Even if I don't want to use it at the time, not having it makes me feel so… I dunno. Out of control, I guess."

Corwin stays silent and I know he wants me to keep talking. And with him, I feel like I can.

"Sometimes the pain is so overwhelming. I feel trapped without air. Cutting… it's the only way I can breathe again. It releases my pain. But it's only temporary. That's why I keep doing it. And so far, I haven't found a better mechanism. I've tried. I really have. I've tried using rubber bands on my wrists, which do hurt if you pull them back hard enough. In fact, I'm often left with bruises for several days."

I hear the echo of my mother telling me that I 'bruise easily' when I show her the bruise on my thigh in the shape of a hand from Ted.

"What else have you tried?" Corwin prompts, pulling me back to the present.

"I've tried writing. I like writing. I feel I can actually understand what I'm thinking when I write it out. But other times I just make myself worse by acknowledging my feelings. Music, I think, is the only thing that really helps me other than cutting. And it's not listening to music. That doesn't help. It's me playing the piano or singing. It's like a balm to my heart," I laugh. "That sounds dramatic, I know. But it's true. The problem is, when I'm in that place where I need it, I don't think to sing. I'm so trapped, it's like I have no voice."

"Hmmm. Do you ever pray?"

I lie in silence for a moment, thinking of the times where I did pray and Jesus came and comforted me, but other times where I'm in so deep I can't even call out for help.

"Sometimes."

"Does that help?"

"Yes. When I do cry out to Him, He always answers, either Himself or through a friend, such as yourself."

"Could you maybe try something for me?"

"Depends on what it is," I say tentatively.

"The next time you want to cut," his blunt words stab me. It's one thing to think the truth; it's another to hear it, "could you text me or call me? I'm here for you, Brie. Maybe you could talk to me about what you're feeling and I can pray with you."

"I don't think I could, Corwin."

"Why?"

"I don't know. It's just too hard to reach out for help. I think it's the most difficult thing to do. I guess it's like giving up control and acknowledging that you can't help yourself."

"I understand. Just something to think about. Another possible mechanism, as you say."

"Thanks."

I relax once more against the warmth of the rock and soak up the sounds and feelings of nature. I leave to go back to Northern later tonight and the thought causes my heart to ache. I don't want to leave him. I want to be able to spend days like these, every day. Yet at the same time, he has his things here with the Christian Union and I know that God wants me at Northern. He's already used my church and people I've met to do amazing healing in my life. But I have so much further to go. And the road doesn't look easy. It never is.

Chapter 25

Normal. Some days are so busy and full of the present that your past has no choice but to watch from the sidelines. You feel normal. You feel as if maybe your past didn't happen at all, maybe it was all just a bad dream. The next day you realize your dream was indeed reality. The small break in your hectic week is when your past sees opportunity to haunt you. It clings to you with full force and refuses to let go.

My feet slap against the pavement as I run across The Green. Birds' morning songs echo around me, but their joyful noise irritates me rather than calms me. I don't stop running until I reach the door of the cathedral. Its size makes it look like a house for giants. But, like the castle gate, there is a smaller door cut out, more human-sized.

I pull at the door gently, trying to avoid being noticed. The door doesn't support me in this endeavor and squeaks loudly as I enter the sanctuary, which is thankfully deserted. My sneakers echo on the stone floor as I step into the center of the main aisle. Stone pillars line either side of the aisle, so wide and tall they are rather intimidating. The ceiling stretches over one hundred feet in the air, yet the stonework carved into each ledge and archway is as intricate as lace up to the very top. Stained glass windows all around give a dim glow to the room. But none of this catches my eye as much as the large stained glass window on the eastern side of the cathedral in the shape of a large rose. The sunlight pours through the window, causing every color to glow with a golden shimmer. Magnificent.

Tears sting my eyes but I'm quick to blink them back and take a seat in one of the middle pews.

I think back to the dream I had last night. I was in a place that looked like New Hampshire, but different. I was in the woods with a stream. There was myself, Ted and possibly my sister and someone else I didn't know, sitting at a picnic bench. I remember asking Ted a question, although I don't remember what that question was now. However, his reply won't shift from my head. He looked at me with a look of shock and disgust and mockingly said, "I was just messing around, Brielle, gee… getting a bit overdramatic."

Thinking about it now, I suppose I am being overdramatic. Nothing ever happened. Anger boils inside me at my own stupidity. I reach into my pocket for my blade and I feel my heart drop as if I missed a step.

My blade is back in my room. I can't cut. Rage turns into panic in the blink of an eye. My air squeezes out of my lungs and I can't replenish it. I grab the journal that I carried out here and rifle through the pages until I find the next blank one. Maybe I can write it out.

May 7ʰ

I'm sitting in the Cathedral, meditating I suppose. Trying to take a step back and see the bigger picture. And I see it. All I see is nothing. It never happened, you idiot! No one touched you, you liar! Keep your mouth shut! I hate myself so much sometimes… I want to hurt myself really bad right now. But why? What reason do I have to hurt myself? What do I have to be upset about? Divorce? Remarriage? Living in the UK? None of these are worth me being this upset. But maybe that is all that is wrong, maybe nothing happened in the past and I'm just homesick for America.

But what about the police documents I found? Did my dad just make up the things he did to me? Was I imagining the whole thing? Did I have some sort of twisted imagination as a child and thought that my dad would molest me when really he was a good dad, a dad who loved me?

But what about Ted? Some of it is true, but it was all my fault. I asked him. Not verbally. No, I must have seduced him. And his violence towards me is just a family trait. He didn't mean it. It was all my fault anyway. I'm blowing everything out of proportion just like he said in my dream last night. I'm weak and pathetic. Nothing ever happened.

I slam my journal shut. My anger continues to simmer beneath my skin but I concentrate on my breathing and try to ignore the fact that I feel crazier than I did before I started writing to myself. Maybe I am crazy...

I sit back in the pew and try to ignore what's going to happen today as well as everything that happened in the past. My mother and Charlie are coming to visit me today. It's one of the last days I have before my major cramming starts for my final exams in a few weeks. Just the thought of exams sends my stomach twisting into knots. I hope my mother doesn't notice my cuts. I've not been able to make it even a day without cutting over the past week. I'm careful to cut in over the top of scars, but there are still a lot of red scabs all up my arms. If she does notice, I will have to make up something pretty fast. I fell over? A wild cat attacked me?

She'll never notice. Never has.

I look out of the window to the cobbled street where Saturday shoppers hustle and bustle their way from shop to shop and large tour groups of Italians and Japanese people push their way past people laden with shopping bags to get up the hill to the cathedral and castle. A 'clunk' in front of me brings my attention back into the little café that my parents and I are sitting in.

I look down and see the tuna fish sandwich I ordered along with a handful of chips, or 'crisps' as the British say. My mother's soup and Charlie's egg salad sandwich arrive moments later.

"Do you want my chips?" I ask Charlie.

"Go on then, if you're not going to eat them."

"Nah, this sandwich is huge," I say, feeling the pressure from my mother's glances at my stomach since she arrived.

An awkward silence passes between us and I resist the urge to continue people watching outside the window to distract myself. My cuts feel like the size of skyscrapers beneath my bulky sweatshirt. Charlie breaks the silence after swallowing a large bite of his lunch.

"So, classes done now, just preparing for exams?"

Thanks for the reminder of my impending doom. "Mmhmm…" I say, taking another nibble at the corner of my sandwich. Another bout of silence fills the air.

"Your sister recently started helping with the children's church and is in the choir."

"Cool." Of course, I am nothing compared to my perfect sister. She's always comparing us, making me feel like I'm never good enough.

We continue to eat our lunch while exchanging casual comments about the weather, or Charlie's latest projects, or some kids that my mother has at her daycare. I think they sense my stress and associate it with my finals, so they stay clear from the subject of chemistry, which suits me fine.

Twenty minutes later, after my mother has had her piece of cake and Charlie has paid the bill, the three of us awkwardly stand outside the café, trying to stay out of peoples' way. Finally, Charlie initiates the goodbye ceremony.

"See ya, sweetheart!" he says, stepping forward to give me a hug.

I next hug my mother's small frame and try to swallow my annoyance at her. After all, she doesn't know what she's done or not done. She has a kind heart and good intentions for the most part. She doesn't know the pain I'm in and I'm not about to share it with her. Therefore, my annoyance toward her is unjustified and completely my fault anyway.

I wave goodbye to them as they head off down the cobbled street. Charlie's tuft of white hair bobs amidst the crowd. I turn and weave my way past the hoards toward the castle.

Memories of the past knock on my conscious thoughts, willing me to let them in. I bolt the door, trying to keep them out, knowing soon they won't bother to knock.

I reach the courtyard and see people either filing in or coming out of the Great Hall for lunch. Arin and Peter will be in there, I presume. They will be having a normal conversation, laughing with each other. They won't be having to fight off flashbacks and focus to stay part of the conversation. I long for that.

I snap out of my daydream and force myself upstairs toward my room. I'm emotionally worn out from the day and I know as soon as I let my guard down the flashbacks will come in force. It's just a matter of time.

I reach the first landing and, as I expected, next to Arin's name the slider is on OUT. I slide mine over to IN and continue up the next flight of stairs. My steps echo around the stone walls. Clomp. Clomp. Clomp.

Clomp. Clomp. Clomp. Heavy steps on the wooden stairs. My stomach squeezes uncomfortably. I sit on a little pink chair, looking out my bedroom window toward the lake. Fall leaves twirl and dance their way to the ground, some landing gently in the water. I hear the footsteps pause outside my door and I hold my breath. The silence drags out and I grab my nearest baby doll, Rose, and rock her gently back and forth in my arms while quietly singing a lullaby.

"It's gonna be okay, little baby… Yes, Jesus loves me, the Bible tells me so."

My door knob turns and the door creaks open. My Dad steps in.

Tears drip down my face and I blink past them to realize I'm leaning against the wall of the bathroom. I have no recollection as to how I got here. Fear and pain choke me and my sobs resound loudly around the empty room.

"I can't do this anymore." I cry out. "I can't!" I slide down the wall and bring my knees to my chest. I begin to rock back and forth and remember my baby doll, Rose. She was such a good baby… never cried. Never told anyone. I did what I was told. I was good. I was good! My heart hammers angrily in my chest as my teeth clench.

"I was good!" I pull out my blade, wrapped up in my jeans pocket. I look at it for a moment, knowing I should call Corwin. But he wouldn't understand. No one understands. I don't even think about it. I watch as the blood trickles down my arm and drips onto the floor. "I can't do this anymore…" I say, my voice exhausted and subdued. "I can't…"

Chapter 26

Hidden. Have you ever lost something? You end up searching for it in every possible place it could be, just to find out it was exactly where you thought it was. You just missed it.

I wonder if people can see my cuts. Do they notice and yet say nothing? If so, what do they think? Do they think I'm crazy? I think that often maybe I am. I keep them well hidden, so there shouldn't be any reason for people to see them, but you never know. Maybe when I'm getting ready for bed, Arin has noticed. Or when blood seeps through my sweatshirt, Peter might have. But no one ever says anything to me. Thankfully. I wouldn't know what to say back.

I have no motivation to get up this morning. Arin has gone to the library to study and I'm left alone with my thoughts. My good day yesterday has been replaced with today. I lie in bed staring at the ceiling, feeling disgusting and dirty. I don't deserve love. But I guess that's the point. Nobody deserves love. Yet God still loves us. It's quite amazing really. But right now, I'm not even sure if I want love. Love hurts so much. When people care about you, you let down your guard, and then you're an open target to get hurt. I want to stay closed. I don't want to be hurt. I feel myself building my walls again, repairing those I've broken. Shutting myself off from even my own feelings. I don't want to feel anymore.

"Gah! Stop thinking!" I yell at myself, breaking the silence of the room.

I sit up and fight a wave of blackness that tries to overcome me as my blood pressure plummets. The room slowly comes back into focus. I blink and see my father's face. A scream escapes my lips and I jolt backward, hitting my head against the cold wall. Pain erupts both in my head and chest. Fear seizes control and starts its process of speeding up my heart and breathing rate. My limbs join in the action and shake. I pull my knees to my chest and bury my face trying to block out the pain. It's no use.

"I don't want to feel!" I cry out, but my knees muffle the sound.

Voices of the police, counselors and my mother echo around in my head: 'Did your father ever touch you?'

"No." I yell out loud. "Nothing ever happened. For goodness' sake, Brie. Nothing ever happened. Get a grip!"

Anger boils up and I know what I need to do. But suddenly Corwin's voice fills my head: 'I'm here for you, Brie. Text me or call me...'

I push the thought away and reach over to my bedside table, pull open the drawer and grab my blade. I unwrap it and hold the cool metal in my boiling hands for a moment. As I look at it, Corwin's words keep flying around my head. I can't think. Panic continues to pound through my veins.

"Gah!" I grab my cell phone and quickly punch in a message to Corwin.

I need to cut.

I press send and toss the phone back onto my bed. There. I did what I was told. I go back to rolling up my left sleeve and think better of it. Summer is coming and I have a bad habit of pushing up my sweatshirt sleeves when I get warm. I roll up my right pant-leg instead. I have the blade corner pushed up against my calf when my phone buzzes, making my whole body jump a few inches in the air. A small nick is left in my leg but it doesn't bleed. I glance down at the phone that glows with Corwin's reply.

Talk to me. Why do you feel you need to right now? God is with you, Brie.

I think back to my recent revelation that God was with me the whole time. He gave me hope. That's what I need right now. Hope.

I pick up the phone but don't know what to say. I can't explain why I need to cut. I just do. Pain. I'm in pain. I need pain. No one can understand that. I'm in pain because I can't stop remembering my father's penis in my mouth. My body does an involuntary shudder.

I just do. I can't explain. I'm in pain. It doesn't feel like God is with me right now. I don't know what else to do, Corwin.

I lay the phone back down on the bed and stare into nothing as I wait for a reply. If he has no solution, then I cut. Several minutes pass. My mind begins to close down from the pain. *Buzz buzz. Buzz buzz.* I push against the darkness and pick up my phone. At first I just stare at the message, not understanding it at all. Then I realize what it is. Bible verses. Corwin has sent me loads of Bible verses. Intrigued, I grab my little Bible from my bedside table and begin to flick to the passages he's sent. As I read them tears drip onto the pages. It's like a soothing balm to my burning anger inside, erasing the pain.

I grab my journal and begin to transcribe the passages for future reference.

"For you created my inmost being; you knit me together in my mother's womb. I praise you because I am fearfully and wonderfully made; your works are wonderful, I know that full well." Psalm 139:13-14

"I will never leave you nor forsake you." Joshua 1:5

"For I am the LORD your God who takes hold of your right hand and says to you, do not fear; I will help you." Isaiah 41:13

Each word I write rings with truth. I am loved deeply by the Creator of the universe! He is with me. Right now, He cares. My tears become sobs and I am overwhelmed with His love for me. Dirty, disgusting me.

I don't know how long I stay knelt on my bed, sobbing. But eventually my tears slow and I sit up. Light. Free. Loved. That's what I feel right now. I quickly pick up my phone and text Corwin back.

Thank you Corwin! I'm loved by God! Amazing! Just amazing! :)

His reply is quick and my phone buzzes before I even put it down.

Praise God! I have been meaning to ask you if you would be interested in coming to New Wine with me in a few weeks. You know that retreat my family and I go on every summer with churches from all over the country? There will be lots of talks and stuff. I think you'd like it.

I recall him talking about it back in the days on the bus to and from school. I smile at the memories. I've never been to New Wine. It's a big camping event for loads of different churches. The closest thing I've ever been to is the retreat with my church here at Northern. I know God did a lot during that time away, perhaps the same will happen again. I have a sudden urge to go to this. I don't even know exactly when it is. But I'm going one way or another.

Yes. I really would like to go. Let me know where and when. I'll be there!

I put my blade back in my drawer and reread the passages in my journal. I smile. Hope.

Chapter 27

Dawn. The night's memories fade in the glory of the sunrise. The Earth basks in the splendor of the sun. The birds resound a beautiful chorus. It's a new day. A new beginning.

Crunch. My mother takes another bite of her Oats & More cereal and chews so loudly, I swear the neighbors can hear. I stifle my annoyance and eat my beans on toast as quietly as possible. I'm not sure how my mother can love cereal so much that she eats it for dinner. She closes one of the books she's reading and immediately picks up the next in the pile. Her daily devotional routine.

I respect my mother's faith. I'm sure that seeing it from a young age had to have had some sort of positive influence in my deciding to follow Jesus myself. For a moment, I feel my heart soften toward her.

Exams have been over for two weeks now and I'm back at home. It's not been easy, but I've been trying to keep to myself and avoid any unwanted conversations with my mother.

"Can you help me with the dishes?" she asks, closing her last devotional book.

"Sure." I follow her into the kitchen. Silence follows us, but it is a comfortable silence. It almost feels as if we have nothing between us.

"I think you've put on quite a bit of weight while you've been at university, don't you?" she comments, breaking the silence, while I help her dry and put away the dinner dishes she just washed. Reality once again slaps me in the face.

I feel the welling up of anger and I swallow it back down. If I hadn't become anorexic a few years ago, I might be much better off right now. But as it is, after you starve yourself for so long and then begin to eat, your body just stores it. It's then really hard to get rid of all the stored fat without falling back into your extremely tempting habits. She doesn't have a clue. I feel disgusted with myself. I want nothing more than to go and vomit up all the dinner I just ate. I even had seconds.

"I'm not meaning to criticize, Brielle," she continues. "I'm just pointing it out. I'm sure you can see it, too."

I glare at her and slam the plates in the cupboard.

"Yeah, Mom. I know I'm fat," I say bluntly, barely controlling my emotions. I feel like I could cry, which in turn makes me angrier with myself for my weakness.

I throw the dishtowel on the side counter and quickly turn, leaving the room before I really lose it.

I walk past Charlie, who is sitting in his usual place, stretched out on the couch with a packet of crisps, watching *Last of the Summer Wine* reruns for the umpteenth time.

My breathing is rapid by the time I reach my room and close the door behind me. I need to cut. My limbs begin to shake. Instead I turn to play the piano in the hope I'll find relief in that, only to remember my mother and Charlie took it back downstairs to the conservatory and there's no way I'm going down there right now. My mother will just try to convince me that she's not being critical and that I'm way too sensitive or something, which maybe I am.

Is it even possible to hate myself this much? I take out my journal from beneath my underwear in the top drawer of my vanity.

My thoughts flow furiously out onto the pages. All the pain from my mother's years of criticism and telling me I'm not good enough well up inside me and spill down my face. I bury my sobs in my pillow. I'm so weary of it all. I'm tired of living with myself. I'm tired of living with this pain. I'm just so tired.

My eyes open. I'm blinded by the brightness of my room, which is filled with the rising sunlight. My curtains aren't drawn. I realize I'm still wearing the jewelry and clothes I had on yesterday. None of this makes sense. With a clear snap the world clicks into place and I remember why I'm in bed like this. Residual pain still lingers heavy in my chest. I look back out the window then at my clock. 7 am, Thursday the fifth of August. New Wine!

I bolt up in bed and wait for my blood pressure to catch up with my movements before scrambling out and rushing into the bathroom to get a quick shower. I have to leave in thirty minutes. I completely forgot!

Thirty minutes later I'm climbing into my Corsa and pulling out of the driveway. It's still rather dark outside. I hope my mother remembered that I was going to this today, otherwise she'll be in a panic when she wakes up and I'm gone, especially after ignoring her for the rest of last night.

Within ten minutes I'm winding my way through the country roads. As I smoothly follow the curves I see the sky begin to soften. Dark blue and black becomes baby blue with streaks of gold, purple and pink. I roll down my window and allow the cool air to temporarily blow the unease of my heart away. I can hear birds chirping in the hedges as I whip by, but all the chatter of nature seems strangely muted, as if it's holding its breath for what it knows is coming. Dawn.

The golden sphere cracks over the fields to my left, piercing the shadows with brilliance. Once it appears, it rises quickly, becoming a full circle hovering over the horizon in majesty.

There's no holding back now. My surroundings become alive. Birds sing and fly overhead. The trees rustle in the wind. Dawn. It's as if the darkness was never here.

I often wish that would happen in my life, where one day I'd wake up to brilliant sunshine and it would be as if my past never happened. But this way of thinking is pointless. The fact is my past did happen, no matter how much I try to convince myself and others otherwise. And not only did it happen but it has affected my present and future. It's an ugly stain which, no matter how hard I scrub at it or try to cover it up, remains.

A song breaks through my thoughts. "What can wash away my sin? Nothing but the blood of Jesus." I recall Tim's prophetic message back in my first year of university. 'Is His blood not enough?' These thoughts stab my heart, but rather than pain, I feel love. I've been stabbed by love.

I see the entrance gate up ahead. My range of emotions settle into unease in my stomach. Something is happening. The question is, is it for better or for worse?

I park where I'm directed to by the stewards in orange vests, turn off my engine and release a heavy sigh.

"Alright God, I'm here. Now what?"

I swing open my car door and slam it shut behind me. Fear bounces around inside me, making me want to just get back in the car and run away. I pull my purse over my head and feel the sharp sting of some of my recent cuts. I suck air in through my teeth. If only I had never been taken and left in this stupid country. If only I had told someone. If only it never happened. If only I had never been born... my final thought lingers in my head as I walk across the car park.

The visitor's entrance is just up ahead, and there, standing with his hands in his pockets, smiling with an impish grin, is my best friend. Corwin. My heart flutters with joy at seeing him. It seems a lifetime ago since we were together out in the open fields of Derbyshire. My footsteps fall faster against the gravel. He takes several steps toward me. Finally, I'm within reach of him. I open my arms and we embrace in a tight hug. It's like my worries flee from me in his presence. He draws back and looks at me in that knowing way. And that's when I realize – it's not Corwin's presence that eradicates the darkness, but rather Jesus shining through him. I can see it in his eyes. Jesus' love burns brightly there and, just like before, I'm pierced by love.

"Hello, my dear friend," I say to him, just barely keeping the sound of joyful tears away from my voice.

"Brie," His face lights up. "You're here!"

"Yep! I sure am." Another jolt of unease comes and I again want to run away. What am I doing here?

We wander through the campground, carefully stepping over tent pegs and ropes. Hundreds of tents and campers spread around us in all directions. At the very center of this mass of people is a large square building, looking like it could hold an indoor basketball court or something. That's where we are heading, I presume.

Corwin talks to me about all the various things going on, about the children's ministries and how his sister and brother are helping with those, and about the talks that are going on. I barely register anything that he's saying. My unease is growing at an exponential rate. I shouldn't be here. I push myself onward, gaining strength from Corwin and our friendship.

We reach the entrance of the building. People are flocking in from every angle. I pause twenty feet away. Corwin turns to face me.

"This is where the morning worship meeting takes place." He looks intently at me for a moment. "You don't have to go. But I think you'll like it."

I look over his shoulder at all the people. They look so happy. So... whole. I feel so broken. I shouldn't be here.

"It'll be okay, Brie," Corwin says, as if reading my mind.

I swallow. My mouth is suddenly dry. I purse my lips and briefly look into Corwin's eyes before nodding and taking a step forward. He smiles and leads me in through the double doors that are held open by two men who are smiling and greeting everyone as they enter.

I feel my muscles tense as we pass them, remembering my father doing a similar job at the church when I was younger. 'Not everyone is your father, Brielle.' I shake off the fear that's trying to take root in my already freaking-out mind.

Corwin leads me to the center of the aisle, about ten rows back from the stage at the front. The inside is very minimal in terms of décor. The breezeblocks have been painted over with a whitish paint and the metal roof and ceiling give the feeling of being in a barn or warehouse of some sort. Folding chairs have been lined up through the whole middle section, leading to at least a hundred rows or so. I spot Corwin's parents as we take our seats. They head over.

His mom sits directly next to me. She has a face that is constantly full of joy and makes me want to smile, despite my emotions. She is small but her outgoing personality outweighs her size, making her presence fill up a room. His father sits on the other side of her. He looks so much like Corwin. Or I suppose I should say Corwin looks so much like him. The same smile. The same life-flowing personality. I love his parents. They are so… caring. Although I am glad his mom is sitting next to me and not his dad. I'm not sure I could handle sitting next to another guy besides Corwin.

"Hi, Brie! Corwin told us you were coming. I'm so glad you could make it. How are you?" Corwin's mom asks me, smiling joyously.

"Hi. Yeah, I'm fine, thanks. I'm glad I could make it too." Okay, so a bit of a lie… I smile just to emphasize it.

"Do you know what other talks you're going to today?" she asks. "You must check out the central book area. They have lots of books for sale and my husband gets a discount, being a minister and everything, so you should definitely check it out. You'll take her, won't you Corwin?"

"Yeah, we can go after the next talk," he responds.

"I don't know what talk I'm going to, actually," I say, responding to her initial question. "I've not really looked."

Corwin takes out a small booklet from his rucksack.

"Here's the list of the talks."

I scan down the list. My heart jolts when I see the name of one of the talks: *Walking through Treacle*. That's exactly how I feel right now. Like I'm stuck. Life is just passing by but I'm trapped in my past, unable to escape. I shake off the strange feeling I get. It's nothing, I'm sure. Yet all the same, I know I have to go to this talk.

"I think I'll go to this one," I say in a small voice, pointing to it.

Corwin nods with his 'knowing' expression. "Good choice," he says simply.

The service starts. A man welcomes us all and we begin the worship. I feel my walls come up immediately. I sing along, but I don't join in. I feel myself guarding my heart fiercely as if it's going to be attacked.

As the thought runs through my mind, I know that's exactly what is happening. God is attacking my heart. I know it. Deep down I know that is what is happening. He wants to do something. But I know change brings pain. And I know what He wants me to do. He wants me to stop cutting. But I can't. I know I can't. I need it. I have to. I can't survive without it. Surely God understands! Panic creeps into my lungs and it becomes more and more difficult to sing. 'I can't give this up, God! I can't!'

I harden my heart further, trying to block out His presence that fills every pore of the room. I steel myself against the light I feel all around me. I can't do this. I can't.

The worship finishes and I breathe a sigh of relief, knowing that it is in music where God meets me the most.

The speaker talks about prophecy and its use in the church. At first I see no real application of what he's talking about in my life. Until he poses the question: "Is it fear that stops us moving further with God?"

He continues to talk, but I'm held up on that question. Yes. It is. And I know it. I'm petrified to let God into this area of my life. I can't give up control. I'll just fall apart! Besides, I got myself into this mess. It's all my fault. God can't do anything about it. I just need to get over it. Right?

Worries spin around my head for the rest of the service. I look down at my fingers and realize I've picked the skin off both my thumbs and my right index finger until they are all bleeding a little. Oops. Corwin follows the direction of my gaze and I see a flicker of pain cross his face. I quickly draw my hands into a fist and stuff them in my sweatshirt pockets. He turns and gives me a sad smile. I feel another stab of love. He cares about me so much it hurts.

I enter through the side door into a room about a quarter of the size of the one we were just in. Corwin showed me to the door but then went off to another talk. I don't even remember what he said it was about. Maybe I should have stayed with him? Without his presence, I feel the fear gripping my throat again. Too late now, I think, as I look around the room for a place to sit, not really wanting to commit to being here but, at the same time, not wanting to stand here looking lost and have some kind person come up and talk to me.

I spot a row in the very back of the room that has no one sitting in it. Perfect. I'm sure not to make eye contact with anyone as I walk by and shuffle sideways halfway into the row. I shove my purse beneath the seat and cross my arms and legs, almost wishing I could curl into a ball without anyone noticing. I keep my head down, again trying not to make eye contact with anyone. This plan fails, however, when I see a pair of legs come and sit down next to me.

I glance toward the person who's annoyingly decided to sit beside me. She is an older lady, maybe in her sixties, with tight gray curls on top of her head.

Please don't talk to me. Please don't talk, I plead with her silently in my head.

"Hello dear." I suppress a groan. "I saw you sitting back here alone and thought I'd join you." Wrong decision, I think to myself.

I give her a brief smile and look away again.

"Ah, my dear. You look like you're hurting. Forgive me for being so bold, but I would like to pray for you if I can."

Stabbed by love. I feel tears sting my eyes at this woman's kindness. Is my brokenness that obvious? Do I look how I feel? I stay silent for a moment, not sure what to say.

"I'm just finding living really hard right now," I finally say, unsure as to why I'm even going along with this.

"I understand. I've been through times like that in my past, too." She pauses for a moment and I look at her. I see a shadow of a haunted past cross her features. "Life is not easy. Jesus never said it would be. In fact, sometimes it's hard to see God in the midst of the storm, but afterward you can see what He has done."

Her words grip my heart. It's like she knows exactly what is going on for me.

'Oh God! Why are you pounding on my heart so insistently? Why would you even want anything to do with me? I can't let go of this. You know I can't. Please! The pain is too much.'

The speaker gets up in the front and starts to talk. The woman stays quiet, respecting my silence. I hear nothing of what the guy up front is talking about. My heart pounds in my head. I feel as though the pain is going to explode out of my chest. All the fear, all the nights I waited for my father to come into my room, all the bruises endured from Ted, they all well up inside me like a fire. I need to cut. Yet I feel God there, tugging at my heart, wanting me to open up and let Him in. But I can't. I need to remain in control. I'll lose it if I open up even a little.

My hands begin to shake and I squeeze them into fists, trying to stuff down the emotions that are boiling to the surface. So many things whir through my mind that I begin to dissociate. I feel myself shutting down all emotions, all feelings and thoughts. Like giant steel doors closing me off from myself...

A gentle hand rests against my arm. It draws me back with a startle. I turn and see the old lady smiling sadly at me.

"Are you here with someone?" she asks softly. I wonder how long I've been gone.

I look around the room and see people getting up and moving toward the door. It takes me a few seconds to work out where I am. Suddenly, the pain hits me again like a train at full speed. My breath leaves my lungs and I squeeze my eyes shut against it all.

"Jesus, I pray for this young lady. Please meet her where she is right now. I pray that Your hand will be on her life and You will comfort her now. You see the pain in her life. Please give her peace. Give her Joy. Amen." She wraps her arm around my shoulder and gently hugs me. I feel my whole body begin to shake.

'Get it together, Brie!' I stuff the feelings back down and look up, forcing a smile on my face.

"Thank you," I say weakly.

"You're welcome, my dear. I'll be praying for you," she says as I stand and move past her, toward the door.

Corwin said he'd meet me here so we could go look at the bookstore. I scan the crowds of people for his face. I know once he's here, I will be okay. My heart pounds in fear when I can't find him. What if he's left me here alone? What will I do? I need to cut.

The thought sears through my panic. 'No, Brie! You can resist. Be strong.' I grit my teeth and continue to look for him. Finally, out of the corner of my eye, I see his beaming face coming toward me. *Corwin.* Relief washes over me and I can tell it reflects on my face. He comes and stands next to me.

"Ready?" he asks, not addressing my obvious distress. He knows me so well.

I nod and follow him through the people. I knock into arms and shoulders, each time becoming more and more tense. Once we enter the bookstore I can barely breathe. Corwin's eyes emit concern but he doesn't say anything. I begin to browse the books, hoping to distract myself. Book. Bookshelf. Table. Carpet. Wall. Window. I begin to chant to myself what I see and I feel my pulse slow and my breathing become easier.

I browse through the titles of the books on the large bookshelf. *What Was Lost, After You Believe, Almost Christian...* nothing really catches my eye. I look along the bottom shelf and my heart skips a beat. A book sits there with a girl on the front. She is curled up with her knees to her chest. I recognize the pose, knowing I've sat in it many times. The title of the book is *VIOLATED: Mercy for Sexual Abuse.*

No! Nothing ever happened. I look at the book next to it. *CUT: Mercy for Self-Harm.* Gah! I feel like my world is spinning. People don't write books like this, especially in Christian circles. Nobody talks about it. Christians don't self-harm. Abuse doesn't happen. I look around to see if anyone notices that the world is spinning. Everyone wanders through the aisles, looking through the books like nothing is going on.

I see Corwin with his dad on the other side of the store. He looks up as I am gazing at him. He smiles but I can't return it. I turn away and look at another shelf of books, trying to shove away the titles of those books from my thoughts. It's no use. They jump out at me. I want to pick them up and see what they are about. But I don't want anyone to see me pick them up. If they do, they'll know everything about me. Nothing ever happened.

"Brie!"

A small scream escapes my lips and I jump backwards into a table. A sharp blast of pain shoots into my hip from the table corner.

"Sorry!" Corwin goes to step toward me and has second thoughts. He knows that in times like this I need space, not comfort.

I laugh nervously, trying to make light of the fact that a few people are now looking at me.

"Did you find anything?" Corwin asks. My gaze flickers to the books behind him and a shudder ripples up my back.

"Umm. Sort of," I say quietly. Corwin turns and looks to where I glanced. I see his lips purse and then he bends down and picks up *VIOLATED*. I look around to see if anyone is watching him. He flicks open the book and begins to read inside. I want him to stop and put the book down. Nothing ever happened. He nods as he reads then closes the book. He looks up at my distraught face and gives me a reassuring smile before bending down to pick up *CUT*. He knows so much. Again, he flicks through the book, reading passages and nodding. After he closes that one he looks up at me.

"I think these books will really help you, Brie. Do you want to get them?"

I turn away from his intense look. I know I should. I know I need help and I can't do this on my own, but denial is so much easier. I can pretend everything is okay. Everything is fine. I'm fine. My stomach twists uncomfortably. I look back at Corwin. He continues to gaze at me in that knowing way.

I bite my bottom lip and move my head just a fraction in a nod.

"Okay." He takes the books over to his dad who is standing in line at the check-out. Crap! My mind frantically races to work out what I should do. Corwin is going to have his dad pay so I can get the discount. But his dad will read the book titles and know everything. I can't let that happen. I hurry over to Corwin, who is waiting at the end of the line. His dad already has the books amongst the stack of others he's picked up.

Corwin reads my face as I hurry over to him.

"It's okay, Brie. He's not going to say anything," he says, reading my mind. "Calm down."

I'm lost for words. I just want to hide in a corner. I'm so ashamed.

His dad walks over to us and hands me a small plastic bag, which contains my two books.

"Here you go, Brie," he says with a smile. How can he smile at me when he *knows*?

"How much was it?" I ask, my voice giving away my fear.

"You can give the money to Corwin at some other point. I'm going to go track down my wife," he says with gentle humor in his eyes as he leaves Corwin and I alone.

"Come on, let's go to the camper. Maybe we can rustle up some lunch. I think we've got cobs or 'rolls', as you say," he laughs as he mocks my accent.

I find myself relaxing and laugh along. His American accent is terrible.

We wander back through the maze of tents to the opposite end of the campsite. The bag in my hand feels like a hundred pounds, just like the weight of my heart right now. I begin to think of how I can separate myself from Corwin long enough to cut. And will he know? Will he see it on my face? Probably. I feel disgusted with how much I need to hurt myself, but I can't stop. There's too much pain.

"Here we are!" Corwin's voice punctures the thoughts that were threatening to overcome me.

I look around and see Corwin's youngest brother, who is the spitting image of Corwin, sitting at a picnic table eating his 'cob' and 'crisps.' Ah… English terminology is such a giggle sometimes.

"Brie!" Mini Corwin yells over, spraying out a few crisp crumbs from his mouth.

"Hey!" I laugh and wave at him.

"Shall we join him and make some lunch?" Corwin asks, stepping inside the caravan.

"Sure," I say, although I feel far from hungry. I know Corwin will insist I eat. He remembers my non-eating days too well, I'm sure.

"Okay. We've got..." he squats down and rummages through the small fridge, "cheese, ham, turkey, tomatoes or tuna."

"Ummm... tuna?"

"Tuna it is. I think I'll join you for that." He quickly moves around the caravan kitchen and ends up with two plates with tuna cobs on them.

We walk out and join Mini Corwin at the picnic table.

"So, how are you doing?" I ask him.

"I'm good. I've been with the kid groups and there's this one little girl, she must be around three or so, who just keeps following me around. She won't stop."

"She must have a crush on you!" I say, biting into my cob.

"Hahaha. Maybe!" he says.

"How old are you now?"

"Nine!" he says with a proud smile.

"Wow! Pretty old!"

I try to remember what I was like at nine years old. Most of what I can recall is how a couple of times a week my mother would pick me up from the bus stop and we'd drive about thirty minutes to see either my lawyer or my counselor at the time.

I remember feeling sick on the bus rides home on those days. As the bus would turn down my street, and I'd see all the mailboxes in a row next to the green jeep, my hands would begin to shake. I would dig my nails into my arms as hard as I could, leaving little reddish-purple nail marks all over. Somehow it would take my mind off what was going on. One time I did it so hard, the mark never left. A small purple crescent shape remains on my arm to this day.

My memories of this habit, which started a long time ago, surprise me. I realize that I learned that pain could clear my head a long time ago. I've been self-harming for over fourteen years. That's a long-ingrained habit to break.

I think of the bag of books sitting next to me with fear. Am I ready to even try to stop? Most of me rejects the idea. Too hard. But somewhere amidst the 'no' is a faint 'yes.' A small bubble of hope. 'Think of the freedom, Brie!'

Mini Corwin is continuing to talk to his larger carbon copy about some other kids in his group. It's now or never. I slip away from the picnic table with my bag in hand. Wandering into the caravan, I find a seat in the corner and sit with my feet tucked up beneath me.

I take out both books from the bag and look briefly at the cover of *VIOLATED*, but quickly put it down. I can't face that right now. I pick up the next book, *CUT*. The girl on the front looks in so much pain. I somehow want to help her but concede that the best way to help her, or people like her, is to help myself first.

I take a deep breath. 'God help me.' I begin to read.

I finish reading the book in just over an hour. I'm known to be a quick reader and the book wasn't really that long. Either way, I'm surprised I finished so quickly. Corwin has joined me in the caravan and sits in the other corner chair with his feet, covered by the crazy socks I gave him for his birthday last year, resting next to where I'm sitting.

I have so many emotions right now that I'm not sure what I feel.

Noticing my movement, Corwin glances up from the book he's reading and gives me a smile. I smile back but quickly duck down and grab my purse, pulling out my journal that I brought along. I open it up to a clean page. I know this is a landmark entry. With a slightly shaking hand I begin to write what my mind cannot think.

August 5th

I've just started reading CUT-Mercy for Self-Harm. I know now that there are some ungodly beliefs I have that I want to overcome with truth. I don't think this will be easy. But for the first time in a long time, I have hope. I truly believe God can help me. When I started to read, I was amazed how much it was talking about me. I have always felt different, like I'm the only one who understands how I feel. But after reading about myself from a book by a complete stranger, I'm convinced otherwise. I think there are a lot of people who are feeling what I feel now. And that makes me sad. The biggest thing I discovered is that my belief, that I need the control cutting gives, and if I give up cutting, I give up control, is a lie. Rather, my need to cut is showing that it controls me. It makes me believe that because I have control of when I feel and when I'm in pain, I somehow have control of the situation so long ago. I feel like I've learned so much, I can't even fully process it all. But these are a few of the lies/truths that I think I need to realize:

Lie: No one knows who I really am or how I feel. No one knows how much I hurt inside.

Truth: God knows better than anyone exactly what is in my heart. He knows me better than I know myself. I can trust Him to handle me and my heart with loving hands of healing (Jeremiah 1:5, Psalm 130:2).

Lie: I must experience pain for the horrible things I have done.

Truth: Jesus Christ has done everything needed to 'take care of' anything in my past, present and future when He paid the penalty on the cross for whatever I might do (2 Corinthians 5:21).

Lie: I am so ashamed of the bad things I have done. There is no way I can be forgiven or loved ever again.

Truth: God chooses to cover me with the blood of Jesus. I can stand before Him without shame (Romans 8:1, 2 Corinthians 5:21).

The book tells me I need to be open and vulnerable. I immediately think of my mother and telling her. But I can't. I can't hurt her like that. She won't be able to handle it. The book also said this wasn't going to be easy. I will be tempted. The progress might be slow. But all in all, I feel it. Hope.

Chapter 28

Wind beneath my wings. Have you ever observed a bird as it takes off into the air? To begin with, it flaps its wings with all its strength. It takes off, continually flapping until it reaches a point where it stops. How does it know that it won't plunge to the ground? How does it know that the wind will carry it? Trust. Sometimes we need to stop striving to fly ourselves and trust that a force much stronger can carry us.

I roll down my window, allowing night air to rush over me. The cool wind chills the tears I didn't realize were streaming down my cheeks. I grip the steering wheel tightly as my Corsa weaves through the hedge-lined roads.

'God, I don't know what to do. I can feel You telling me to give it all to You. But I can't. If I let go, I'll fall apart even further! I can't lose control. I can't!'

I choke out sobs and try to blink the tears away so I can see the darkened roads. The sound of my cries amidst the roar of the wind in my ears unnerves me. I can't lose it. I put my stereo on and music pierces the night. I let the noise calm me, distracting me from my own thoughts. I glide around the corners smoothly, allowing my breath to mimic the long drawn out sweeps of the car. The words of the song suddenly reach my conscious thoughts:

"And I'll praise You in this storm, and I will lift my hands. For You are who You are, no matter where I am. And every tear I've cried, You hold in Your hand. You never left my side. And though my heart is torn, I will praise You in this storm."

With a rush of emotion, I begin to cry again. But this time it's not out of fear but out of joy.

'You never left me! Not once. You're here asking me to lift my hands to You and allow You to take control of all of me.'

I feel my heart race with conviction. I know what I should do. But I don't know whether I can.

I turn right down my street and pull into the parking space next to my parents' car. All the lights of the house are off except for the one lamp in the front window. This could either mean my parents are asleep or waiting up for me. I quickly check my face in the rearview mirror. My eyes are puffy and watery looking. There's no hiding the fact that tears have been shed. I rub away the flecks of black that are scattered beneath my lashes from run off mascara, hoping that my mother's not waiting up for me. I grab my purse and my bag of books and silently head in the back door.

I creak open the door that leads from the kitchen into the living room and, with a rush of relief, find a vacant room. They're in bed. I switch off the lamp that stands on a table that I would sometimes hide beneath when my dad came home. A shudder ripples up my back and I force the thoughts away. 'Focus, Brie. Light, books, chair, stairs, door, bed, mirror.' I look into my vanity mirror. My tear-stained eyes look back at me. I grip the sides of the cabinet and focus on my breathing. In and out. In and out. My eyes hold so much fear, but mixed in is resilience. Fight. I won't give up.

My thoughts go back to what I read just hours ago. The truths. The lies. It's hard to believe that all this time I've been listening to lies. They didn't feel like lies. And what about the truths? There's one undeniable truth that fills my heart with both uncontainable joy and unexplainable fear and it is that God loved me so much that He sent His son to die on a cross and shed His blood for me so that I can know just how much He loves me. It's crazy. Crazy love. And what this means is that Jesus really did pay it all. That I don't, and never did, deserve this pain. I'm free! I've just not embraced my freedom. It's like the chains have been broken but I remain in prison, afraid of what I will encounter if I leave the world I've always known. A world of pain, fear and shame. Now God is calling me to step out of my prison and trust in His saving power.

My whole body begins to shake. I fall onto my bed, face down on my pillow. Hot tears soak into the fabric and my heartfelt cries are muffled.

'God, I give it all to You. Please come free me from this pain. Set me free from the fear and the shame. God, I need You! I give You control.'

"Good morning, *Brie*." My mother emphasizes the fact that she is conforming to addressing me by my nickname. "How was your conference yesterday? Or whatever it was with Corwin."

I step down the last few steps and plonk myself on the couch facing my mother. I'm too dazed to answer right away. I woke up this morning to light. Not sunlight. No, it was a typically cloudy English day, threatening to dump water on us any second. Rather it was like a light inside burning so brightly I couldn't help but lie there in bed and grin. I even did a little happy wiggle. When I stared at my reflection I saw the change in my eyes. The pain was still there but hope was welling up.

"Good," I finally reply. "It was really good." Part of me wants to tell her all about it. How God has transformed me overnight. But I can't. If she had even a peek at what is behind the wall I hold in front of her she would fall apart.

"How's Corwin?"

"Doing well, I believe." I smile thinking of him and how he always knows what I need at the right time. I needed to go to New Wine yesterday. I know deep down that this is a major turning point in my life.

'But how long will it last, Brie? Last time, after you tried to end it all, you got better, but you were back to cutting in no time,' a little voice prods me, planting doubt in my mind. Maybe this is only temporary? Nothing good can last.

No! I try to capture the thoughts like the book said to do, to see them as lies that are not what God thinks. I repeat the scripture in my head: "We take captive every thought to make it obedient to Christ," from 2 Corinthians 10:5. These are not thoughts from God and therefore I won't listen to them. If only it were that easy. The voice gets louder as if trying to overcome my defense. *'Jesus,'* I silently cry out. It's like the magic word. The voice diminishes and peace once again settles over me.

My mother is reading her stack of devotionals while I'm having this mental battle. I try to curb my annoyance at her obliviousness. It's my own fault she doesn't know.

Pushing it all from my mind I get up and raid the kitchen cupboards for some breakfast. Nothing sounds appetizing to me. I close the cupboard ready to just skip breakfast but I catch myself. I can't go back to that.

"Gah! Cereal will do," I mutter to myself, grabbing a bowl and spoon. As I reach for the milk in the fridge I feel a twinge in my arm from some of my recent cuts. A wave of shame sweeps over me. Will I ever be able to stop?

I remember the vision God gave to me so long ago, of the boulder with all its scars and how He sees it for what it will be. How one day it will be beautiful. 'God, when will I be beautiful?'

Chapter 29

Amazing Grace. In the Chinese language, there is no direct translation for the words amazing grace; instead they use the phrase 'qi yi en dian', which means bizarre favor. His grace truly is breathtakingly bizarre.

The cold air bites at my exposed legs and toes as I slip out of bed and pad across my room. I begin to rummage through my sock drawer and freeze as my hands find a small folded piece of paper.

How long has it been? I automatically look down at my arm, ignoring the wave of shame that flows over me at the sight of all the scars. My heart aches and my hands grip the sides of the drawer. How I wish I could go back to New Hampshire. Wake up one day and have all this be a dream. I quickly put the blade back in the drawer and put on my slipper socks and fluffy robe before heading downstairs.

A small smile touches the corners of my mouth as I step into the living room. I've not needed to cut for so long. God has truly achieved a miracle in my life. Even after all the times I've failed and fallen so short of what I should be. *His mercies are new every morning.* The scripture floats into my mind, erupting a fountain of joy and peace within me. I bypass the kitchen for the piano after a quick 'good morning' to my mother and Charlie who are sitting watching *Time Team* reruns, of course.

I put on my headphones, so as not to disturb them. My fingers automatically begin to play a song I wrote so long ago. *Amazing Grace.* Yes. That is exactly what this is. God has been so gracious. He has started a healing in my life, and if the scriptures are true, which I believe they are, then God will continue the good work of healing He has begun.

I sing the lines of the song in my mind as the notes ring out in my ears. 'Sing Alleluia. Amazing Grace.'

As the last notes are played I know what I must do. The final cut.

I get up and grab a bowl of cereal before I forget to eat.

"Mom…" I say, between mouthfuls of oats.

"Yes, dear." Her voice is kind and I feel slightly relieved. Maybe she'll react better to what I have to say if she's feeling well.

"Would you let me get a tattoo?"

Shock is definitely the first emotion that flashes across her face, but it doesn't last long. She composes herself and slowly says, "Why?"

I choose my words carefully. "Well, I've wanted one for a long time now and I want a meaningful one. One to remind myself of all God has done for me."

She remains silent for a while and I pray she doesn't ask for the specific details.

"I suppose I'd be okay with it. It's up to you."

I feel like I could fall off my chair in surprise at her nonchalant attitude toward me getting a *tattoo*.

"Where will you go?" she asks.

"There's a place near my old bus stop. I used to pass it on the way to school." I've been thinking about it for a long time now, but now I know exactly what and why.

"When are you going to get it?" she asks, still not freaking out. Charlie is just ignoring us and continuing to watch the guys dig in the dirt.

"I was thinking maybe tomorrow. I've only got a week before I go back to Northern."

My stomach does a little leap with the thought of a new semester so close on the horizon.

"I can't believe summer has come and gone. I'm going to miss you," she says and I actually believe she is sincere. She does love me in her own way. And she's letting me get a tattoo!

I gobble down the rest of my cereal and rush upstairs to get ready before she changes her mind. I can't believe I'm doing this.

'Don't think. Just do it, Brie.'

"Ready?" the rough looking skinny guy speaks to me from the doorway to the back room.

I take a deep breath. From this point on, I am putting my trust in God and His grace. This will be the final cut.

"Yes," I say, more boldly than my legs feel. I get up and follow him into the back room, which is very well lit.

He shows me the trace he's made and I squint at it against the blinding lights.

"Perfect," I say.

"Alright then. Sit down on this bed here and lean onto the stool with your arms."

I get onto the bed and struggle to suppress a shiver.

"I'm okay," I say to myself.

"You alright there?" the guy asks.

I'm thankful for his rough appearance. For some reason, I'm more comfortable with people who actually look like they could hurt you than those who look safe.

"Yep, I'm ready."

"Okay." *Buzz…*

My whole body freezes in shock. I had been mentally preparing myself for the pain, but completely forgot about the noise. The sound sets me on edge and I force myself to relax and take deep breaths while closing my eyes.

Time seems to drag on forever. I sing my song in my head. When is he going to start? A few moments later his voice interrupts the middle of the third song I'm singing silently to myself.

"Three quarters of the way done," he yells over the noise.

Three quarters done? I didn't even realize he started! I can't feel it. I force my mind to pick out the sensation on my back. Slowly bursts of sharp pain come through to my consciousness but it's bearable.

"Done," the guy says. "Let me just grab a bandage to cover it. Make sure you apply the nappy cream like I told you before. It'll help it heal a lot faster." He steps away and I mentally note to pick up some diaper rash cream on my way home.

"Dang!" His voice makes me jump. "I've never seen a girl sweat this much!" He chuckles and I feel my cheeks go red. "I can't get the bandage to stick." He gets a towel and wipes my back. The area around the tattoo is sore, but I feel happy. I feel branded in love.

"You're good to go."

"Thank you very much," I say and head out onto the main high street. My heart feels light as a feather. I can't believe what I just did. A huge smile spreads across my face. I feel freedom. I'm free from cutting, I know it. God has set me free from the bondage of self-harm. And I shall never ever forget how it was His grace that brought me through. It is written on me. 'Amazing Grace.'

PART 4

I hear him call my name.

"Brielle!"

I look up and see him on the cliff ledge. My heart leaps in my chest. I long to be with him, but my eyes focus on the massive cliff face before me. I could never climb it. I'll never be strong enough.

"The joy of the Lord is your strength, Brielle!"

A fire kindles in my heart and bursts forth into song.

I look back at the beach. My house is already destroyed by the incoming tide. It is time to leave the past behind me and press on toward the goal. I walk up to the bottom of the cliff face. Its height is staggering. I grit my teeth and place my hands in grooves above me. I pull with all my strength, but it's not enough. I lose my grip and fall back to the sand with a thud. I look down at my right hand. It's cut and bleeding.

"I'll never make it!" I cry out in despair.

"I am the Lord your God, who takes hold of your right hand and says to you, do not fear! I will help you!"

His gentle words speak to me in the quiet of my heart. I'm overwhelmed by love. Through healing tears of joy, I stand again and begin to climb.

Chapter 30

Pimples. The more you get, the more makeup you wear to cover them up. The more makeup you wear, the more pimples you get. The cycle is endless until you decide to stop trying to cover them up. Only then do they heal.

Time has flown. It seems just yesterday I was at Northern, hanging out by the river with a Pimm's and small disposable grills, laughing and chatting with friends. Here I am, about to encounter the next chapter in my life. My final year.

I hand my passport to the woman behind the little podium. She looks at me, then at my passport and then at my ticket. *Bang, bang, scribble.* I'm clear to go through. I take one step forward, then turn. My mother and Charlie stand on the other side of a sea of barricades waving and smiling at me. My mother makes the sign for 'I love you' in American Sign Language to me. She used to do that when I was a little girl and I would get on the bus, sit next to the window and wave goodbye to her. A lump instantly comes to my throat and my eyes sting. I force a smile and wave goodbye. Taking a deep breath, I turn and drag my little suitcase through toward the security check.

I decided that I would complete my masters research at a different university. A program that Northern's chemistry department offers. It's known as an international year of study. I decided to do my international placement in my home country. I applied to many universities across America, but it seems that not many people are willing to have you come and study and research while receiving no tuition fees. Who'd have thought? However, fortunately one researcher did. Professor Li, in Detroit. Detroit. Yep. That's what I said. Detroit. The place where no one lives. Apparently, the population has shrunk from two million to eight hundred thousand in not so many years. My imagination paints a picture of abandoned houses and drive by shootings. Beautiful.

The positive side to all this is I'm finally leaving my prison for a significant period of time. I will be spending the next eight months in my homeland. My excitement to leave England behind me far outweighs my fear of being shot. I think.

◆

We make the final descent below the layer of clouds and over the checkerboard of Detroit. I can't stop a smile spreading across my face. I'm here! I'm actually here! This is a new start. I'm leaving my past behind. Three thousand six hundred and eleven miles behind, to be exact. I checked.

The de-boarding is at its typical snail's pace, which is frustrating for my bouncing stomach. I can't tell whether my nerves are from excitement or fear. Maybe both. Professor Li told me she'd pick me up. She's kindly allowed me to stay with her until I find a place. It's difficult to look for a place when you're on the other side of an ocean. I've seen a picture of her. She looks Chinese and her name sounds Chinese. But you never know. This is America. She could be third generation by now.

I stand next to the carousel that should have my suitcases on them. I spot my polka dot duffel bag first and slide it off without much trouble. Next I see my giant pink suitcase heading toward me. Ugh. It's heavy. It even has the little orange label: Warning Heavy. I get my 'light' packing skills from my mother. I take a step closer to the carousel and grab the handle of the bag.

"Can I help you with that, ma'am?"

I glance to my side and see a gentleman, probably in his sixties, offering to help me. My heart breaks a little. People are so kind here. That would be such a rare occurrence in England. I want to give the guy a huge hug for such a beautiful welcoming. Instead I shake my head.

"No, you're good. I think I can get this." I push out a bunch of air and heave the bag off onto the floor with a *thunk*. "Thank you though. Have a great day!" I say to the gentleman and turn with my three suitcases wheeling behind me through the frosted glass doors. I scan the crowds for someone who resembles the picture of Professor Li. A small woman with short black hair steps forward and I realize that's her. Her face is the same, but in the picture her hair was very long.

"Are you Brielle?" she asks me as I draw nearer.

"Yes, I'm Brie. You must be Professor Li. It's nice to meet you." I prop up my giant pink suitcase and shake her hand.

"Did the travel go smoothly?" she asks, but I can tell the conversation is forced for her. I feel suddenly nervous, realizing I have no idea what I'm doing. I'm in a new place and know no one. I am about to stay with my newly acquainted professor and her cat until I can find a place to live.

We exchange pleasantries but the twenty-minute car ride back is quiet, which suits me fine. I spend the time looking out the window at the scenes unfolding before me. It's only once we're off the highway, which is basically like any other city highway here in America, that I begin to see some of the Detroit I imagined. Suburban houses stretch for miles with every other one looking completely abandoned and the rest only looking half lived in. Older brick buildings on street corners are covered in graffiti. People stand outside in small groups talking or smoking or both. Grates on the streets steam, just like on TV. We turn down a street lined with trees already painted in fall colors. Professor Li clicks a button in the car and a black gate outside begins to open. We pull through and park.

I heave my luggage out of the trunk. They actually call it that here. I turn around and follow her up the path toward a row of brick houses. I didn't realize they had brick houses in America. They are quaint, old-looking with large bay windows. She walks up the wooden stairs at the end house and I follow her, making a load of grunts and thunks as I do so. We step inside and I suddenly feel like I'm really in a movie. The kitchen has the look of a New York apartment having one wall completely bare brick with various artsy pictures hanging on it. Baskets containing various vegetables and herbs hang from the ceiling. Pottery from different countries is scattered around the windowsills and the kitchen counters.

I hear a rustle near my feet and see the fattest cat I've ever seen sniffing my bag.

"That's Pilikia," she says, referring to the giant brown poof that's looking at me with curiosity bright in its eyes. "It means trouble in Hawaiian."

Hawaiian... hmm... maybe she's Hawaiian. That could work too. I follow her through the kitchen, past the living room with small chairs around a very ornate rug and up the stairs where she stops at the first door.

She opens it and steps in. It's a white-walled room with more oriental pictures hanging around and is well lit by two large bay windows that look out onto the tree-lined street. The floor is a dark wood that looks like it is original to the house. There is a bed, chair and small trunk. Two large sliding doors to my right presumably hide a closet.

"I hope this is okay for you. Through that door is your bathroom. You'll be sharing with Pilikia." She indicates the wooden door behind me. "He likes to lick wet toes, just so you know." I try not to laugh and instead nod solemnly. She leaves without another word and I'm left standing in the middle of the room with so many emotions, I feel practically nothing. I drop to my knees at the window and slide it open, breathing in the fresh fall air. Birds chirp, the sun shines and the wind rustles the leaves. Perfect. Just perfect.

I double-check the door. Yep, it's locked. A crisp gust of wind squeezes through the gaps in my scarf. I tuck the ends into my red wool coat and hurry down the steps.

Professor Li left hours ago. I swear she never stops working. It's 7:30 am now. I should be at the lab in thirty minutes at a nice walking pace. I turn around the corner and exit via the side gate, which is locked with a padlock at all times. The gate closes with a large squeak and a bang. I hope I don't wake the neighbors, not such a great first impression. Another gust of wind blows down the street, rattling the leaves above me and sending a flurry of yellow and red raining down around me. I grin and do a small twirl along the path. I love fall. I take off down the street past a small coffee shop where several people are in line for their morning drink.

As I round the corner onto the main street I spot a woman standing at what I presume is a bus stop. They're not the same as they are in England, but it says 'bus stop' so I can't argue. She's wearing a baggy sweatshirt and ripped up jeans. Her thick black hair is pulled back and braided against her scalp. Her expression is fierce and stone-like, looking off down the street. As I draw closer she side-steps to the left as if to stay away from me. Funny. I was scared of her. I'm a white-skinned country girl on the streets of Detroit. She could take me down in seconds, I'm sure. I pass a hairdressers called Dying for Color, an amusing name, I must say, and the girl's now about ten feet away. She glances toward me and I feel like I've been struck. It takes everything in me to keep walking. In that brief moment I catch her eye, I feel the weight of her brokenness. A torn family. A father who beats her and her mother. A life where she has to act tough or die. A soul that cries out in pain. Tears sting my eyes.

'God! How can this world be so broken?'

Here on the broken streets of Detroit, you will find your healing.

The words are bold and loud in my mind. They ring with truth and authority. My heart beats fast in my chest. I look back at the girl whose back is to me. I'm not broken. I'm fine. I don't need healing. I'm free. I'm in America. The past is the past. I shake myself and concentrate on getting to the lab. I have research to do and a thesis to write.

***

Hope Community Church.

I click on the first link of my Google search. This is the one the guy said, I think. I emailed the president of the Intervarsity (American version of Christian Union) here in Detroit months ago to ask about churches in the area. He recommended Hope Community Church. However, I'm beginning to realize that places aren't as walkable around here as they were back at Northern. Google Maps shows the walk to be an hour and a half from Professor Li's. I guess I could do that if I have to. Having no car is a bigger problem here than I would have thought. I click on the 'contact' link on the church webpage. There's a space to fill out your name and contact information and write a short message. Everything in me avoids asking people for help, especially people I don't even know, but my fingers seem to think otherwise. I quickly type out my name and email address and in the 'message' section I inform them that I just moved here to study in Detroit and that I don't have a car but would like to come to church on Sunday.

I hit send before I can think about it. I lean back in my chair, which sits looking out of the window in my temporary room, feeling shocked about what I just did. I reach over for the newspaper Professor Li gave me. She pointed out the housing section. I glance down the list of apartments. Most are too far away from the labs and the rest seem expensive or too big for just me. A quiver of fear shoots through me. What if I can't find a place? What if I can't afford any of them? What will I do? I'm so out of my depth here. Back at Northern it was easy. I had friends to share a house with. Here I'm alone.

My laptop makes a little bubbly sound notifying me that I have received an email. I click on it. It's from Hope Community Church. That was fast.

Hi Brie,

It's great to hear from you and thank you for your interest in coming to join us for our Sunday morning service. A member of our church is a med student at the university and he lives near there also. I've already talked to him and he said he's willing to give you a ride. His number is 958-276-5454. You can give him a call on Sunday morning and confirm with him details. Hope this helps.

Love in Christ,

Tyler

I quickly reread the email. I didn't expect them to reply at all much less this fast. I copy the number and save it in my phone. Am I really just going to call a complete stranger and ask for a lift to church? I guess I'll find out on Sunday! I turn back to the newspaper and apartment hunting.

I munch away on my mandatory breakfast. Reese's Peanut Butter Puffs. Man, I've been missing out while being stuck on that little island. They taste delicious; however, they settle uneasily in my stomach. I look up from the counter where I'm sitting on a barstool. The wind whistles outside the kitchen windows, but there's no rain. That makes a nice change.

Professor Li, or Stacey as she prefers to be called, is in the lab again today. It's Sunday. She really doesn't know how to take a break. It makes me feel like I should be in the lab as well, but I remind myself I'm only a master's student, not even a PhD. I can take a morning off at least.

I check my watch. 8:45 am. Worry tightens my stomach again. All I seem to be doing these days is worrying. I worry about how

I'm going to complete my thesis and pass my classes. I worry about finding an apartment and having enough money to live on. And deep down, although I'd admit it to no one, I worry my dad will find me. He always finds me.

However, the worry that lingers in the forefront of my mind is calling this guy about a ride to church. I've decided to wait until nine. Church doesn't start until ten thirty so if he sleeps in I don't want to wake him.

I slowly finish my cereal and wash my bowl and spoon, checking the clock every thirty seconds. It seems like the longest fifteen minutes ever. Finally, the stove clock displays 9:00 am. I take my phone out of my pocket and find his number; with a trembling finger, I push call and wait anxiously as the phone rings (with an American ring sound, which is quite comforting). Three rings later I'm beginning to think he's not going to pick up. Suddenly a scratchy sound emits, followed by a muffled, "Hello?"

"Hello?" he says again more clearly.

"Hi," I say, suddenly unsure of what I'm going to ask. "Uh. I emailed a guy by the name of Tyler at Hope Community Church a few days ago asking if there was some way I could get a ride to church. I just moved here and am without a car. He said he talked to you and gave me your number to call." I end the sentence weakly, having run out of words.

"Oh, yeah. Brie, was it?" He continues without pausing for a response. "Yeah. Tyler mentioned you lived near the college. To be honest I completely forgot about it and I would have normally already left for church a few minutes ago because I help set up the sound equipment, but as it just so happens I dropped a pot of yogurt all over the floor and I just got done cleaning it up when you called. So, if you don't mind getting there super early, I can pick you up in say ten minutes?"

"Uh." I'm a little taken aback by how this is all working out. "Yeah, I'll wait on the corner of Third and Fairfield."

"Sounds good. See you soon." He hangs up and I stare at the brick wall of the kitchen for a moment before the realization dawns on me that I have to be ready in ten minutes. I fly up the stairs and grab my Bible, notebook, and purse, check my hair, brush my teeth and then run down the stairs past Pilikia, and shove on my sneakers and red coat. I double-check I have everything then look at my watch. I have two minutes before he should be here. I quickly shuffle out the door and lock it.

I hear a footstep near me and I freeze, panic suddenly seizing my chest. He found me.

"Mornin'!" a man says from the porch beside me. He must be Stacey's neighbor. My heart still beats wildly, but I force a smile.

"Good morning!" I say and skip down the steps, whipping around the corner and out the gate. One minute. I walk across the road and wait on the corner in front of Luigi's Italian restaurant. Several cars come down the street, but none of them is... I realize I don't even know his name. I rack my brain through our conversation and my email from Tyler. I don't recall his name being mentioned.

A white car pulls up in front of me and I assume this must be him. He looks about the same age as me. He wears a light blue button down shirt and he smiles at me, a smile genuine enough to put me at ease somewhat. I step over and open the car door.

"Are you Brie?" he asks.

"Yes," I reply and get in. His hair is sandy brown and cut short, nothing like Ted's. I breathe a little easier.

"I'm Phil. I realize I never introduced myself on the phone. It's nice to meet you."

He extends his right hand toward me. I shake it, a little surprised by the gesture.

"It's nice to meet you too."

I buckle up and he heads down the street past more old-looking brick houses next to brightly colored square buildings selling groceries or alcohol. We pass a run-down looking laundromat and a café called Thistle. A strange name, I find, since it's a Scottish plant with sharp prickles. To me, cafés should be cozy.

"So," Phil says, startling me. "Oh, sorry. A little jumpy there?" He has a friendly tone.

I give him a small smile and even smaller laugh.

"So, you said you just moved here. What brought you *here*?" he asks, in a way that makes 'here' sound like an insane place to be.

"I'm doing my research project abroad for my master's degree in chemistry."

"Abroad from where?"

"England."

"England? Wow, that's far. You don't sound British," he notes.

"No. I've lived there for over ten years and never picked up the accent."

"Oh. What took you over to England?"

I once again go through my list of options on what to say and, as usual, go with the 'my mom married an English guy' one. It seems the easiest to understand and has the least amount of follow up questions.

"Oh. Cool," he says in response.

"What about you?" I ask, changing the focus from me to him. "Are you from here?"

"No. I'm from a place called Grand Rapids over on the West side of Michigan."

I realize I don't know anything about Michigan geography.

"I came here for med school."

"Gotcha. I presume you want to be a doctor then?"

"I do."

I smile, despite my insides freaking out. He's a doctor! No, he's a doctor in training. But doctors know things. 'Don't freak out, Brie. He knows nothing.'

"What year are you in?" I ask, trying to sound calm and collected.

"I'm only in my first year. It's pretty tiring."

He talks to me about his classes for a while. I listen and take in the sights as we drive by. Broken. Abandoned. That's mainly what I see. That's what I expected. However, what I didn't expect to see is life. Pockets of buildings up and running. Artwork sprawled across abandoned buildings, making the broken look beautiful.

We make a right down a street called Hopeville Ave. It's a stunning street, lined with giant golden-leaved trees and large mansion-like houses on either side. Rich people must live here, I think to myself, but then realize that, like the rest of the surrounding areas, most houses are abandoned and in dire disrepair. My heart breaks.

Phil turns left into a parking lot.

"This is it," he announces.

I slide out of the car and follow him across the street into what looks like a school. We step through the front doors. Yep. Definitely a school. Children's artwork mixed in with class pictures line the walls above children's height coat pegs.

Phil leads me down the corridor and opens a heavy wooden door for me. I step in and see an assembly hall with a stage at the far end of the room, past rows of wooden fold-down seats that run downhill toward the stage.

"Hey, Phil!" A tall black guy with no hair comes up and gives Phil a manly hug. Phil turns toward me.

"This is Brie. She just moved here from England to study at the university for her masters in chemistry."

"Hey Brie!" He steps forwards and I freeze. What is he doing? Before I have time to step back he engulfs me in a hug.

My mind swirls into panic. My breath leaves me and I feel memories knocking at my consciousness.

"I'm Tyler. You emailed me. I'm glad you came." He steps back. He must see my distress because he adds, "Don't worry, we're all family here."

Great. Just what I wanted. Family... not.

Tyler introduces me to the rest of the music and tech crew. I catch another Tyler but don't retain any of the other names.

Phil leaves me at the back of the room and starts helping the guys set up the speakers.

I spot a girl a few feet away putting pieces of paper inside booklets. I step over and she looks up. Her hair is pinned back but several loose curls fall, framing her face. Kind large eyes look at me and her mouth stretches into a wide smile, forming soft dimples in her cheeks. She emits joy, is the first thought I have.

"Hi!" she says to me. Her voice is almost giggly, confirming her joyful demeanor. "I'm Grace."

"I'm Brie," I reply. "Do you need some help?"

She glances down at the piles of paper and booklets in front of her.

"Sure!" She splits her stacks in half and I kneel down on the floor across from her.

"I'm just stuffing the bulletins."

I immediately imagine stuffing turkeys at Thanksgiving and suppress a giggle, hiding it behind a smirk.

"What?" she asks. I look up to see her beautiful smile, which is rather contagious.

"Oh. I just found the term 'stuffing bulletins' rather amusing. It makes me think of Thanksgiving turkey," I giggle and Grace laughs too.

"So, I heard Phil say you're here from England?"

"Yep. I've come for eight months to research."

"That's cool. I just started studying law here."

"Oh, neat. I momentarily thought of doing law but decided against it, although I'm not sure why. It might have been good. Is there any specific type of law you're interested in?"

"At the moment, international law. But I also have interests in sex trafficking laws. I'm involved in an organization called 'SOAP' here in Detroit, that tries to help women out of sex trafficking."

I nod and smile as she talks but my mind is whirring. What if she can tell? She obviously knows things about girls who have been... well, whatever. I continue stuffing flyers and Grace is quiet for a moment. I push away all my intrusive thoughts of the past. This is a new start.

Tell her.

The voice is strong in my head. Tell her? No way! I came here to escape my past, not to blab it all to the first person I meet.

"Are you okay?" Grace asks me, her infectious smile causing my face to mirror hers.

"Yeah, I'm fine thanks."

I place my pile of stuffed bulletins next to hers.

"Thanks for your help, Brie!"

"No problem," I reply.

I notice a few more people filtering in and Grace goes over to give them a bulletin. I take one from the pile I stuffed and find a seat in the middle of the room. I take off my coat, glance around, smile at the couple down the row from me and then begin to read the bulletin.

They're studying Genesis right now, it appears. That should be interesting.

More and more people arrive. Some smile at me and say hello. But none sit next to me. I suddenly feel rather alone. I look back and see Grace passing out bulletins. I wish she'd sit with me. I spot Phil and a guy of similar age shuffling up the row toward me.

"Hey, Brie. Mind if we sit next to you?" he asks.

"No. Go for it," I respond, happy to feel less like a person to avoid. Sometimes I wonder if people can see how disgusting I am.

"This is my friend, Mike. He's also a med student. Brie just started doing her masters in chemistry here," he informs Mike. "She lives near us. I gave her a ride this morning, but she had to come in super early with me so I could set up. Do you think you could give her a ride next week?"

I love how he assumes I'll be coming back. Not that I mind.

Mike responds right away. "Sure. That's no problem as long as you're okay riding in my rocket."

I glance at Phil to see whether he's being serious or not. Mike continues, seeing my lack of comprehension, "It's a big van with personality."

I smile and nod, suddenly missing my little Corsa. "I see. Thanks. That would be awesome. I don't have a car here nor do I have an American license."

"Where are you from?" Mike asks.

"England."

"Oh, cool. Well, welcome!" The music starts and we stand to sing. I don't know the songs but pick them up quickly, adding in harmonies. It's been a while since I sang and I'm filled with joy in doing so.

Tyler gets up at the end of our worship and explains what the little piece of paper that I was stuffing in the bulletin is for. Apparently, it's for anyone to write down a praise or a prayer request and then they read it out from the front. Someone then will volunteer by raising their hand to take the card and commit to praying for that request for the whole week.

I find the idea awesome and terrifying at the same time. I can see how it would draw the church body closer, but also how open and vulnerable you'd have to be. No way would I ever do that. Tyler reads out a few that have been collected. There seem to be similar themes to the requests.

"Prayer for finding a job."

"Prayer for sick loved ones."

"Prayer for safety of family – gunshots fired on street last night."

"Prayer for sister who was raped."

I'm suddenly on edge with the last words. How can people say it so easily?

The prayer requests are passed out to various people scattered around the hall.

Tyler then begins to announce the offering. I automatically reach for my purse. In England I was putting in ten pounds a week, so I guess that would be twenty dollars? The worries that have been consuming me come at full force. I don't even know if I have enough money to live on. How can I give even twenty dollars in the offering?

Give forty.

As with the words 'Tell her,' these words are clear and convicting.

Forty? That's way more than I would normally give, even when I'm financially stable. I don't even think I have forty dollars on me. I check my purse. I have three tens, a five and five ones. Forty dollars exactly. I take out all my money. The basket is coming toward me. Now is the time to decide. Trust God with everything or try to control it myself? I smile to myself. Stupid question. I *know* I can trust Him.

I place the forty dollars in the basket as it goes by. Instead of an increase in worry, I feel a washing away of fear and a deep sense of peace settles within me. All will be alright.

Tyler begins to teach from Genesis. He talks about how guys need to fight for their women, just as Jacob fought for Rachel. I realize that many of the insecurities women have are often because they are the ones doing the pursuing and the fighting for the man. Huh. Interesting.

We conclude with a couple more songs. I glance over to where Grace is sitting a few rows back.

Tell her.

The conviction weighs heavily upon my heart. I can't! I want to leave it behind. Besides, she's a law student and will have no time to meet with me.

'Tell You what, if she has time for a coffee (which I seriously doubt) this week, I'll tell her. Otherwise, I'm keeping my lips sealed.' I deal with God.

Mike and Phil begin talking with some guys sitting behind us. I slip out of the row and beeline for Grace, determined to show God I'm not about to say anything.

She smiles at me and I smile back, however I stay focused on my task.

"Hey Grace," I say with confidence, knowing the outcome of this conversation. In fact, I feel rather smug. Ignoring this not-so-humble attribute, I continue, "I know you're super busy during the week but—"

"Yeah, but would you like to meet up for some coffee or something sometime this week?" she cuts off my planned conversation.

I stare back at her with my mouth agape. Blink, blink. Blink. My mind tries to catch up with what just happened. I feel like God just slapped me in the face. I desperately want to break into hysterics. I manage to keep my giggles down and casually reply.

"Uh. Yeah... yeah, that would be good..." God, what are You up to?

"How about Thursday at 4 pm at the Starbucks across from the science building on campus? Does that work for you?"

"Um. Yeah. Okay." I still can't grasp how this just happened. My sentences are lacking words, not to mention structure.

"Great. See you then. It was nice meeting you, I look forward to our coffee date!"

I smile. Ha ha. You think that now... just wait until you find out about who I really am.

Mike appears at my side as Grace disappears.

"Would it be cool if I give you a ride home? That way I can work out where to pick you up next week. I already told Dave."

Mike's long, thin frame is very unintimidating and I feel myself relax slightly. Slightly.

"Yeah, that's fine. I'm ready when you are."

"Okay. Shall we?" He motions toward the big doors at the back of the hall.

I follow him out of the school and back across the road into the parking lot. He walks over to a large green van, appropriately dubbed 'the Rocket.'

"Hang on a minute, I have to open the passenger door from the inside." He climbs into the driver's side and opens my door with a loud 'squeak' and 'pop.'

I gulp and give him a wary look. Never mind being shot on the streets of Detroit, I'm not going to make it home in one piece if I ride in this thing.

I look back toward the street and see the trees blowing in the wind. It's been nice knowing you, world! I smile and hop in to the Rocket.

Chapter 31

Faithful. In our society, the word faithful usually follows the prefix 'un-.' *'My husband has been unfaithful,' or 'She's such an unfaithful friend, I can* *never count on her.' Today we struggle to trust anyone, knowing the vast* *majority of people are unfaithful to their word. However, there is One who* *never breaks His promise. One who is constantly with us, helping us. He is* *the Faithful One.*

"Let us hold unswervingly to the hope we profess, for He who promised is *faithful." Hebrews 10:23*

I know this is true, but, after searching for a place to live here in Detroit to no avail, I'm beginning to doubt God's provision for me. I take a deep breath and close my Bible. As Job said, "Yet will I trust in Him." The stairs creak behind where I sit at the kitchen table. I jump and turn around. Stacey's feet appear as she descends the stairs. What day is today? It's not like her to be home still. It's 7:30 am on a… Thursday!

"Good morning," I say.

She smiles but says nothing. This isn't surprising. After just a couple weeks I have learned that she is a woman of few words.

She rummages through the fridge and pulls out an assortment of vegetables and promptly begins chopping them over the counter.

"Have you had any luck finding a place?" she asks me, catching me off guard with a mouth full of Peanut Butter Puffs. I crunch on them quickly and forcefully swallow.

"Um… no. Not really. The places are either too far to walk to the lab or are too expensive."

She nods her head fractionally. "Well, I've got plenty of room here if you'd like to stay. You could pay me fifty dollars a month to cover water and electric?"

She continues chopping and I struggle not to jump up and dance around praising God.

"Uh, yeah. That would be amazing! Thank you!"

She nods again and I grin as I continue to eat my cereal. God is faithful.

I place the little blue vial into the heater/shaker and cover it all with aluminum foil before hitting start. Light might be good for most of the planet, but for my reaction, not so good. I check my watch, 3:45 pm.

Ugh. 'God, what am I doing? I can't do this. Really, I can't.'

My meeting with Grace is in fifteen minutes. I walk out of the lab, remove my lab coat and safety glasses and wrap up in my big wool coat.

"Leaving already?" my Chinese lab mate, Xue, asks me.

"Yeah, just a little early. I've got the reaction heating overnight. See you in the morning for our team meeting," I tell her and walk out of the office. I take the four flights of stairs out rather than using the elevator, or, as I like to think of it, a small metal box suspended on steel ropes that anyone could get stuck in.

I emerge outside to crisp sunshine, something I haven't had the privilege of seeing lately since I've been staying in the lab past dusk every day.

The coffee shop Grace and I are meeting at is just across the street. I still have five minutes. My hands get more and more shaky every step I take closer to the café.

I try to swallow my fear but fail to calm myself in the slightest. I get in line once inside, deciding to get my coffee and wait at a table rather than have that slightly awkward line conversation with someone I barely know.

"What can I get for you?" the smiley coffee girl asks me.

"I'll have a medium black coffee with a squirt of pumpkin spice please." Mmm. I love fall.

I take my hot cup of coffee and find a table for two empty in the middle of the room. I position myself so I can see out of the large floor-to-ceiling window. At least I can visualize escaping.

My breath suddenly becomes constricted and my legs join in the shaking. I look to the large school-like clock on the wall. 4 pm on the dot. I hear the door open behind me. Turning in my chair I see Grace wearing a white fitted coat and pink scarf step inside. She spots me immediately. I wave and indicate that I've already gotten my drink.

She grins, her cute dimples appearing once more, and gets in line.

I let out a slow shaky breath. I don't think I can do this.

'And surely I am with you.'

The end of Matthew 28 rings out in my mind. God's not going to let me fall.

I smile a little and take a sip of coffee. Hot coffee. I set it back down, mildly annoyed at the number of taste buds I just mutilated with the scalding drink. Grace comes over, coffee in hand, and takes the seat across from me.

"Hello!" she says, removing her coat and scarf, allowing her perfect spiral curls to fall fluidly around her shoulders.

"Hi!" I smile. "How are you? How's your day been so far?"

"Oh, I'm good, thank you. My day has been busy but productive. How about you?"

"That's the best type of busy. Mine's been okay. Just been working in the lab all day."

A small silence passes by and I feel the weight of conviction like a brick in my chest. Alright, alright. I'll tell her.

"So." I start feeling my legs turn to jelly and I'm thankful we're sitting down. "I wanted to talk to you about something." Grace smiles with a hint of foreknowledge. She can't know, I remind myself. "I don't really know where to start," I continue slowly.

My gaze is locked outside the window. I pull it back and look at my coffee cup, which I turn slowly around in my hands, waiting for it to cool. I sneak a peek at Grace who is smiling, waiting patiently for me to continue. I take a deep breath. I can't do this! I let out the air through puffed out cheeks. 'Just do it, Brie.' I close my eyes for a brief second of composure then look up to Grace's encouraging smile.

"When I moved here I had planned on telling no one about this. I thought 'the past is the past.' And I thought it would be easy since I am far away from anyone involved or anyone that knows. However, it seems God has a different idea. So here I am…" Oh boy. I puff out my cheeks again, and then take a tentative sip of coffee. Bittersweet and pumpkiny. Perfect.

"So basically…" I feel myself become more animated as my feelings begin to detach. It's almost like I watch myself talk about someone who isn't me while I hide in the corner and cover my ears.

"From as early as I can remember until I was eight, my father abused me." I pause, even while I hide in the corner covering my ears, I know the next word will impact me like a knife. "Sexually." I suppress a shudder and quickly continue.

"All was okay after he left until my mom and I moved to England where it started again by an older cousin of mine. He was a little more… rough." Again I suppress a shudder. "Anyway, this led to anorexia, self-harm and stuff, which I'm now healed from thanks to God. I can't say my old habitual urges are erased completely, but their temptation has a much weaker hold on me now. So, yeah. That's about it."

I look up from my coffee cup that I realize I'm talking to and stare at Grace. Her face is unreadable. Is she sad? Disgusted?

"You are very brave, Brie. I know that took a lot of courage to say."

I begin to nod, then realize what she's saying. I'm not brave. I'm a coward who couldn't even fight back. I shrug instead as if it's nothing. Which it is. Nothing. Nothing ever happened! My old voice comes back screaming and I'm thankful to Grace for continuing to talk. I try to listen to what she's saying and tune out the screaming in my head.

"...Tyler's wife, Kelsey, is a counselor. Or at least she was, she doesn't work now with the baby."

I try to catch up. Tyler... the pastor? Or maybe it's the other Tyler. Yes, I saw him on Sunday with a woman who had a baby in her arms.

"She might be willing to meet with you and maybe point you in the right direction on what to do now. Shall I ask her for you?"

"Umm." I hadn't planned on telling one person, much less two. "Sure," I say, completely unsure.

"Hey, would you like to have dinner at my house tonight? I'm not sure what I'm going to make, but we could make something together?"

"Uh, yeah. That sounds fun." I can feel my shaking subside and the screaming in my mind fade away. "I don't have a car though," I add.

"Oh, that's okay. I can drive you home afterward." She smiles and somehow I know this is to be the beginning of an amazing friendship, but also the start of a steep climb toward healing.

◆

After meeting with Kelsey and telling her briefly my story, she gave me an assignment. It is to grieve the things I lost in my childhood. I need to admit the hurts I have and stop detaching from my emotions. Easier said than done. I came up with two lists.

Reasons why I'm hurting:

1. *My dad wasn't a good father*
2. *My mother didn't protect me.*
3. *I was kidnapped and taken to a foreign country into a worse situation.*
4. *My mother expects perfection from me. I'm never good enough. I'm too fat. I'm not top of the class. I can't play the piano well enough.*

What I need to do:

1. *Journal*
2. *Grieve for what I lost as a child.*
3. *Do things that I missed out on as a kid with innocence and freedom. Things such as swinging on swings and finger painting.*

Grace told me that she'd help me with all this. We decided to meet up every Thursday evening and talk and do some fun childish things together. She gave me a book to read called Redeeming Love by Francine Rivers. It's about a woman who was abused and made to be a prostitute. I can relate to many of her feelings. But unlike her, I don't think that I will ever find someone to love me for me.

Xue and I return to the lab after an intensive Zumba session. I've been going three times a week for about a month now. At first I was hesitant. They make you move your hips a lot and I feel uncomfortable doing so. But through my weekly Thursday evenings with Grace, she's helping to encourage me to not detach from my body. I didn't realize I did this before, but looking back on when Ted would touch me, I realized I didn't feel much. I would feel pain, yes, but even then, I would block it out of my consciousness. And I now struggle with feeling anything. If I hurt myself, I can just push the pain away and feel nothing. So I've been working on taking note of every part of me. I notice now that I'm doing much better in Zumba. I'm really getting the hip-shaking thing down and instead of feeling shameful and disgusting, I feel free and happy.

"I've got to go run an NMR down in the basement," I say to Xue, grabbing the little tube from my bench.

"I've got to talk to Dr. Lawson, so I'll come down with you."

"Alright. But I'm taking the stairs."

We head down and I quickly submit my sample and get the

results a few minutes later. Not exactly what I was hoping for. I'll have to do some more analyses to confirm I made the right thing.

I walk down the hall toward where Xue is talking to Dr. Lawson. A sharp pain shoots through my back on my right side. I take a sharp breath in. Dang. I must have pulled a muscle or something during Zumba. The pain pulsates and fades. I slowly release my breath.

"You okay?" Xue comes out to the hall and sees me holding my side.

"Yeah. Just pulled something in Zumba, I think."

"We should take the elevator back up."

I start to protest but another intense pain stabs me. I grit my teeth and follow her, breathing in shallow breaths like a woman in labor. What the heck did I do?

The elevator door shuts with a 'clank' and my heart rate takes off to the races. I grip the railing on the side of the elevator tightly as it rumbles and shakes its way up the four floors. The pain doesn't let up this time and between the intense pain and the panic of being in a tiny metal box, I feel like I'm going to pass out. The doors 'ding' open and I step out, still pressing my hand against my right side.

"Are you okay?" Xue asks me, her voice thick with concern.

"I think I just need to lie down for a moment." Instead of going into the lab I go straight down the hall where there's a small lounge with comfy chairs.

I push two of them together and lay down on my side across them. The pain remains. I adjust my position hoping to relieve it somehow, but nothing works. The pain is so intense it is difficult to breathe. What's happening? My hands shake and I don't know if it's from the pain or just that I rode in an elevator. Breathe in. Breathe out. I try to calm myself but fail.

I hear voices. It's Xue and our other lab mate Shanthi, a girl from Sri Lanka who never fails to make me smile.

"Brie, are you okay? Do you need something?" Shanthi asks me, kneeling down in front of me with worry etched across her face.

"No. I think I'll just go home." I try to stand and another bolt of pain rips through me. I grit my teeth and suck in the air. "Maybe I could use a ride home."

Shanthi nods and goes to get her keys. I slowly stand and realize I really need to pee. I hobble over to the bathroom across the hall and gingerly go into a stall. Xue follows me into the bathroom and waits by the sink. The pain seems to be getting worse and worse. I turn around to flush the toilet and see the toilet bowl full of blood-colored water. I feel the blood drain from my cheeks. What's happening? Am I dying? I think I am. I'm peeing blood! God! I don't want to die right now. Or maybe I do. Maybe that will be the best. I quickly flush the toilet. My shaky hands fumble with the stall lock. I step out and Xue takes in my pale face and shaky hands.

"What's wrong?" she asks as I wash my hands.

"I'm peeing blood." I struggle to keep my voice calm and not freak out.

"I think you need to go to the doctor," she says, and I feel another wave of pain mixed with panic. I lean against the counter for support.

"I can't," I say and head out into the hall. Shanthi is there and Stacey is behind her. She also appraises my slightly hunched over appearance.

"She's peeing blood. She needs a doctor," Xue says to the others.

This can't be happening. This has to be a dream.

"I can drive her to the hospital, Stacey says."

"I can't. I can't," I say, but they're not listening. Shanthi goes and grabs my coat and bag and Xue hooks her arm through mine and guides me back into the elevator while Stacey goes and gets her car.

At this point I don't even care that I'm in an elevator. The pain is so intense. This can't be happening. This can't be happening. Shanthi joins us in the lobby and they help me put on my coat before braving the cold air that chills the late afternoon.

We slowly make our way to the road that passes in front of the café Grace and I were talking at a few weeks ago. This is a dream. It must be. A really bad dream. Stacey's car pulls up and we get in, Xue helping me into the front seat. I buckle up and place my shaky hands onto my lap.

Stacey, Xue and Shanthi talk and I barely register anything they are saying. Sharp scraping pain claws at the lower half of my body. I concentrate on the road and the cars flying by on the freeway. We drive for about twenty minutes, or so it seems. I have little idea of time right now. The pain doesn't lessen.

We pull up outside a small hospital. The name of the hospital is lit up on a blue and white sign. My breath leaves me and I will myself to wake up from this nightmare. I can't do this. I can't go in.

Xue opens my door and I step out and we head through the automatic doors. I'm no longer aware of what's going on. It's like a dream that's just happening; I'm not really in control at all.

I find myself sitting at a desk in front of a black woman, nicely dressed in a floral-patterned ruffle shirt. She smiles a professional smile and asks me to fill out the form she places in front of me. I watch myself do so. I feel trapped inside my body. I watch myself write BRIELLE JOY in the little squares at the top of the page. I don't even register myself filling out the rest of the form, but the next thing I know the woman is taking the sheet back and telling me to follow her through another set of doors.

Xue, Shanthi and Stacey have gone somewhere. I don't know where. I'm confused and terrified.

I'm now in a small doctor's office. Equipment lies everywhere I look. Flashes of other doctors' offices rapidly fire through my mind and I struggle to know where and when I am.

A man in blue scrubs suddenly is in front of me. I recoil against my chair. Where did he come from? Who is he? He speaks to me and I can't work out what he's saying. I look around and realize the door is shut. I'm trapped. A wave of panic engulfs me. I feel myself slip away into darkness.

A hand touches my arm and I snap back to the little doctor's office. The man is talking at me again and he puts a blood pressure cuff around my arm and begins to pump it so it squeezes my arm. Ted's hand grips my arm and he smiles at me. I try to pull away, but I'm trapped in this little room. The man takes away the blood pressure cuff.

He speaks to me again and I look around for Ted who was just here. My heart is beating so fast I can hear blood whoosh past my ears. The pain in my back is practically forgotten with the panic I feel in my chest. The man stoops so he's looking right at me. Ted's face flashes again and I suck in my breath.

"Do you suffer from panic attacks?" the man asks. I look at him and try to work out what he's asking. Panic attacks? Yes? No? I don't know. I don't know what I'm doing. All I want to do is get out of here. I don't know where I am. I grip the edges of my seat and look at the closed door. Can I reach it before he stops me? Doubtful.

As if reading my mind, the man opens the door and stands in the doorway speaking to me again. I don't know what he says but I stand, in the hope he's allowing me to go free. He walks next to me and my fear heightens. Where am I going? He doesn't lead me out, instead we head down a hallway and he indicates to the room on the right. The room is white like the rest of the building. The smell of hospital is strong in here. It smells like disinfectant. Another flash of the past. The man says I need to put on a little gown that's on a bed in the room and pee in a little pot that he sets on the counter. This can't be real. I need to take all my clothes off? Dread. I know what's coming. I can't. I can't do this. I turn to the man and he must see the absolute fear in my eyes, but instead of letting me go free he explains that I can keep on my underwear for now. For now. I want to scream but he leaves me alone in the room. I just stare at the little gown and the pot.

I once peed in a pot at university. My dance team would get a five-pound reward for every person tested for STD's. All you had to do was pee in a pot. It was weird and awkward. I was pretty confident that I had no STD's so I didn't fear that. However, when the results came in the mail a few weeks later I realized I could have and wouldn't know. I opened the letter with my heart racing. Negative. I didn't. Relief. But this is now. And I don't know what's happening.

I take the small pot into the bathroom and pee into it. The pee is still blood red. I go through the motions and wash my hands. I'm dreaming. I slip off my jeans, sweatshirt and T-shirt and realize I don't know what happened to my red coat. I put on the little gown that they wear in the movies. This is a dream. More like a nightmare.

The man comes back in and tells me to wait on the bed. He takes the pot of bloody pee and tells me the doctor will be right with me.

"Female?" I ask. I'm surprised at my voice. It's like someone else just spoke. I look around the room, confused.

"No, there are no female doctors on staff tonight," he says and walks away.

I pace around the room. My breathing rate is so fast I'm sure I'm going to pass out. I try to focus. I count the tiles on the floor. One hundred and twenty-five. I count the number of dots on the tissue box. I name things in the room, but realize that it makes me panic more. I'm in a hospital! People walk past my room. My apprehension increases. I sit on the very edge of the bed, swinging my legs wildly beneath me. I feel as though my dad is going to walk through the doorway any minute. I look down and see my hands covered in little red crescent moon shapes from my nails.

A half an hour passes. I can hear a small boy in the room next door reading a book out loud to an older man that I presume is his dad. It's a book about a dog that wanted to go out and play.

"Please can I go outside?" the little boy said, reading the book out loud. I empathize with the puppy. I want to leave.

Suddenly a man in a white coat appears. I try to pretend he's a chemist but the stethoscope around his neck gives him away. A flash of my father's silhouette opening my bedroom door... the doctor has dark hair and handsome features. I have nowhere to run. He takes a rolling stool and sits in front of me.

"Hello, Brielle. I hear you're in pain. We're going to see if we can make you feel better." He talks to me as if I'm a child. "That's a pretty bracelet," he says, pointing to my wrist. I look down and see the bracelet Charlie gave me before I left England. I count the number of beads on the bracelet. Thirty-one.

The doctor suddenly moves toward me and I try to back away, but I can't.

"I'm going to listen to your chest, Brielle." He raises his hands and moves them toward my chest.

My dad is putting his hands on my chest saying, 'lift up your shirt just like when the doctor tells you to.'

The doctor gets off his stool and sits on the edge of the bed next to me and starts gently hitting my back asking me if it hurts.

Ted is hitting me, gradually getting harder and harder. "Does it hurt yet?"

The doctor asks me to lie down on the bed.

Ted stares at my naked body lying on the bed with a sadistic grin on his face. I know what's coming so I close my eyes and drift away.

The doctor is at the doorway asking a nurse to come in, but I'm only half aware of what's going on. I try to concentrate on the flowery border that runs around the walls.

I feel the doctor pull up my gown and flashes of my dad race through my mind. I feel like I'm going to explode in panic. My body cringes as the doctor touches me. I can't feel much but I can tell he's touching me. I block out the feeling. I want to fly over the treetops. I want to fly away... I try to push away, but I can't. I'm trapped. Panic chokes me and the doctor is asking me if I feel safe at home.

Where's home? I wonder. I don't respond. He then asks if I was abused as a child.

My father crouches down in front of me and looks me in the eye. "You shouldn't tell anyone. It's between you and me. Our little secret."

I shake my head at the doctor. I just want to get away from him touching me.

He talks to the nurse as if I'm not there and they suggest an IV. Needles? I sit up suddenly. I can't stay. A wave of dizziness comes over me and I have to lie back down.

The doctor tells me to stay lying down and assures me that he'll not give me an IV if I drink all the water he gives me. He tells me he thinks I have kidney stones.

Kidney stones? Is that bad? I don't even know what they do about them.

"Would you like one of your friends to come back here with you?" the doctor asks.

I nod. Somehow, I'm unable to speak. He leaves and the nurse comes over to the bed where I lie.

"You need to allow the doctors to do what they need to do. You want to get better, don't you?" She doesn't wait for a response. "It'll be easier if you cooperate," she says and I feel like she's angry with me, reminding me of the many counselors and police who would ask me over and over again if my father ever touched me, if I had ever seen parts of naked people. They would seem frustrated when I said no or just didn't answer. I want to disappear. I want to wake up.

The nurse leaves and I go over to my purse and get out my phone. I quickly text Mike, who's been giving me rides every Sunday to and from church. I know he's a med student and he seems to know a lot. I ask him what the treatments are for kidney stones. He replies shortly after, saying that they either let them pass out on their own or sometimes have to do surgery.

This was not the response I was looking for. Surgery! I feel my chest rise and fall even more rapidly than before.

"Knock, knock!" Shanthi is in the doorway. I find myself just smiling seeing her. "Are you okay?"

I shake my head. I'm petrified.

"The doctor just came out and said he'd never seen a patient panic so much. He asked us if you'd gone through anything traumatic recently. We're all super worried about you!"

I try not to cry. I really just want to leave. Shanthi senses my mood and she smiles and says, "It'll be okay. I heard you and Xue went to Zumba today!" I nod. "I wish I could have gone, but my experiment is taking forever. Remember yesterday when I was dancing in the lab and I knocked over that bucket of dry ice and knocked the flask into the sink and broke it? Oh dear, that was so embarrassing!" I start to giggle. She mocks what she was doing, dancing around the room and that's when the doctor comes back. He smiles and sees me smiling. "That's better," he says and hands me a large Styrofoam cup of ice water. "You've got to drink all that.

We are going to give you a CAT scan." A what? I look at Shanthi, wide-eyed. The doctor catches my look and tries to assure me it's non-invasive and will be fine. It doesn't feel fine. They're going to put me in a tube! A tiny tube which I'm probably too fat to fit in. "You can't panic. You're going to have to calm down," the doctor tells me. Panic? I'm not panicking visually. I'm calm. I'm not even speaking. What is he talking about? I feel like I'm doing so well. I've not run away yet.

As he leaves, a nurse enters with a phone in her hand.

"Your mother is on the phone." I roll my eyes.

"Hello?" I say, my voice cracking.

"Brielle? Are you okay? Lynn and Laurie called, telling me that they had gotten a call from your professor saying you were in the hospital with suspected kidney stones." Lynn and Laurie, my cousin Alex's sister and mom had been put down as my emergency contact. At least they were in the country, albeit in the next state over. I plan on visiting them in a couple weeks for Thanksgiving.

"Mom, I'm fine. Really, I am."

"Lynn and Laurie are willing to drive over. They could be with you by the morning."

"Seriously, Mom. I'm fine. My lab mates are here with me. I'm feeling better now. Anyway, thanks for calling, but I have to go."

"Okay..." She sounds unconvinced and uncertain.

"Tell Lynn and Laurie not to come. I'll see them in a couple weeks. Bye, Mom."

"I'll call you tomorrow. Bye."

"I love you," I add and hang up. I feel a fire burn in my chest, unspoken anger at her. I'm not even sure of the reason behind it.

Minutes turn to hours while Shanthi sits in the room with me. She chitchats while I've shut down emotionally and physically. I'm exhausted from the pain, the fear and the constant tightening of my muscles.

Unfortunately, as I give up the fight and numb myself, the flashbacks come more readily. Shanthi will be there one minute and the next it's my father. I can't stay in either place longer than a few minutes. I clench my jaw and force myself to remain unreactive to my surroundings. I want to get out of here and I can only do that if I don't panic so they'll give me the CAT scan.

The male nurse appears in the doorway and I startle. 'Dangit, Brielle. Not cool.' I attempt to smile and I almost see a trace of a smile on the nurse's face.

"Alright. Are you ready?" he asks me. "You're not going to panic on me, are you?"

My mind is freaking out but I purse my lips and shake my head.

"Okay then. Follow me."

I hop off the bed and look at Shanthi.

"Yes… she can come down with you," he says, and I hear the amusement in his voice.

I totter down the hall in my socks and gown. I hum Jingle Bells to myself and try to block out all the hospital stuff around me. After a few turns my nerves step it up. I have no idea how to get out of here. The nurse stops outside a pair of green doors with various radiation hazard stickers on them, making me think of the NMR room in the basement of the lab.

I grasp onto that thought. I'm just going inside a NMR machine. I'm a human tube. But I'm so much bigger! What if I get stuck?

The nurse tells Shanthi to wait here and he leads me inside where a small bed lies in the middle of a well-lit room. At the foot of the bed is a circle only about two feet deep. At least I won't be fully trapped

"You've got to lie down on that on your back with your arms above your head and be very still. Do you think you can do that?" He talks to me like a child.

I nod.

"Good. Don't panic on me now. Up you get." His words trigger memories in my head, but I squeeze my nails into my palms, keeping the flashbacks at bay.

I force myself to lie down on the bed. As soon as I'm lying flat I begin to have body memories. They come in the form of intense pain down below and an asphyxiating feeling like I'm being crushed. 'Focus, Brie. Fly away.' The nurse goes behind a little cubicle with a window and soon the machine turns on with a loud whooshing sound. I close my eyes and as the tube moves over me I pretend I'm flying above the treetops in New Hampshire with the red and golden leaves fluttering below me.

"Breathe in," a woman's voice says to me soothingly. I do as she says, realizing I have not taken a breath in for a while.

"Breathe out," the automated woman's voice says after a few seconds. I exhale slowly and feel more peaceful than I have all evening. The voice repeats itself several times.

"Alright. You're all done. See, that wasn't so bad, was it?" The nurse comes over. I sit up quickly, leaving the treetops behind and replacing it with blinding light and small stars, which appear in my vision. I think I stood up too quick.

He leads me back out to a waiting Shanthi and together we go back to the white room. After what seems like a second eternity, the handsome doctor returns.

I'm exhausted and afraid, but I'm able to stay present and focused on what he is saying.

Conclusion: I have kidney stones. Good news: no surgery needed. He say's they've already passed through my kidneys and I'll just have to pee them out. Great... He gives me a prescription for some antibiotics 'just in case.'

"You're free to go," he says, leaving me beaming.

Chapter 32

Reality. It is something that most people try to run away from. They bury themselves in work or entertainment, futile attempts to avoid painful realities. There is no running. There is no hiding. The truth is the truth. Reality wins every time.

I exit the frosted glass doors of Chicago's O'Hare airport with my little suitcase in tow. I scan through the crowd's faces until I find them.

They both stand there with huge smiles on their faces. I dash over and wrap my arms around Alex's neck with a grin and a giggle. Then I turn to Lynn. My twin. We share a bond as sisters although we have barely spent any time together in life. Our personality, voice and laugh have people raising their eyebrows at our similarity. I just laugh and her laugh joins in. It's so good to see them.

I walk out to the car in between the two of them. Just like I felt a couple of years ago, with them I feel safe. I can feel my fear ease and my muscles relax. Breathing in the Wisconsin air as we travel North toward their hometown, I'm amazed at how easy it is. To breathe. It's like a weight off my chest. With them I don't need to worry.

Lynn and I talk and giggle for the whole two-and-a-half-hour trip.

Instead of staying with Alex, this time I'm staying with Lynn at her mom and stepdad's. Since Thanksgiving is taking place there, it made more sense. Besides, I wanted some girl time.

Alex drops us off at the house. It's been awhile since I've been here and I struggle to make out the house in the dark. An American flag is illuminated against the night sky.

I follow Lynn into the dark house. I don't expect Laurie and her husband, Marshall, to be up but, as we giggle our way into the large living room, Laurie and Marshall sit on the couch, each with a book in their hands. They waited up for me. A grin spreads across my face and I run over to embrace Laurie in a huge hug.

Just as Lynn is like my sister, Laurie is like my American mom. She treats me like a daughter and I love it.

Marshall gets up and comes over to give me a hug. I hug him briefly, forcing myself not to freak out.

I've not known him for long because I've not been back to visit here much since I left for England. But from what I've seen of him I can conclude several things.

One, he's a southerner. Like Virginia southern. His drawl is thick and I have to often mash my lips together when he talks so I don't burst out into a laughing fit. Two, he has little concept of my personal space bubble, having absolutely no problem talking to me only one foot away. And three, he's a really nice guy, but that gives me little reason to trust him. Aren't they always nice at first? After all, my father loved me a lot. I try not to impose my prejudice against men onto Marshall, but it's difficult. He often comes up behind me and squeezes my shoulders, causing me to instantly freeze and focus on my surroundings so I don't flashback. Of course, he doesn't know my past. Neither does Laurie. Lynn, however, knows a little from the last time I was around when I shared with her some of my past.

After thirty minutes of 'life catch-up' we all conclude that we should head to bed.

I'm sleeping on a trundle bed in Lynn's room while I'm here. I walk into her room and smile. If there's one thing someone should know about Lynn, it's that she collects ducks. Not the live quacking kind. No. Rubber ducks. Armies of yellow rubber duckies line her shelves everywhere I look. There are tiny ones the size of a fingertip, to big ones as large as my head. She's a serious fanatic. And with this many in one room, it's kind of creepy.

We get ready for bed and turn off the light. I snuggle comfortably beneath a feather quilt. The darkness doesn't bother me here. Lynn and I stay up talking for another hour before we finally drift off.

I'm safe.

"Happy Thanksgiving!" I say to Lynn, seeing that she is awake. I spring out of bed and take a couple steps, pausing at the door as I wait for the wave of dizziness to pass before tottering off downstairs in my PJ's.

"Happy Thanksgiving!" I announce to the household. Laurie, Marshall and Alex are all there in the living room waiting for us to get up.

"Happy Thanksgiving!" they respond.

I couldn't wipe the grin off my face if I tried. It's been eleven years since my last Thanksgiving in America. I look out the back window at the stunning fall colors and the three pumpkins that Lynn, Alex and I carved last night. My heart aches as I think over those eternal eleven years of waiting to be here.

If only. If only my dad was a good man. Fact: my dad was not a good man.

The rest of the day is consumed with Thanksgiving festivities, including the Macy's Thanksgiving Day parade, preparing vegetables and of course, the Thanksgiving dinner.

My smile remains intact all day and I rarely have to work to keep it up.

But every day has a night.

I can feel it. The darkness trying to engulf me once again. Pushing away unwanted thoughts is becoming challenging. But I must push on. I must.

In the book I'm reading, *On the Threshold of Hope,* they call me a survivor. I don't feel like one. I feel like I just let it all happen.

I hear a bang outside, which startles me. I look around to see 2:00 am illuminated on Lynn's clock. Her silhouette is lit by the moonlight filtering in through her blinds. Her breaths are deep and steady. I look back to my journal, lit up by a small flashlight. The darkness of the room suddenly feels heavier. I can almost hear breathing behind me. He's coming…

I get out of the blue bathtub and wrap my Precious Moments towel around me. I hear my dad's voice coming closer. 'Not now,' I think. I imagine myself going and playing with my Barbies and dollhouse. 'Just let me play, Daddy,' I plead silently. He's just outside the door. I run into the closet with slatted doors and crouch beneath the shelf holding all the towels. He comes in and must know where I am already. Closing the door behind him, whoosh, click, he peers through the slats. Smiling. Opening the closet door, squeak, whoosh, he gently pulls me out and at the same time takes my towel away from my shivering body. I didn't realize I was cold. He begins to dry my hair with it and at the same time he gently strokes my body with a grin on his face.

My mother's footsteps can be heard in the hallway. His face drops and he hastily puts my towel around me once more.

"There we go," he says, as the bathroom door opens and my mother questions what is taking so long…

I silently scream into the darkness.

The Thanksgiving festivities end too quickly. I'm back in Detroit, needing to be in the lab as much as possible, cramming in work before Christmas is here.

It's late one Monday night. Stacey is upstairs watching TV and knitting, relaxing for a change. I sit at the dining room table, which Pilikia is laying on, staring at me like I'm food. Fat cat.

I'm still undecided on what to do at Christmas time. Laurie and Marshall would love me to join them in Wisconsin. I'm sure it would be good, yet I find myself checking flight prices to New Hampshire.

My mind wanders back to the last day I was there. It was just before Christmas…

I run along the back of the church to where my best friend, Hope, is standing in the doorway. Her freckled face smiles at me.

"I can't believe you're going for a whole three weeks!" she says to me.

"I know. But it will go fast, I'm sure. Then when I get back we can have a sleepover at my house," I grin at her.

"I wish your mom would let you have one at mine."

"She doesn't ever let me have one anywhere else. I don't think she trusts your dad." My mother had become extremely overprotective of me.

"You'll come back, won't you?" Hope asks, suddenly serious.

"Of course!" I say, "I promise."

It was a promise I couldn't keep. I never returned. The memories leave moisture pooled in my eyes. I blink them away and stare at Pilikia still watching me.

I have to go back.

Chapter 33

Closure. It's something we often desire. When relationships end abruptly, we feel ill at ease, off balance, as it were. When traumatic things happen unexpectedly and leave your life drastically different in mere seconds, you're lost floundering with the pieces that are left, unaware of how you'll ever move on.

I watch the snow swirl down from the sky and instantly melt on the road next to where I stand outside Chicago's airport.

"We better head home before this picks up much more," Marshall drawls, looking up at the blinding white sky. "It's been good to have you home for Christmas, kid. You're like my own daughter." He comes over to me and gives me a hug. I'm finding myself beginning to relax around him. So far, he's not hurt me. "Love ya, kid," he says to me, as he hops in the van and pulls away.

My heart chokes up with emotion for the second time today.

Just before we left the house, I received a voicemail from Jeff and Jenni, the couple I'll being staying with on my visit to New Hampshire. Jeff ended the message with: "I love you, can't wait to see you."

It seems absurd that *I* would have all this love. All these people who care about me, who treat me as their daughter, but in a good way. The way my father should have treated me.

I shift my tear-filmed eyes from the falling snow and walk into the terminal. I'm beginning to feel like I spend all my time in airports. Always going somewhere. Running away from my past or chasing it, I never know which.

I look out the little window next to me on the plane. I see the barren winter forest stretch out for miles, over hills and valleys. Lakes pop up occasionally, frozen in the snowy air. New England. My home. Oh, how I've missed it! My heart aches sharply with all I lost here.

I think of seeing Jeff in under half an hour and I can't describe the number of emotions that run through me at the thought. I was struggling to explain to Marshall and Laurie my relationship to Jeff. It's rather complex, yet not really at all. Just different.

Jeff is a little older than my sister so I imagine he's in his late forties. He was in the Navy, like my dad. And it was through my parents that he met my family. Apparently, he would stay with them (my mother, father, brother and sister) long before I was around. For me, he was there from early on, a big brother while mine was far away.

My parents had an apartment in the basement of our house. Numerous families came and went when I was young, and I'm not exactly sure when Jeff came to live there, but I was probably around four or five.

He was a shorter, more stout man than my father, with a funny laugh. He always joked around with me. He often joined us for dinner and my mother treated him like a son.

One of his 'hero' moments for me was a time when I lost one of my baby teeth at the dinner table. I put the tooth on the side of my plate. Unfortunately, I forgot about it and my mother scrapped it into the trash when clearing up. I began to cry, afraid that the tooth fairy wouldn't come if I didn't have my tooth to put under my pillow. So Jeff got up, took off the lid of the trashcan and stuck his arm in. A few minutes later he pulled out my tooth!

The memory puts a smile on my face and I see that the tops of the trees are closer now. I'm almost home.

I walk as fast as I can without running. My suitcase *k-chunks* rapidly behind me as I drag it at full speed over the tiled airport floor. I'm so excited that I don't know if I want to laugh or cry.

I scan the faces up ahead and it only takes me a second to spot him.

Jeff hasn't changed a bit. He's a little balder and gray. But he's got the same jolly smile. Tears prick my eyes and a giggle bursts from my lips as I fling myself into his open arms.

"Ellie," he says softly into my hair as he hugs me tightly.

The name my father called me shocks me to the core. I forgot Jeff also called me this. For a moment, I'm haunted by memories, but only for a moment. I pull back and see Jeff and remember that with him, I'm safe. He takes my suitcase from me, still grinning.

Bubbles of laughter keep popping out of my mouth, which is stretched into such a large smile my cheeks are already aching.

We don't speak. We don't need to. I walk next to him to his car and I pretend for a moment that he's my dad picking me up from the airport after being away from home for a long, long time. I'm home.

Our drive home is full of conversation, mainly from him, he's quite the talker. We talk about work and stories he has from there. Anticipation of returning to my hometown sends butterflies to my stomach. This all feels so surreal.

The road here and scenery are all so familiar. Even the sound of Jeff's voice makes me feel so comfortable. It's like the world has been spinning out of control for eleven years and suddenly everything is right again.

I realize why I try to never think about Jeff and all I lost after being taken from here. I lost too much for my heart to handle. The pain simmers beneath the surface and I swallow it back.

"Jenni and the girls should be getting home soon. They have not stopped talking about you for a week straight. They are so excited you're coming."

"How old are they now?" I ask. I've not met them yet. Jeff and Jenni got married shortly before I left the country. I was the flower girl at their wedding.

"Six and three."

"Wow." It's all I can say. I've missed so much.

"Do you want to swing by your old place before we go home?"

The question freezes my whole body. The idea terrifies me, but I feel I have to.

"Sure," I say, completely unsure.

I keep my eyes looking out the window. We pass a familiar cliff face on the highway and my stomach squeezes uncomfortably. We're almost there. A few minutes later we exit the highway, turn left, curve to the right and drive straight for several minutes. My body recognizes the turns of the road and my eyes recognize the houses that we pass by. The Christmas tree farm is up here on the right. Sure enough.

I smile faintly at the memory of my mother's and my first Christmas without my dad. I suggested we get a small tree, but she was insistent on us getting a big one like we normally did. We trudged through the snow, which was up to my knees at the time, until we found the right one. She used a handsaw and worked really hard to cut it down and then drag it out. I learned then that women could do anything men could do.

The car turns right at the little stone well covered in mounds of snow. My heart beats fast. The little row of mailboxes is still there. We turn left onto the dirt road. We are thrown around in the car as it goes over the giant potholes.

"Guess they don't keep it up as well as they used to," Jeff says. I try to smile, but I fear I'll puke if I open my mouth. I push away memories of the trips to the dump in my dad's truck.

The woods surround us. All the trees are naked but I can imagine them full of the green leaves of summer or golden leaves of fall. The house emerges from behind the wall of trees like a mirage or a ghost.

It looks exactly how I remembered.

Jeff stops the car and turns off the engine. Dogs bark as we get out.

"I know the woman who lives here. I'll just go explain why we're out here," he says to me, and heads up the driveway.

I stand rooted in place. Everything is the same. I suppose they've cut down a lot of trees near the house, making it seem much bigger. My tree house is also gone.

I can't stop my eyes from flickering up to the top left window. It's like a haunted room. I can imagine myself sitting there on my little pink chair, looking out the window, wanting to escape my life.

Wind whirls cold air over my face. I close my eyes and remember running through the woods around here. So many memories.

"Not much has changed, has it?" Jeff asks me.

I jump as I open my eyes. I was far away for a moment there, somewhere in my past. I finally work out what he just said.

"Nope," I say simply.

"Well, Jenni is home now. Ready for the attack of the girls?" he jokes.

I suddenly remember why I don't go near children, especially little girls. I don't know if I can do this. I gulp and give him a tight smile before getting in the car with one last glance at my bedroom window.

"She's here!" I hear a girl scream as I get out of the car. Oh boy... I prepare myself as I walk up the front porch steps of Jeff's very Victorian-looking house. It's a blue two-story house with white trim. I vaguely remember Jeff and Jenni being really into Victorian everything.

I spot Jenni's flaming red hair at the door. She opens it and embraces me in a hug. I feel a wave of heat and I hear the crackling sound of a log fire.

"Hey there!" Jenni says, taking my red coat and scarf from me. Jeff enters with my suitcase.

"Daddy!" A high pitched squeal followed by an "Oooofff!" from Jeff as two little people zoom past me and fling themselves onto him.

Tears immediately threaten to spill down my cheeks. He holds the youngest, whose hair burns like her mother's, in his arms and the older one, whose hair is bright blonde, clings onto his leg. She positions herself so that she hides half behind her dad.

"Ashley, Amber, this is Ellie."

I give them a little wave.

Ashley, the older one, suddenly grins and moves away from her dad.

"Do you want to see what Amber and I made with Mom today?" she asks me excitedly.

I can't help but smile. "Sure!" I say enthusiastically. Amber wiggles her way out of Jeff's grip and follows her sister out of the living room. They come back moments later, each with a little bouncy ball in hand.

"We made bouncy balls!" Ashley says, holding hers in her palm, outstretched so I can look at it.

"Ooo! Beautiful colors."

"Yeah. And they bounce really high, too! Watch!" She throws the ball downwards and it bounces off through the living room. Amber squeals and giggles as she tries to get it. I look up at Jeff and Jenni watching them, and I realize I have nothing to fear about these girls. They are happy. They are safe. They are loved.

I spend the rest of the evening talking to Jenni and Jeff while Ashley sits on my feet and Amber curls up on my lap.

They ask me to read them a book before bed. I agree and Ashley gets *The Aristocats*. I put on my best French accent and read the book animatedly to them. They listen intently and giggle at the funny parts. Within a couple hours the two small girls have captured my heart.

Jenni herds them upstairs to bed. Amber is staying in her sister's room so I can have her room. She was more than excited about giving up her room for me.

Jeff and I sit around the fire and talk. It's small talk at first, but, as time goes on, questions burn in my chest. He knows a lot about what happened, I'm sure. Things I can't ask anyone in my family. I steer us deeper and deeper.

"Do you know much about what happened with my dad in all that craziness?" I ask him.

"I know a lot, yes. I've never been sure how much you knew or remember, so I avoid talking about it. I don't want to bring up painful memories for you."

I nod and stare into the fire as I continue to talk.

"My mom doesn't even know. I kept our secret. I didn't even tell when they asked…"

Jeff nods as if he understands. "Everyone presumed you just didn't remember or nothing happened. But I knew. If nothing happened to you, you wouldn't have been the way you were."

"What do you mean?" I ask, turning to look at him intently.

"Well, for one, you never once asked about your dad or ever even gave the impression of missing him."

My mind goes back to that day…

I remember having heard my parents talking late into the night. Eventually I had fallen asleep. My mother awakened me the next morning. She sat on the foot of my bed like my father would at night.

"It's time to wake up, pumpkin," she said softly. Her voice sounded funny and very unusual. I got up and my mother placed my soft pink blanket around my shoulders. She bunched it tightly around me.

"Come downstairs, I have something I need to say to you."

I followed her down the stairs, taking care not to slip on the wooden staircase.

"Have a seat," she told me and I chose the rocking chair.

I curled up so my knees were next to my chest and wrapped my blanket around them, cocooning myself against what my mother was about to say. I didn't know what it was, but her voice and actions made me think something was very wrong.

"Pumpkin," my mother started, and paused as if she was unsure of how to speak. "Pumpkin, your dad... well, he's gone. He's not coming back."

I looked up at her to see her face contorted in a strange way. My dad was gone? He wasn't coming back? I remembered the times where he would go away with work for a short time and how much I loved it when he was gone. This was like that, but forever, right? I looked out the window. The sun was just beginning to illuminate the tops of the trees in the forest. And that's what I felt like. My darkness was ending.

"Do you understand, Brielle?" my mother asked me seriously, forcing me to look at her.

I nodded. Yes, I understood...

"And another thing that was strange," Jeff continues, snapping me out of my memory, "was the way you acted around men. You were terrified, not just shy. You were okay with me, but I was around often." He squeezes his eyes shut for a moment. "I'm sorry I never did anything. I saw things when I stayed with your family when your sister still lived at home. It seemed strange at the time, but I didn't think much of it. Your dad was a respectable guy. He was like a father to me. He fooled us all..." His voice breaks a little.

He swallows and goes on, "We had to change all the locks on the house when your mom kicked him out. The dogs would go crazy a lot during the night. I think your dad was out there in the woods. I once heard him trying to break into the basement window. He ran away when I turned on the light. After that I started sleeping with a gun and I set up an alarm that would turn on a light in my face instead of setting off a noise that would scare him off.

"If he ever dared come around here now, I'd shoot him without blinking. He's not going to get near my girls. I'm so sorry, Ellie. I'm sorry I didn't do anything."

"That's what my dad would call me. Ellie," I simply reply.

"Oh. Sorry. I can call you Brielle."

"No. No... I like you calling me Ellie. It makes me think of you now, not my dad. Happy thoughts," I smile at him. "I should get some sleep." My head feels overloaded with thoughts and emotions.

"Alright, sleep well, Ellie," Jeff says to me as I pad silently up the stairs.

I get ready for bed in a daze. Thoughts of seeing my old house, of finally being back here in New Hampshire and of my dad and all he did swirl around my head. I flop onto Amber's bed and turn out the bedside light, willing myself to stop thinking and get some sleep.

I hear the bitter wind outside the window whistle through the trees. I close my eyes, but immediately see my father opening my bedroom door.

A gasp echoes across the room and I bolt upright.

"He's not here, Brielle. It's okay," I whisper to myself.

I lay back down and roll over, peering out the window at the world outside. The winter woods are illuminated by the moon's reflection on the snow. The moon itself, a reflection of the sun. I just gaze at its beauty for a moment, absorbing God's perfect alignment of the solar system.

I turn and plop my head on the pillow and catch a glimpse of the headboard on Amber's bed. I feel my breath catch in my throat.

This was *my* bed. This would have still been my bed if everything had been different.

It's the thought that breaks my dam. Tears begin to pour out of my eyes, splashing onto my pillow, which becomes sodden in minutes. My body shakes violently as I silently scream and cry into the darkness. My tears continue until I begin to worry they will never stop. All I can think is, "This should have been my bed."

"Have fun!" Jenni says to me, as I step out of the front door.

I hear Ashley and Amber whine at their mom, "Why can't she stay and play with us?"

I bite back a smile before skipping down the porch steps. Those girls have demanded my attention every waking moment and I've been happy to give it to them. However, my day's plans will give me a much-needed break.

I run to the driveway where a large black 4x4 Jeep sits waiting. The driver's side door opens and out steps Hope. My mind flashes to that last day at the church all those years ago. She hasn't changed. She still has a full beautiful smile across her adorable freckled face. Golden hair still drapes over her shoulder.

I run to her and we embrace in a silent hug. Words cannot describe this moment. Words are not enough to express the extent of how much I've missed her. We giggle since words fail and I climb in the passenger side of the Jeep.

"So, how's it going?" she asks, as if I'd seen her just last week. I understand her tone. To me it feels like we've never been apart. I smile. Not even an ocean of time can separate the bond of friendship we share.

We talk, we laugh and we pretend that the past eleven years of separation never occurred.

"So, where are we going?" I ask her.

"Well, Jason wants to hang out too, so we'll head over and pick him up. Where we go is up to you. What do you want to see while you're here?"

I smile at the thought of seeing Jason, who, like Hope, is a lifelong friend. All our mothers were close friends and we were practically raised together.

I think about how little time I actually have to spend in this dream world and I feel that familiar painful tug at my heart. I swallow back the emotion.

"How about we go to Spofford Lake?" I suggest, as we pull down the familiar road that Jason lives on, right across from my old school. Its giant brick three-story structure emerges into view with a rush of memories. Hope pulls into Jason's driveway, but my eyes remain glued on the school.

"Sounds good. It's been a while since I was last there." She parks the Jeep and hops out. I follow suit, finally tearing my eyes from the flood of memories.

The screen door bangs against the side of his house as he steps out. I jump at the sound but am immediately filled with a rush of joy at seeing him. My once weedy friend, Jason. He's now over six feet tall with broad shoulders and muscles that look… fwah! Crazy.

"Jay! What happened?" I tease him, as I run up to his outstretched arms.

"Hey, Brielle," his voice is deep but soft. My heart settles. He's still the same friend… just bigger.

"Let's hit the road, peeps!" Hope calls out. We climb into the Jeep, Jason taking the back seat.

For the first ten minutes of conversation I'm constantly turning back to talk to him. It's all so surreal that I'm here in a Jeep with my two oldest friends.

Unfortunately, the twisty mountain roads catch up with me and I resort to just staring out the window at the bluest blue sky as a backdrop to the frosty sunshine forests.

Spofford Lake was our typical summer retreat. We'd come as often as we could convince our moms to take us. We'd play in the water and explore forest hideaways.

I catch the first glimpse of it over the peak of a hill. The sun glints off the water's surface in a direct path down the center of the lake. My heart flutters with excitement. What a beautiful day.

The road twists and turns for what seems forever before we finally reach the lakeshore.

As soon as we're there, I jump out of the car and rush toward the water. It's not frozen over. In fact, today is unseasonably warm. I stop inches before the lapping waves hit my sneakers. I take in the scene stretched out before me. The calm. The beauty. I close my eyes and let the sun dapple my cheeks. I hear footsteps behind me.

I turn around and see Hope and Jason smiling at me. My smile stretches beyond happy. Tears of joy well up in my eyes.

We don't speak. Instead we wander over to 'our spot.' It's a large flat boulder at the shoreline where we'd sit and dry off after swimming.

I sit down with my legs hanging off the side over the water. Jason and Hope sit on either side of me. I breathe in the cool air and just soak up the blissful atmosphere.

"I can't believe I'm here," I finally say, breaking the comfortable silence.

"I know. Neither can I," Hope says, staring out over the lake.

"It's been forever. I can't believe you just disappeared," Jason says, sounding hurt. "One day you were here, the next my mom told me you'd moved to England and were never coming back."

I purse my lips and try not to cry. I feel their pain. I feel mine.

"My mom thought she was doing the best thing for me…" I take a deep breath. "Do you guys know anything about my dad?"

Jason shakes his head.

"No. Not really. What happened?" Hope asks.

"Well, he cheated on my mom. And the police suspected him of murdering several women in the area. He also tried to kill my mom to get to me. And the part that not many people know is that… well, he was…" I swallow and look over the lake at the shimmering sunlight, "abusive to me… sexually," I add, in almost a whisper.

"What?" Jason exclaims. "That's sick."

I nod in agreement, thinking he's talking about me.

"I can't believe he would do that to you. Dang. If he was here I'd pound him to the ground!" Jason begins to rant and I realize he hadn't meant I was sick, he was referring to my dad. I feel my brow furrow in confusion. Everyone seems to have this odd reaction and I just can't really grasp it.

I turn to Hope. Her eyes are downcast.

"I don't know what to say," she says at last. "I never knew."

"Yeah, I know. I was good at keeping it secret. I thought I was doing the right thing. Even when the lawyers, counselors and police asked me about it, I never told."

I feel slightly freer, getting that off my chest. I tell them about the problems I dealt with and that I am dealing with now because of all that happened.

They listen, often shaking their heads in disbelief.

"I'm glad you're here," Hope says.

Jason gets up and starts throwing rocks into the lake.

The subject lightens as we talk about old friends we had and things we used to do.

I told them the truth and they still are beside me. I'm overflowing with love and happiness. I'm here. They're here. The world is beautiful.

Chapter 34

Shrapnel. A bomb explodes. Shards of metal and debris cut into your flesh, leaving gaping wounds. Time allows your wounds to heal and the shrapnel remain forgotten. It can be years before you discover that beneath the scar tissue lies parts from the initial blast that your body has now accepted as part of you. Only a surgeon can remove the pieces that do not belong. Only God can remove the lies our minds have accepted as truth.

The silence is tight in the car. Familiar scenes of the highway in New Hampshire fly past the window, but rather than surreal excitement, I feel deep sorrow. Even Jeff's jolly demeanor has faded the closer we've gotten to the airport.

We left Jenni and two crying girls on their front porch over an hour ago. Hope and Jason said goodbye to me last night. I couldn't stop the tears. Once again, words were not enough. Our tightly held hugs were an attempt to convey the extent of how much we didn't want to let go, but it wasn't enough. I watched her Jeep taillights disappear into the forest through blurry eyes. My choking sobs rang out around me. It's not forever, I'm trying to tell myself.

Jeff attempts several times to lighten the atmosphere by talking about work or his girls. But every time, the conversation flops with a thud. No amount of small talk is going to change reality.

Jeff exits the highway and my heart begins to race.

Wait. I want to go back. I can't leave again! What if I never come back? What if it's another eleven years? Please, turn around!

My eyes begin to fill with my silent plea.

Jeff seems to sense my mood and his lips squish into a tight line.

The airport quickly comes into view. Jeff pulls the car up to the first terminal door and jumps out of the car, retrieving my suitcase as I slink out of the car, using every ounce of resolve I have.

Jeff drags my suitcase and I walk with lead feet into the terminal.

I check in at the kiosk hoping for some reason that I can't leave. Instead the machine spits my ticket to Detroit into my ungrateful hands. Jeff follows me to the security check, but this is as far as he can go. I look at the line of people waiting to be scanned in the metal detector, then out of the window at the gray clouds. Anywhere but at Jeff. Tears well up in my eyes. I know they'll spill out momentarily. Jeff outstretches his arms and I fall into them.

"Ellie. Ellie. I love you so much, Ellie," he says softly into my hair as he strokes my back like a little child. My tears drip onto his sweatshirt. He steps back, his eyes also brimming with tears.

I'm too choked up to speak. He gives me a small smile and I wave, turn around and join the queue of people as a fresh wave of tears pours down my cheeks.

An older lady in front of me looks at me with kind eyes full of sympathy. This just makes me worse and my tears become sobs. I glance back around and see Jeff still standing there with tears in his eyes.

I had no idea it would be this hard. For eleven years, I mourned leaving my home and my country without warning and without a choice. I thought that maybe if I had chosen it, it would have been easier. Standing here waiting to leave by choice, I realize it's not much easier, yet somehow I know, this is not where God wants me. The woman in front of me smiles at me again and a scripture warms my heart.

"For I know the plans I have for you," declares the Lord. "Plans to prosper you and not to harm you, plans to give you hope and a future." Jeremiah 29:11

And it is that hope of the future that causes me to smile while tears continue to flow.

"You know that's a lie, right?"

I switch my gaze from the synthetic pink flower in the vase sitting on the kitchen table to the tree branches barely visible outside the window as the last rays of pink and orange give way to deep blue.

Do I know that's a lie? Do I know that all men are not like my father and Ted? Yes... and no. I glance back to Grace and see her patiently waiting for my response.

"I guess," I finally say. "I don't know... I guess I think all men have the potential to be like them and some just choose not to act upon it. I guess I believe that men only think about sex and the problem is, that's pretty accurate, from what I've heard, or at least it is a common thought for them."

"Do you think sex is a bad thing?" Grace asks.

I feel my nose wrinkle in disgust at the thought of sex.

"Yes."

"But that's not true. You have a very distorted view of sex. God created sex to be between a man and his wife. He created it to be good and beautiful."

I cringe at the fact that God even created such a revolting thing. I feel like I've somehow failed at understanding it altogether. What's wrong with me? I know many people my age can't wait to have sex, or at least look forward to it. For me, it is a dreaded thing and the idea of marriage is terrifying. Grace observes my mental battle for a while before interjecting.

"Brie." She waits for my attention to focus on her. "What your father did was wrong."

A shiver runs through me and I feel the need to correct her. My father loved me, he was just showing me that he loved me. She continues, oblivious to my discomfort.

"God created a father to be a protector of his children, to love and honor them."

Yes, yes. And my father did! He would get the big bad snakes and kill them. He built me a tree house. He would carry me around. He loved me!

"God did not intend for a father to have sexual relations with his daughter."

I can hear the disgust in her voice and I feel dirty and revolting. I feel the urge to hurt myself. Instead I lean back in my chair and slip my hands beneath the table so I can dig my nails into my palms. The small amount of pain temporarily relieves the welling up emotions inside me. Grace allows for a moment of silence and I feel the need to apologize for letting it happen. Instead, Grace breaks the tension by getting up and retrieving the freshly baked cookies from the stove.

"We'll come back to all that another day," she says, putting the cookies on a plate. "I can see that's enough for tonight." I'm not sure what she's 'seeing,' but I wholeheartedly agree. "There was something else I wanted to discuss with you." Her tone suggests this isn't going to be an easy discussion.

"Sunday's sermon," she says, and I feel panic grip my stomach. I don't need reminding about Sunday's sermon...

Mike had picked me up outside Stacey's as usual. We discussed what we had done over Christmas break. I was still a little raw from the pain of leaving New Hampshire, but I was enjoying being back in Detroit.

We got to church and I said hello to a few people I had gotten to know a little bit, but avoided most of the men. Dissociation had become common recently, and around men it was even more prominent.

Mike and I sat in the middle back of the hall. Worship was great and prayer was good and eye opening. There is so much brokenness in Detroit, it is a little overwhelming at times. Then it came to the sermon. We were still in Genesis.

Tyler had seemed more subdued than usual as he got up to preach.

"Genesis 34," he said and began to read, commenting that Dinah meant 'justice' and she was Leah's daughter.

I was filling in the date and the chapter we were on in my notebook and I had just finished writing *Dinah=justice* when Tyler's words caught my attention.

"Violated her. Or humbled her."

I looked up to see if I'd just misheard him. He went silent for a moment and I could hear my heart thudding in my chest.

"He raped her." Tyler's words hit me like a dagger. Pain exploded in my chest. My whole body froze. He kept talking.

"Rape. Rape. Rape."

Every time he said it was more painful than the last. I just wanted to run out. I wanted to scream at him to stop. I wanted to deny it. He said that there were people in the church who were victims of sexual molestation and abuse. I kept thinking 'not me, not me' over and over again, trying to dodge the harsh reality of his words. But I couldn't. They hit me square on and left me bleeding. I spent the rest of the service somewhere else in my mind.

Mike accidentally brushed against my arm and snapped me back into reality. When I looked down I saw my notebook page full of deep impressed drawings and doodles. I slammed the book shut so no one would see and then I noticed both my hands were covered in red nail marks. I quickly shoved my red coat on and hid them in my pockets.

I told Mike I'd wait for him outside but he said he was ready straightaway. The ride home was tense. My mind was still screaming. My heart was still bleeding...

Now here's Grace bringing back the memories of this painful experience. I try to mute any expression on my face.

"What about it?" I ask flatly.

"Tyler's sermon gave the impression that there are possibly several people who've been sexually abused."

I cringe at her harsh words but force myself to move swiftly past them. Several women's faces come to mind, who, like Jade and numerous others, I can 'tell' have been sexually abused to some degree.

"It's statistically likely," I reply casually.

"You mentioned when we first started meeting how you thought it would be good for you to be able to meet with and talk to other survivors."

I nod and look out the window again at the tree, which is now only a faint shadow in the darkness.

"I think this is possibly a need that should be addressed in our church family," Grace says, pulling my attention back. "What do you think?"

I look at her directly. I think of all the implications of how I might have to talk about my past, about the pain of recalling memories, about the struggles with denial. I really want to say it's a bad idea. A bad, bad idea. But the women's faces come to mind again. Each with secret hurts buried deep within. Hurts that need a gentle Savior to come and heal, to set them free from the torture of silence, and I realize this isn't about me wanting to hide from my past, it's about God using it to help others through theirs.

I take a deep breath, fully realizing all the possible effects of my next words. "I think you're right."

Chapter 35

Bravery. Dragon slayers, bear fighters, ancient warriors and firemen running into a burning building to rescue a trapped child are the images that usually come to mind. Usually bravery is recognized as an act that puts someone in extreme danger for the help and benefit of others. But sometimes bravery is much more subtle and often overlooked by society. Sometimes bravery comes in the form of shattering the silence.

I sit back in my desk chair and stretch my arms over my head. My eyes flicker to the clock at the corner of my laptop screen. 5:01 pm. Already? Instantaneous knots form in my stomach. How can time be moving so quickly?

I lean forward again and finish typing the introduction to my thesis that I've been working on for what seems to have been hours. A long time for only one page. I'd been hoping to get another NMR run, but it'll have to wait until tomorrow. I shut the lid of my laptop and slide it into my book bag at the same time as I grab my monkey earmuffs and red coat.

"See you tomorrow, Xue!" I say to the wall of my cubicle.

"Zai xian!" a voice on the other side replies.

I speed down the four flights of stairs and step out into the cold evening air. Dusk is already here.

I hate short winter days when I arrive at the lab in the dark and leave in the dark.

My shoes slap against the sidewalk at a relatively fast pace and another burst of nerves wrack through my core.

My mind has done a good job today at keeping my thoughts occupied with chemistry and my thesis. But now as I draw closer to Stacey's I feel my guard begin to ebb.

I can't believe the day is upon me. Thursday evenings are normally ones I look forward to. My dinner dates with Grace. Even though the accompanying conversations are often difficult, the overall time is encouraging and fun. And over the past couple months we have discussed this day coming, I just can't believe it's actually here.

Since our first discussion, not long after Christmas, about the need to address the hurts of sexual abuse in our church, the ball has really been rolling. Grace has been keeping me up to date weekly and has been asking for ideas and my opinions on things.

She and Kelsey teamed up, both having a desire to see healing for women in the church with a past of sexual abuse.

They asked the leaders of Hope Community Church, and after getting the go ahead, proceeded to meet and come up with a plan on what to do. It was decided that they would start a group that would meet at Kelsey's on Thursday evenings for eight weeks. I recommended it take place in one location, a safe space, where women can open up in a familiar and comfortable environment. Hence the group was dubbed 'Safe Space.'

As time passed, I became more and more anxious to start. They decided to only announce it one time in church. It was to be a very closed and anonymous group. Grace and Kelsey prayed and fasted, waiting for God's direction to start.

Finally, two weeks ago, it was announced in church as a group to address the hurts of sexual assault. Grace had given me a heads up, but the impact of the announcement still left me feeling queasy and wondering what I was getting myself into. They'd waited so long I was only going to be able to attend six meetings before heading back to England.

I shut the kitchen door behind me, blocking out the cold, and quickly unload my stuff onto the nearest stool. Pilikia pads up to me and rubs his nose against my leg.

"Hello," I say to him, bending down to give him a quick pet on the head. I rush upstairs to my room and shove on a bulky sweatshirt and check my hair, which is edging on the wild side of curly from the wind whipping through it.

I look at my watch. 6:00 pm. Grace is picking me up at 6:30. Just enough time to eat. Eat? Who am I kidding? I can't eat. I feel like I'm going to vomit as it is.

I go downstairs and pull out my laptop and begin aimlessly surfing the Internet at the kitchen table while Pilikia stretches out beside me.

At 6:20 I close my laptop and eat a cracker. I pace around the kitchen several times under the puzzled glare from Pilikia. My phone buzzes in my pocket.

Grace: On my way.

Gulp! Butterflies scatter through my body, which I'd almost had under calm control. My hands shake as I put on my coat, scarf and earmuffs. Will I say it today? What will people think? How are they coping with life? Do they struggle with the same things I do? Will I cry? Will I laugh?

Beep!

I grab my keys and hit the lights. I force myself to concentrate on locking the door and getting out of the gate before I hop in Grace's car.

"Hello dear!" she says, leaning over the middle armrest to give me an awkward car hug. Physical contact is so rare for me, it feels good, filling me with a little more calm.

"How are you?" she asks.

I give her a grin that feels stupid-looking on my face.

"Fine!" I say brightly. Too brightly. My freaking out is leaking out.

"Nervous?"

"Uh. Yeah. Big time," I nod, my stupid grin still plastered in place.

"It'll be okay," she says with a hopeful smile.

"Do I have to speak?" I ask, as we draw close to Kelsey's.

"No. You don't have to." She pulls up outside the large house, switches off the car and turns in her seat to face me. "It'll be okay, Brie." She grabs my hand. "Really, it will. Come on."

She gets out of the car and I step out, unsure as to whether my legs can carry me. They're so jittery, I feel like they're either ready to sprint away or collapse into a heap. I manage to follow Grace up the front steps where Kelsey has already opened the door and is greeting us.

"Hello, hello. Glad you could make it," she directs her greeting toward me.

I slip off my sneakers in the breezeway and follow Grace through into the house. As soon as I step foot inside I'm engulfed in, for lack of a better word, cozy.

A crackling fire resides in a hearth to my left causing the air to be thick with warmth. A few candles flicker on the large wooden coffee table in the middle of the living room, giving off aromas of apple-cinnamon spice, which mix in with the smell of baked goods wafting through from the kitchen. All the colors are warm browns, creams and greens, like an enchanted forest.

"Can I take your coat?" Kelsey asks me. I hand it to her, my jaw tight and my smile still in place.

"Would you like something to drink? Coffee, tea, hot chocolate perhaps?" she asks, as she hangs up my coat in the hall closet and heads into the kitchen.

I clear my throat and follow her into the kitchen. "Coffee please."

"Alright," she says brightly, grabbing a mug. "Decaf or regular?"

I hear a knock and the sound of Grace opening the front door. Greetings are exchanged and my legs feel extremely wobbly. I lean against the countertop for support.

"Umm... regular please," I say, trying to block out the new voices that resound from the living room.

Kelsey places a few scoops of ground coffee in a cafetière, reminding me of Arin and the castle. A sharp pang of longing hits me unexpectedly. I miss her more than I realized. Corwin and Peter all flash through my mind. I miss them all.

Kelsey hands me a mug with rounded edges that fits snugly in my palms, then her attention is drawn to the doorway.

"Hello! Welcome. I'm glad you could make it," she says to a girl about my age with sandy brown hair. She wears a blue and yellow sweatshirt from the University of Michigan. She looks as nervous as I feel and I'm suddenly filled with empathy and compassion for her. It's like I want to run up and give her a hug and tell her it wasn't her fault and that she's loved more than she knows.

"I'm Kelsey."

"I'm Hailey," she says, in a voice that sounds unsure.

I resist the odd urge to hug her and smile at her instead, my nerves and fears vanishing. "I'm Brie," I tell her.

"Would you like a drink?" Kelsey rattles off the options again while I remain leaning against the counter, filled with awe at my drastic and immediate change in feelings.

This isn't about me, it's about them. I satisfyingly plunge the coffee and pour myself a cup. The rich aroma just adds to the coziness. I take my coffee into the living room where Grace is talking to two other girls.

One stands with her back to me and is about my height, but extremely thin with dark brown hair up in a ponytail. The other is older than me, possibly in her forties with a head of red curls.

She smiles at me. I recognize her from church and remember the strange tug at my heart when I walked by her during communion one week. I thought little of it at the time. But with her standing in front of me now, I know we share pains of the past.

"Brie, this is Alice and Claire," she motions to the dark-haired girl and red-haired woman. Alice turns around. Her delicate features frame large brown eyes that seem burdened with sorrow. Again, I want to reassure her somehow. Give her hope.

"I'm Brie," I smile, and place myself on the end of the squishy green couch nearest the fire. That's all it takes – the girls follow suit and take seats that have been placed in a circle.

Kelsey and Hailey join us, Hailey taking the seat next to me and Kelsey taking more drink orders. The silence is only broken by the crackling fire. It's strange being in a room with people you know nothing about except that they've been sexually abused, quite an intimate detail.

Kelsey comes back bearing drinks and a loaf of banana bread on a platter. She sets it on the coffee table and speaks through my rather awkward realization.

"Nicole should be here soon," she says, and at first I don't think I know who that is, but I then recall being introduced to a woman named Nicole. She had a confident demeanor and tight blonde curls springing from her head.

A few moments later, in which there was bread eating and compliments to the baker, Nicole enters. She's exactly the woman I'm imagining. Her confident demeanor is still apparent, but I see the reserve in her eyes. She smiles, while at the same time scanning our faces warily, and finally joins the circle in the chair nearest the door as if to place herself near the escape.

Grace clears her throat and begins with a small welcome.

"So, before we start I want to just go over a few things. The lawyer in me wanted to make a contract that we'll all sign and agree to for these sessions. The agreement is as follows:

"We commit to God and one another for these eight weeks to: build trust and maintain confidentiality, show respect for one another's needs and differences, inform others if we need to leave the room, feel free to tell our stories in whatever manner we feel most comfortable." She takes a breath and glances around the circle. "Remember that we are not here to judge how others have coped and we are to encourage but never push others to share. Remember that emotions are good and encouraged and realize that not all emotions expressed are toward one another. We commit to not minimize others' or our own stories because of differences and to reach out for help during the week if needed. Please practice self-care and check in with one another about this each week. And finally, we commit to believe the truth of the Gospel and allow our sisters in Christ to challenge us in the healing process."

As she reads the list my heart begins to pound. I focus on Grace and try to ignore the others, not wanting to make them uncomfortable by looking at them.

"I also want to define sexual assault according to the law. I think it might help some of you to hear this." She takes a quick glance around the circle before proceeding. "Sexual assault is any type of sexual contact or behavior that occurs without the explicit consent of the recipient. Falling under the definition of sexual assault are sexual activities such as forced sexual intercourse, forcible sodomy, child molestation, incest, fondling, and attempted rape."

As she rattles off the definition I find myself feeling more and more uncomfortable. The words, while less harsh than Tyler's a couple months ago in the sermon on Dinah, are like small jabs to my heart. They hurt and I will her to finish. My lips stretch out into a smile and I hide it behind my coffee cup. I resist laughing as hard as I can. Finally, she finishes and a heavy weight descends. That was hard to hear for the rest of them as well, I'm sure. The silence drags on for what seems forever and a small giggle erupts from my throat, which I proceed to cover with a small cough and take a sip of my coffee.

Kelsey eventually speaks.

"We thought it would be a good idea to just quickly introduce ourselves. I'll start."

"My name is Kelsey, I'm married to Tyler and we have a six-month old baby named Lisa. I'm originally from Halifax, Canada. Tyler and I moved here a couple years ago."

Claire goes next.

"I'm Claire. I'm originally from Virginia. I've lived in Detroit for two years now. I have two kids who live with their father. And I am getting married to Anthony in the summer. He has a son, Anthony Jr. And, yeah, that's me."

"I'm Grace. I moved to Detroit for law school in the fall. I grew up in Haiti with my parents, who were missionaries," she ends with a dimpled grin.

We seem to be going in order, which means I'm next. Hmm... what to say...

"I'm Brie." I flash a quick smile while working out my story details, how much or how little information to share. My life is not simple, to say the least. "I came to Detroit in the fall. I'm here for eight months as part of an international research project for my chemistry degree. I've spent the past eleven years in England, and before that I lived in New Hampshire. I started coming to Hope Church where I met Grace. Oh, and a bit of a warning…" I pause, realizing this could sound weird, but I feel myself about to burst into giggles any second. Grace has been encouraging me to share this; she thinks it's a wise move. "I've recently started to laugh at seemingly inappropriate times. Like I really wanted to laugh the whole way through Grace reading that definition. It's possibly a defense mechanism from my past. So yeah… just in case I laugh, please don't think that I find it funny." The girls smile at me. Nicole is the only one to comment.

"Thanks for the heads up. I appreciate it." The rest of them nod in agreement.

Phew… I sip my coffee, my hands shaking slightly.

"I'm Hailey. I graduated from college last summer and just got a job at a bank nearby. Last Sunday was actually my first time at Hope. I finally decided to come with my boyfriend, who has some friends who go there. I've been away from church for quite a while now, so it was good to be back. And the first thing I hear about is this group. I knew instantly that I had to come." She smiles slightly and takes a gulp of her hot chocolate.

"I'm Alice," she speaks extremely quietly and sweetly. "Umm. Me and my husband have been coming to Hope for about six months off and on. We just started coming more regularly. We have a baby girl named Emily. She's about the same age as Kelsey's," she smiles at Kelsey. Her face lights up momentarily when talking about her baby, but she finishes and retreats once more.

"Well, my name's Nicole," she says matter-of-factly. "And I don't really know what I'm doing here." She laughs a little, sighs and continues. "I moved here a year ago with my two kids." She avoids looking at anyone when talking and suddenly my heart goes out to her. "We moved here after my divorce…" She purses her lips and gives a nod as if to say she's done.

Grace gets the cue and moves ahead. "We've got about thirty to forty minutes before we wrap up. There's no pressure, but this is what we're here to do, to talk about what happened. So, if anyone would like to start us off, feel free."

Sharp silence. Not me. Not me. My heart races in my chest. Adrenaline courses through my veins. Not me. Silence.

"I'll go," I say, releasing a burst of air that is pent up in my lungs. I'm shocked at my own words. "Pull the Band Aid off quick, right?" I laugh and a couple others smile. "Oh boy. Hmm… well, where to begin?" I feel myself detach and watch from the 'corner' again as my hands and my face become more and more animated. I avoid looking at anyone, but occasionally glance at Grace for encouragement to keep going. I tell a quick summary of my dad, moving to England and Ted.

"So yeah. That's me," I laugh and the room goes quiet. Each of the other four girls besides the leaders, Kelsey and Grace, has a somber look on their face, like I've just shared some really sad news. Kelsey and Grace are studying each person, taking in their reactions.

"Anyone else like to share?" Grace asks. Silence.

"I'll go," Hailey says beside me, breaking the silence and making me jump. Thankfully my coffee is over half gone, so none is sloshed out of the mug.

She takes a breath and swallows. I bet I can imagine what's going on in her head right now. Again, my heart swells with compassion for her. I almost want to give her a shot of bravery, to shatter the silence. But she doesn't need it. She begins to speak in such a way, it's as if she's talking to herself, like she's ignoring our presence. There again, I can understand.

As I listen to her recall sexual abuse by her cousin at a young age and how she began to sleep around in her teens, searching for love, my heart breaks.

"And I know, this isn't exactly sexual abuse… but when I was with my last boyfriend… there were times where…" Hailey takes a deep breath. "…where he wouldn't take no for an answer…" She doesn't need to explain further. A chill runs down my spine. How can people be so evil and selfish?

Grace talks very directly toward Hailey. "It wasn't your fault, your boyfriend raped you. That's not okay, whether you were sleeping with him willfully at other times; it's not just something he can take. You have the right to say no."

Tears leak out of the corners of Hailey's eyes and Kelsey picks up the tissue box from the coffee table and offers her one.

"Thank you for sharing," Kelsey says. I look around at the other girls. Each looks solemn, as if they're each realizing we're not alone in our pain, but how we wish we were so that others wouldn't feel this pain. "We have just about time for one more share if anyone's feeling brave enough," she says with a smile.

"Umm." Shock kicks me out of my pondering mind. Alice clears her throat. She's the last person I would have expected to be brave enough to share. "It happened the summer before college." Her voice is still frail and I strain to hear her over the crackling fire. She looks down at her lap as she talks in a detached 'story-like' way. "I was at my friend's house, hanging out, swimming." Her voice quivers and I can feel her pain. I can feel what's coming. I'd prefer it if she wouldn't continue, but she needs to. I brace for the impact. "My friend went inside and I went into the pool house... a friend of ours... he followed me in. We had both been drinking. He pushed me to the ground and... and he wouldn't stop." Her words come out so faintly they are hard to make out, but the impact is obvious. She sits with her arms wrapped around her middle. It's the typical stance for trying to keep yourself together when the world seems to be falling apart. She tells us how more things happened later. I can hear the guilt in her voice. She blames herself. But it wasn't her fault!

I begin talking before I can stop myself.

"It wasn't your fault." I look at her. She glances up at me. "I know you think it is, you might say it was because you were drunk, but it wasn't your fault. You tried to fight. Who knows what would have happened if you continued? Please, please don't blame yourself." The words ring true in my head, but I realize, I think the same thing. What a hypocrite I am.

"Thank you for sharing, Alice," Kelsey speaks through the heavy silence that hangs in the air. "We're going to close by just meditating on this song."

She grabs her laptop and begins to play *The Real Me* by Natalie Grant. The song soaks into my soul. I look around the circle as we listen. Each of these precious women are here for a reason. As I think about the fact that only one of the five of us have been in Detroit for over a year, I am struck by God's perfect timing. If we had started the group when I wanted to, Hailey would have never been here, and never able to share and heal. I'm convinced that God has an amazing plan in store for each of these women in front of me. For me too. A grin escapes onto my lips, not one from nerves, but one of joy.

The song ends and Kelsey closes us in prayer.

"The last thing I want us to do before we leave is for each of us to find a space in the room." We spread out a little. "I want us to breathe in and draw our arms up," she demonstrates, "and breathe out and let them fall down by your sides. And while breathing in and out say: Father, I am Yours."

"Father, I am Yours," I say it along with the others, but my voice catches on the word father. It seems strange to call God father when to me the word father has a very bad connotation. I shake off the uncomfortable feeling and proceed to say goodbye to the girls.

"So, what did you think?" Grace asks me as we get into her car.

I turn to her and feel tears prick my eyes.

"Amazing. God is so good. At first I was scared, but then my heart broke for each of them and the pain they were in. I know that as much as I care for them and want to see God heal them, God wants to also heal me. I'm no longer scared. I'm excited!" I end with a giggle and a little dance in my seat.

"That's great! You were very brave to go first and I think the girls understood why you laugh. I'm glad you said something."

"Yeah. Me too."

She pulls up outside Stacey's.

"I love you, Brie Joy!" she says to me, giving me a hug over the armrest.

"I love you too, Grace. See you next week. I can't wait!"

I walk into the house baffled at the drastic change in my heart since I left a couple hours ago. God is good.

Chapter 36

Disappointment. We avoid it like the plague. As long as we keep the bar low for people, they will never disappoint us. Never expect anything from them, and they won't let us down. Don't voice your wants only to get them ignored. Yet then we are upset when we receive nothing from relationships. They begin to feel like we're giving and giving and getting nothing in return.

I feel as if I'm losing it again. My workload for my thesis is so heavy right now, plus I leave soon to go back to England. And with all the stress comes my past.

Thursday night at Safe Space was so hard. Nicole and Claire shared. As Nicole spoke, flashes of my dad would race through my head. I think she is beginning to see how her past has affected her now and the alcoholism and promiscuity she constantly falls back into. Claire… her story is so very similar to mine with my father. It felt as though she was telling my story. The big difference was that at the age of nine, she was brave enough to tell her mom. I was not. During the session, I kept dissociating and Kelsey tried to get me to focus on the candlelight, but it didn't work.

Sunday, Tyler was preaching and kept mentioning 'those of us who've been molested.' I hate it when he does that. It hurts! He also posed the question: "What if your abuser came and told you he was sorry and you could see he was sincere. Would you forgive?" In some ways, I feel as though I've forgiven my father and Ted, but can I truly forgive if I'm not angry at them, if deep down I feel like I deserved it so they didn't do anything wrong?

All day I've not felt able to focus. I feel like the water is coming at me from all sides. Rising fast. I don't want to swim again. I'm too tired. But oh the change God is working in me! I suddenly have a deep desire to have children. Something I thought I would never desire in a hundred years. I helped at Sunday school with Grace and I loved it. What is wrong with me? I really am losing my mind. All I need to remember is God's got it.

I tear my eyes away from the tree outside that I've been staring at from the chair in my room for quite some time. I gather my gym clothes. Stress continues to weigh heavy on my shoulders. Maybe I can pound some of it out on the treadmill since I'm not going to get anywhere with my thesis in this unfocused state of mind. I race down the stairs past Pilikia, giving him a brief stroke, and out the door.

It's unseasonably warm, almost too warm to wear my sweatshirt. Almost. I'm definitely not going to take it off. But I feel like I could! Gah. Sometimes I'm surprised at how much I still hate myself.

I walk quicker, pushing myself with anger toward the gym. I reach the large building with huge glass windows, behind which people are running, biking and weight-lifting like hamsters in a cage. Most of me doesn't like the gym and the coldness of the atmosphere, but I need to do something. I go in and head straight down the stairs toward the locker room. I round the corner and almost bump into an older man walking toward the bottom of the stairs. The smell of sawdust fills my lungs and I feel the world spin away...

I run as fast as I can down the hill from my house to the barn. My purple and pink bike is at my side. The front tire is flat. I swing open the barn door and the smell of sawdust hits me. Mom said Dad was out here working in the workshop.

"Hi Ellie!" Dad says with a grin.

"Dad, can you pump up my bike tire please?" I ask him.

He kneels down in front of me, still grinning. He looks behind my shoulder and then back at me. My insides go to ice. His grin has changed. I know what's coming.

"Of course I can, Ellie," but instead of reaching for the bike, he reaches for me...

I flash back into the basement of the gym. I stagger my way to the locker room, trying desperately to cling to the present. Pain erupts inside me and I slump onto a bench. Focusing on the floor I begin to count the floor tiles until the smell of sawdust is out of my mind. I hate realizing just what a mess I am. The pain is so intense I want to shut off. My old urge to cut surfaces and I grit my teeth.

"No!" I say under my breath. I stand up and begin changing into my gym clothes frantically.

Within minutes I'm upstairs on a treadmill pounding my feet to the beat of my iPod. Anger continually boils up and I push it out through my breathing.

What is wrong with me? Why can't I just get over it? Why do flashbacks haunt me so much? I must look like a crazy person. Maybe I am crazy...

I turn the speed up further until I'm running at a reasonable pace.

Pound, pound, pound. I hate you, I hate you, I hate you.

My phone, which is tucked into the little holder on the treadmill lights up and begins to buzz. I glance at the screen without breaking my stride.

"Mom Calling"

I suppress a groan and ignore the call. *Buzz buzz. Buzz buzz.* Pound, pound, pound.

A voicemail message appears on the screen. I slow the treadmill down and listen.

"Hi, Brielle. It's your mother! I haven't heard from you in over a week. Just wondering how you are and what you're up to. Is your thesis going well? I can always try and proof read it for you. I know how much you struggle with grammar and spelling, although I may not be much help with the chemistry terms. Anyway, give me a call!"

I slam the phone back into the holder and turn up the speed until I'm practically sprinting. There are no words or even thoughts that come to my mind concerning how mad I am at her. I don't even know why I feel this way. Her voice sends blasts of anger coursing through me. Her concern about my work, reminding me of how stressed I am with my thesis, and then criticizing my failures in grammar and spelling. Gah!

I see the woman next to me look over and I realize I released my angry sigh out loud. Oops.

I shut off the treadmill, quickly dismount and head to the locker room once more. My 'stress relieving' activity has failed to relieve any stress; in fact, I feel more stressed than when I came. Hopefully my girls' night in with Grace tonight will help me.

We decided to have a chill out night together since our weekly Thursday evening meetings have turned into Safe Space meetings. It could not come at a better time.

"I think you're expecting too much of yourself."

I re-adjust the red fuzzy blanket I'm curled beneath and proceed to weave the edges through my fingertips, trying to understand what Grace is saying. She continues when I fail to respond.

"It's not just going to go away in a night. You know full well that it takes time. Look how far you've come! Even just in your time here in Detroit, I've seen such progress."

I look over at her curled beneath her pink blanket and smile. She's right. I do feel like I've changed, grown.

"But I keep having flashbacks. I feel crazy. I am crazy."

"You're not crazy, Brie."

"I am!" I sigh, not wanting to admit this to myself, much less someone else. "I got my medical records from the night I was in hospital in the mail today. I needed them to submit to my insurance company in England." I puff out my cheeks and release a slow breath.

"I read them. Grace… they diagnosed me with PTSD." I look up at her. "Posttraumatic stress disorder," I clarify, in case she doesn't know what that means. "I mean… I know I check the boxes… people have suggested it before… but seeing it there on paper as a diagnosis from a medical doctor… I knew I hated them," I end in a mutter, my stomach twisting uncomfortably. How did they know? I didn't tell them anything.

"Brie. It's okay. This is a normal response for people who have been through something as traumatic as you have."

I cringe away from her words. She continues, ignoring my discomfort.

"But this doesn't mean you are crazy. It means you are reacting as would be expected."

"Mmm," I shrug, and change the subject. "I got a call from my mother today."

"And? How did it go?" she asks.

"Well, I didn't actually talk to her, she left a message. I just get so angry at her and I have no idea why."

"Don't you?"

I frown, unsure of what she means.

"I don't think I do... I mean, she's always so critical of me. I just can't handle it. Aren't parents meant to love you no matter what, not expect you to be perfect?"

Grace remains silent.

"I mean, she doesn't know anything about me. She never has. She's been blind to my life for twenty-two years. How does she think she can try and be a part of it now, acting all caring? She never cared. She was never there for me." My chest rises and falls rapidly. My head begins to spin.

I suddenly realize I have all this anger pent up for her over my past. I'm not even remotely angry at my father, I'm mad at my mother for marrying him and having me and not knowing that while she slept in her bed, her husband was... doing stuff to his daughter! And I'm not mad at Ted, I'm mad at my mother for marrying Charlie, taking me to England and putting me back into that situation. I'm so mad at her. I swallow deeply and pull the tears back that threaten to spill out of my eyes.

"I really think you need to tell your mom what happened," Grace says after a few minutes.

I know she's right. But that's impossible. I can't do it. I can't.

Chapter 37

Goodbye. One of the hardest words to say. It speaks a volume of emotion and yet is not even close enough to express your heart. Somehow you never escape goodbyes, no matter how hard you try. They're inevitable.

I look around at each of them: Alice, Claire, Hailey, Kelsey, Grace and Nicole. We've been through so much together, fighting the hauntings of our past, shattering the silence. Tonight is my last night with them. Tomorrow I fly back to Wisconsin before departing back to England. I can't believe how much I'll miss them.

I take a deep breath and begin to speak.

"So, this is the Psalm I wrote, as Kelsey encouraged us to do last week." I open my journal to the right page.

"The days were long. The nights were longer. Where were you, oh God?

The storm surged and the waves rose above me. Where were you, oh God?

My heart feels heavy and I can barely keep my head above water. My past haunts me day and night. Its darkness creeps in and steals my joy. It extinguishes the light of truth and replaces it with lies.

My abusers laugh at me. They mock my weakness. Their words taunt me constantly. Where were you, oh God?

You were there. There in the darkest night, you were there, my Lord. You gave me a hope deep within when all others stole it away.

You gave me dreams of You and Your kingdom when my nights were filled with terror.

You raised me out of the ocean depths and gave me strength to make it to shore. You gave me back my joy! You take my hand and lead me on.

The road is hard, but You are with me, just as You always have been."

I close my journal and look around. Many of the girls have tears in their eyes and for once I understand. 'God, you are so good, so kind, so loving.'

"I'm going to miss you all so much," my voice cracks with emotion.

"We're going to miss you too!" Claire says, standing up and coming over to my seat and giving me a big hug. That's it. Tears flow readily now. "But this isn't the end. We'll see each other again. Either in this life or the one to come." She sits back down and Kelsey hands me the tissue box. I take it gratefully.

"Yeah, you're right. It's still so hard to leave you all."

Sad smiles surround me.

"But you're right, I'm not saying goodbye, I'm saying see you later!" I laugh and they join in. Oh, what beautiful flowers have sprung out of the cracked and broken earth that was our pasts.

"Lynn!" I run to her, dragging my much larger suitcases behind me this time. "Hello." I grin at her. "I'm back!"

"Hey," she smiles at me. Again, that comfort and sense of belonging that I get when I'm with her and her family washes over me.

"Thanks for picking me up."

"No problem."

We're quiet for a moment. Both of us know our time together is limited. I leave to go back to England in a few days.

I glance at her as we walk over to her car and begin to laugh. Within minutes we're both crying and holding our sides from laughing so hard. So us. Time may be limited, but we'll sure make the most of what we have.

"Hello," Marshall's voice resounds from the living room.

"Howdy!" I reply, bounding into the living room after leaving my suitcases by the door.

Laurie stands and gives me a big hug.

"Hi 'Mom'," I say.

"You girls probably never stopped talking all the way here!"

I grin and look at Lynn.

"Nope!" We both giggle.

"And they're off," Laurie says in good humor.

We spend the rest of the evening talking away. Well, mainly Marshall talking and Lynn and I bursting into fits of giggles every few minutes. I go to bed amongst the army of ducks, with my sides hurting and my cheeks aching, but also with a heavy heart.

I know I only have a couple days here with them, and the weight of knowledge of what I must do is burdening my thoughts.

I lay restless on the trundle bed for what seems an eternity before I speak out into the darkness.

"Lynn?"

"Mmm?" She's not quite asleep, and I feel bad for disturbing her, but I feel like I'm going to explode if I don't talk.

"You know all the stuff I told you a while back about my dad and Ted...?"

"Yeah," she says, a little more awake now.

I take a deep breath. "I think I need to tell my mom. It seems insane. I used to promise Corwin this would never, ever happen. Ugh... anyway... I think I'd like to have a practice run on your mom, my 'USA mom.' What do you think? Would she react badly? Should I tell her or not?" Just saying that out loud brings a wave of nausea over me. I'm dreading this with every fiber in me.

I hear Lynn roll over in her bed so she's facing me. "It's up to you. I don't think she'd react badly. But I dunno. I think it's a good idea as a trial run. Maybe help you work out how to say it the best way."

"Yeah... that's what I thought too." I sigh and roll over onto my side. "Thanks, now to see if I can get some sleep. I can't believe I'm going to do this. Will you be there with me please?"

"Sure."

284

"Night, sis!"

"Night."

Morning comes quickly. My heart pounds through breakfast. Laurie notices my peculiar manner.

"Are you okay?"

"Me? Yeah, I'm fine!" I say with a mouth full of Kix, the cereal she brings in especially for me. It makes me feel like a little kid again.

"Alright…" she says, totally unconvinced.

I wolf the rest of my cereal down and clear away my bowl into the dishwasher. I slam the dishwasher and Lynn walks in. My eyes flick between them.

"Might as well get it over and done with," I say. Lynn gives me a little nod and looks nervously at her mom, who's eyeing me cluelessly.

I feel the nervous chatter and giggles bubble up.

"Well," Giggle. "I wondered if I could make you my guinea pig?"

"For what?" Laurie sounds so much more serious than I'd like.

"Uhhh… well…" I wander into the living room and take the seat nearest the window. Lynn follows and takes the seat nearest to me. Laurie follows suit with a confused look on her face, taking the couch across from both of us. "Ugh. I don't know if I can do this…"

"Do what?" she asks, with a thread of impatience weaved into her tone.

"I want to tell you something, kinda like a trial run for telling my mom. Please don't freak out though…"

"I'll try," she says, still having no clue what I'm talking about.

I take a deep breath and let it out slowly. Then repeat. I look out the window and my legs begin to shake followed by my hands, which I proceed to stuff under my legs.

"Uh." The silence in the room sounds like screaming. I can't do this. *Jesus, help me!* "I don't know how much you know about my dad…"

"Not much."

"Alright. Well… basically, I never told my mom this, but he… he sexually abused me," I stutter out, detaching as I say it.

"How often?" she asks, in disbelief.

285

"Until I was eight. Quite a lot," I say in a monotone. I add a laugh at the end, which produces a glare from Laurie. "Sorry. I laugh because I don't cry."

"And you never told anyone?"

"The police tried to get me to talk, and so did the endless number of counselors. But I didn't. He told me not to. I was afraid I'd hurt my mom. I still am afraid. I'm pretty sure she won't handle this well."

Laurie shakes her head. I can't tell if she doesn't believe me or is just shocked.

"Then... they took me to England. As you know." Laurie looks up at me with a look that says 'There's more?' I take a deep breath again. "It started all over again... this time with a cousin of mine." She frowns. "From the other side of the family," I hastily say before she thinks she knows who it is. "So, yeah. It stopped when I left home. So all's good," I end with a nervous smile and glance at Lynn, whose face is unreadable. The silence chills me to the bone. What if she doesn't believe me? What if she gets mad at me? What if she now looks at me differently? What if she tells other people?

"I can't believe this happened." She looks at me and I see hurt in her bright blue eyes. "Not that I don't believe you, I do," she adds quickly, "but I knew your dad. I never thought him capable of such a thing. I guess it's always the ones you don't expect. I'm sorry this happened to you."

I nod, not really sure how to respond. I feel a little better having that off my chest, but I keep glancing between Lynn and her mom, just waiting for her to flip out.

After a few minutes, I ease back into my chair. Maybe she's not going to flip out.

"I think your mom definitely needs to know."

"Hmmm... I'm not so sure. I don't think she'll handle it very well."

"She may not, but you're her daughter, she should know."

I sigh. "I know... I know." She glares at me. "I will! Eventually..." Her glare gets sterner. "Okay, okay. Soon." I laugh.

"Shall I keep this from Marshall?" she asks.

"Umm… it's up to you. If you think he should know, then feel free to tell him, I don't mind. But I don't think I can tell him myself."

"Okay."

She stands up and I get up and give her a hug. Her embrace is tight and long.

"Wanna go out to lunch, sis?"

"Sure." Lynn says, getting the hint that I need to get out of here.

"I think that went well, don't you?" I say to Lynn as we go out to her car.

"Yeah."

"Phew. Ahhh! I can't believe I just did that. Next is my mother… Do you think your mom will tell Marshall?"

"It's hard to say."

I nod.

"Where shall we go for lunch?" I ask with a grin, an obvious change of subject.

We walk through the back door a few hours later with hands full of shopping bags. I stocked up on marshmallows to take back to England. At least they're light and might not put my luggage over the weight limit.

The house is quiet. Too quiet. It puts me on edge. Both Laurie and Marshall's cars are in the driveway so they should be home.

As I round the corner into the living room I hear muttering immediately stop. The atmosphere is heavy and I know Laurie told him. He looks at me with a broken expression on his face. I look away and instead fix my gaze on Lynn beside me, who is also taking it all in. She gives me the smallest smile and I sit down in my usual chair.

"I want to hug you, but I know that's probably not the best thing to do right now, but I'd like to," Marshall says firmly to me. Good ol' Marshall, straight to the point. "As you can surmise, Laurie told me. As appalling as this is, it does not surprise me. These things happen more often than any of us care to think. I'm broken for you, to think that it all happened to you. I think of you as my own daughter and I'm mad. I'm mad at what they did to you."

I can feel the smile fixed in place on my face and a small laugh begins to build up in my stomach. Oh no, Brie. No, no. Not now. Don't laugh. I replay what he all just said. He's upset. He shouldn't be. It's no big deal. Oh crap. Here it comes.

Laughter escapes my mouth. I laugh and laugh until tears begin to pour from my eyes. The room is deadly still besides my hysteria. Not even Lynn joins me this time.

After a few moments, once I catch my breath, I settle down and avoid eye contact. I don't know how they've reacted to this outburst.

"Brie." Marshall waits until I look at him before he continues. "I'm not going to say much more on the matter, I can see that it's upsetting you. And I can see how deep the pain is for you, that's obvious by your laughter and I'm sorry. I will be here for you for whatever you need." He tightens his lips and gives a nod. Laurie remains quiet and I sneak a peek at Lynn whose expression matches that of her mother's. Unreadable.

Marshall's words echo in my head and in my heart, causing my chest to ache with the care he shows. I don't want to cry, so I stand up and go to Lynn's room and begin to get ready for bed.

I can't believe what happened today. I can't believe I did that. I leave tomorrow. I'm going back to England.

My world seems to spin as thoughts whip around my head. I crawl beneath the covers and put my headphones in, hoping that the music will push away all my thoughts and I'll be able to sleep. It works. Within minutes I feel myself drift away into a peaceful sleep.

I can't even think straight. It's all gone so fast. I'm here in Chicago's airport waiting for my flight back to England. I just said goodbye to Lynn and Alex, who gave me a ride to the airport. It was so hard. I hate leaving them, especially when I don't feel I have anything to look forward to. Tears threaten to spill out. I was going to study for my upcoming exams while I waited in the terminal, but I am too tired and upset.

I am so sad to leave America, but I know God will work everything out for good. I am making the decision to embrace the road He has set before me, for with Him no enemy can stop me. Fear not for He is with you!

I look out onto the setting sun. It is the last sunset I will see in America for quite some time. My heart aches with the apprehension of the homesickness that is to come. I try to look at the positives: I get to see my mom and Charlie and Arin and Peter...but I just can't bring myself to be excited about returning.

Nevertheless, God gives us trials to mold us into working tools. So as the sun sets, I open the next small chapter, or rather, end the long first chapter of my life in England.

Chapter 38

Survivor. The term often used to describe someone who has been through something traumatic such as war, or an earthquake or a shipwreck. It is also used to describe a victim of sexual abuse. The term is to honor the strength and the courage it took to continue living when your world was destroyed.

"Your righteousness reaches to the skies, O God, you who have done great things. Who, O God, is like you? Though you have made me see troubles, many and bitter, you will restore my life again; from the depths of the earth you will again bring me up. You will increase my honor and comfort me once again. I will praise you with the harp for your faithfulness, O my God; I will sing praise to you with the lyre, O Holy One of Israel. My lips will shout for joy when I sing praise to you—I, whom you have redeemed. My tongue will tell of your righteous acts all day long, for those who wanted to harm me have been put to shame and confusion." Psalm 71:19-24

I hear Charlie leave through the back door and out the side gate. He's going to help our next-door neighbor who's got a leak in their kitchen. I pace back and forth across my small bedroom. I've been back in England for two days and I feel as if I'm going to explode.

This is the perfect opportunity. I may not get another chance. I leave for Northern in the morning. I have to do it now. I pace a few more times before stopping in front of my mirror.

A girl with brown curls that fall to her shoulders looks back at me with piercing blue eyes. Not the eyes that once were cold and dead with fear, pain and sadness. They now have a spark. Courage. I take a deep breath and step out of my room.

I'm not sure if my legs will hold me as I walk down the stairs to the beat of my pounding heart.

My mother is sitting in her usual chair with a few books on her lap. The room is dark, aside from the little light beside her.

"Hello," she says, tearing her gaze from her book to me.

I feel as though, if I were to speak, I would vomit. Where is the giant hole in the Earth to swallow me whole when I need it? So instead of speaking, I merely sit down on the couch across from her.

She can obviously tell something is up, just as Laurie could a few days ago. She shuts the books she's been reading and places them all on the table beside her.

"What's up?" she asks, directing her full attention to me.

I squirm in my seat, wanting to be anywhere but here. I purse my lips, wishing I could go back in time and remain adamant that I would never tell her.

"Mom, I need to tell you something."

She steels herself as if she knows what is coming. My words feel like lead as they come out.

"Mom, remember ages ago when you told me my dad was a pedophile?" I look up and see her face freeze. Will she laugh like before? Will she believe me? Will she break? I continue, knowing I can't stop now. "Well... I didn't say anything at the time, but I know. You see, I never told you... I never told you because he told me not to, I didn't want to hurt you!" Emotion envelops my words and I struggle to keep the tears back. "I'm sorry I never told you. But Dad did things to me. He did sexual things to me and I never told anyone. I know the police and everyone tried to get me to talk, but I couldn't." I avoid looking at her, instead focusing on the light beside her. I quickly continue, I must get it all out. "And then it was good. Just me and you for a few years. Everything was good besides the lawyers and all that. But then you took me here... and... and it started all over again. Ted... he would do stuff to me. But don't worry, he stopped. All this made me pretty messed up. I hid it from you well, so don't feel bad for not noticing. I was recently diagnosed with PTSD."

"What's that?" she asks, her voice rough.

"Post-traumatic stress disorder. It's common for people who have been sexually assaulted. But God has been doing so much healing in my life. Truly amazing things. I'm sorry I never told you. But I needed to. Please don't think I blame you in any way. It's not your fault."

"Well, it's not your fault either!" she practically yells at me. "I thought I had protected you from him. I tried, I really did. I knew what he was capable of, so I kept an extra eye on you. I don't know how or when it could have happened!"

I feel as if she does not believe me, but I remain quiet, knowing she needs to let it out.

"You know your uncle, his brother, was also put in jail for raping two teenage girls? I think something must have happened when they were younger. I suspect they abused their sister too... she's never been quite right. And Ted! I can't believe it. How dare he hurt my little girl. I want to knock his block off."

"Mom. Please don't. I've forgiven him, so can you. Please don't do anything. Try not to treat him any differently than you always have. He needs love, Mom."

"I don't know if I can do that."

"Try, Mom, you have to try."

"I've told you before how your dad tried to kill me, to drown me?"

I nod, trying to keep up with her change in subject. "Well, for a long time before you were born, I wouldn't let him touch me. He was abusive toward me. He would try to sleep with me, but I wouldn't let him. Then one night I felt God told me to surrender. So I did. And that was the night I conceived you. You were my miracle that God promised me nineteen years before. A woman prophesied over you when you were born that you would be a shepherdess. I can't believe how much I've failed you."

I continue to look at the light. She sits there, I can feel her eyes on me and I finally look her in the eye. And that's when I realize. She's broken too. Just like Jade, just like that girl I saw outside the train, just like the girls in Detroit. Broken. How could I have never seen it before? My heart breaks for her.

"Mom. You haven't failed me. I love you, more than you will ever know!" I stand up, tears freely flowing down my face now, and I don't bother to wipe them away.

She stands and we embrace for what feels like the first time. The first time there are no walls between us. She weeps in my hair and I comfort her.

"I love you too. So, so, so much!" she whispers at me. And I believe her.

My life has changed. Over the past two days, my life—well, I've become freer than I ever expected. Yesterday I told my mom about my dad and Ted. I can't believe I did it. After twenty-three years of secrecy, I finally told her. It felt like a weight had been lifted from my shoulders, a weight I wasn't even aware I was carrying. All I can say right now is, 'Thank You, Jesus!'

I'm back at Northern with a thesis to print and more studying to do than I think is actually possible. Arin and I have created a study timetable and stocked up on cookies (or 'biscuits' as they call them). My mom tried to talk about my past some more when she dropped me off here, but we're not there yet. She wanted details that I don't think are necessary to give her. She doesn't need to hear what happened; it wouldn't benefit either of us to tell her. But still, I feel as if our relationship is on the mend, or rather forming since you can't have a relationship formed on lies, which I did my whole life.

I close my eyes and let the sunlight soak into my skin. The wind ruffles my curls around my head. I breathe in and out, trying to comprehend what just happened. I feel numb. I have no idea what I'm even thinking.

I open my eyes to the bright sunlit treetops that line the river below my dangling legs. The blue sky is a stark contrast to the green-leaved trees. The cathedral glows golden beside me. I'm here. The place I've shed my tears. The place I've poured my secrets out onto the blank pages of my journals. The place I've cried out to God for help. The place I've been still and taken a step back from life and all its craziness.

I'm here. On my wall. Today I finished my degree. My final exam, while extremely difficult and stressful, is over. As I stepped out of the chemistry building doors, I shed two tears of relief. It's done!

I have so many emotions right now, but all I want to do is sit here in blissful beauty and worship my Lord.

I begin to sing. I sing out over the treetops. My voice resounds against the cathedral's mighty walls and flutters to the river below. I sing worship; I praise Him for all He's done. So much!

My praise is cut short by a voice calling my name.

"Brie!" I turn and swing my legs over the wall landing nimbly on my feet. "Brie!" I look down the hill toward The Green and see Arin dashing toward me. I smile at my friend, who's been there through all the ups and downs of chemistry.

"Brie. We did it. We're done! I can't believe it. Ahhh!" She runs up and gives me a hug. I can't help but smile. We really have. Joy fills my insides, but with a hint of anticipation. Now what? Most of my friends have decided to stay on for PhDs. I don't want to do that, and I have no idea why not. I think of the group in Detroit. If only I could do that sort of thing forever. To help women who have been through sexual assault and to tell them that there is hope and healing in Jesus Christ. The uncertainty of the future troubles me.

"I think I need to go take a nap. Maybe you, Peter and I can go out later and celebrate?"

"Sounds good." she replies.

I head back to my room and settle down on my bed, my mind still racing. As I sit there, memories come to steal my joy. It seems like once again, when I'm up in the highest spirits, then do I fall the farthest.

The pain of my past, while much less than before, still pierces me with sharp, jagged edges. Will I ever be truly free?

My phone buzzes on my bed beside me. I look at the screen then close my eyes and shake my head. Corwin, Corwin, Corwin. Oh, what timing! Of course.

I begin to read the text, with each word my heart swells and breaks and at the same time, is filled with hope.

'I release over you the deep heart of peace of Heavenly Dad right now. He says to you in this moment that 'Brie, you are my daughter, you're really precious to me and I never have and never will leave you!' He has hugs for you this afternoon. Reach out and touch His heart for you. You are released by the blood of Jesus to know the heart of Abba Daddy. There is more for you. I stand against any lie, against your mind that would prevent you believing these truths and I decree a supernatural encounter with Dad right now, however you were feeling beforehand, whatever you've thought as you read this. You are free to be loved. There is more for you! Be loved! Freedom!'

Tears roll down my face and I continue my song of praise to my Father. Oh how wonderful He is! He knows me and He knows my thoughts. He is here with me and He loves me. I race out of my room to the piano. Words are not enough.

◆

I sit in a sea of black. Friends and fellow chemists surround me. My black gown feels heavy on my shoulders, but I feel free from the weight I've carried for so long. I look up to the ceiling that rises about a hundred feet above me. The detail on every inch of it is exquisite. My mind wanders from the speech of our university's chancellor to imagining the work and time it took to build this enormous cathedral one thousand years ago. It was built in an attempt to reflect the majesty and glory of God. While it doesn't even come close, it is stunning nonetheless.

It was four years ago that I was sitting in here in my black gown, excited and nervous about what university life held for me. Hoping that by escaping the reality of home, I'd escape the reality of my past. But God had a different plan in mind. He took me down a road of pain, of facing my past, of hurt and anguish, but overall, of hope. He was there, every step of the way. Every cut, every nightmare, every flashback, He was there, ready to embrace me in love and guide me through the darkness with a gentle hand. He placed friends in my path so I would not have to do it alone.

I think back to the way I began, in total darkness. I see the lights He placed around me, in Arin and Peter and in my church. My heart swells in my chest with the gratitude I have for them all. I think of Jade and of my time in Detroit, of the women who shared their pain so that we might heal and grow together. I think of the miracles God did, of how free I am now! And it hits me. God brought me to Northern, not to get my chemistry degree. No, that was the means by which He got me here. God brought me here to heal me. God brought me here to do a miraculous transformation in my life. God brought me here to save my life. He brought me here that I might have life!

"Brielle Joy," the person on the stage calls out from the podium. I stand with shaking legs and make my way out to the front before thousands of people. I plead desperately with myself not to fall flat on my face. Step, step, step. My high-heeled shoes echo on the stone walls.

"Congratulations." The chancellor takes my hand and shakes it. I can't help but beam. I turn and face my audience. I spot my parents a few rows from the front, both of them beaming at me with love and pride.

I take a deep breath, glance up to the ornately carved ceiling and smile. I don't know what God has in store for me next, but I *know* I can trust Him to continue the good works He has begun.

I am a survivor. By the grace of God, I have survived.

About the Author

Brielle Joy graduated with her master's degree in Chemistry and moved back to the United States with the hope of helping survivors like herself. In 2014 she co-founded a non-profit organization to help bring hope, freedom and healing to survivors of sexual exploitation through Christ. Today she continues to bring hope to survivors of both sexual abuse and sex trafficking in the United States and beyond. In 2015 Brielle married a wonderful man, something she never thought would be possible, but that's a story for another time.